Clues to Achieving Consensus

A Leader's Guide to Navigating Collaborative Problem Solving

Mirja P. Hanson

Rowman & Littlefield Education
Lanham, Maryland • Toronto • Oxford
2005

Published in the United States of America
by Rowman & Littlefield Education
A Division of Rowman & Littlefield Publishers, Inc.
A wholly owned subsidiary of
The Rowman & Littlefield Publishing Group, Inc.
4501 Forbes Boulevard, Suite 200, Lanham, Maryland 20706
www.rowmaneducation.com

PO Box 317
Oxford
OX2 9RU, UK

British Library Cataloguing in Publication Information Available

Library of Congress Cataloging-in-Publication Data

Hanson, Mirja P., 1955–
  Clues to achieving consensus : a leader's guide to navigating collaborative
problem solving / Mirja P. Hanson.
      p. cm.
  Includes bibliographical references and index.
  ISBN 1-57886-270-1 (pbk. : alk. paper)
  1. Consensus (Social sciences) 2. Problem solving. 3. Community. I. Title.
JC328.2.H36 2005
658.4'036—dc22

                                                              2005006348

∞™ The paper used in this publication meets the minimum requirements of
American National Standard for Information Sciences—Permanence of
Paper for Printed Library Materials, ANSI/NISO Z39.48-1992.
Manufactured in the United States of America.

Contents

Figures and Tables

FIGURES

TABLES

Foreword

A major difficulty in problem solving is that all too often, the managers and administrators make decisions affecting the workers or the service providers. Furthermore, the workers make them with little organized input. This often creates a downward spiral of "don't bother me with your management problems, as my thoughts don't count anyway."

This book provides the model to break that spiral and actually reverse it—a consensus decision-making process. The advantages are backed up with hands-on examples of successful implementation. Problems for the skeptics are included, which makes easy and interesting reading for both workers and managers.

A team consisting of a cross section of the workplace could develop a prescriptive process to improve their final product, while developing a feeling of direct contribution to that improvement process. Development of a consensus-based decision-making model, based on information in this book, will improve morale as the service providers, whether they are teachers or widget makers, will have a direct action on the decisions which affect the work they do.

Each of us serves as a worker or a manager in our various positions in life. Mirja Hanson has defined these roles as sponsors, facilitators, and participants. She has provided game plans and rules for each, with further examples from actual worksite experiences.

It is my hope that today's workplaces, schools, and other organizations will consider the decision-making model outlined in this book. I believe the end product will be improved by its use. The future of my grandchildren depends on it.

Jim Luoma
Superintendent of Grand Rapids, Minnesota, Public Schools, retired
Minnesota State Colleges and Universities Board of Trustees,
Past Chair

Preface

This book is about getting things done. It is for leaders that want to get results, for participants that don't like to waste time, and facilitators that want to meet leaders' and participants' needs. It is a guide to effective action in school districts, agencies, companies, organizations, and communities by using consensus decision making.

I wanted to publish a different book—something like the "Seven Easy Steps to Solving Complex Social Problems." How pleasing it would be to equip school administrators, public officials, teachers, managers, and other leaders with a formula for resolving difficult dilemmas such as graduating all school students with high test scores, maintaining service levels without raising taxes, decongesting highway commutes, curbing violence in neighborhoods, resolving land use disputes, eliminating homelessness, turning around rural economies, eliminating mercury in lake fish, caring for our elders, and other pending issues.

However, with a growing urgency to work out solutions to complex problems and no miracle cures in sight, time has come to resort to powerful old remedies. It is time to solve problems by cooperative means—to amass the views, concerns, passion, intelligence, resources, and power of affected individuals and organizations and tackle messy problems that cannot be addressed by one person, function, organization, community, or jurisdiction.

Even hard realists endorse collaborative decision making as the best hope for sound solutions. At the 1995 Annual Meeting of the American Association of School Administrators, Sorenson delivered a no-nonsense paper offering considerations for "avoiding disaster while sharing decision making." At the end, however, he concluded that "considerable risks for stakeholders notwithstanding, collaboration; bold support from school boards, central office administrators and parents; and open communication about the important business of education, hold the best hope to improve our public schools in a way that is supported by all those who value education. One must believe that people of goodwill, working for the common good, will make good decisions"(1).

Collaborative problem solving is a return to the core principles and practices of democracy that many communities and nations have practiced for several centuries.

For philosopher John Dewey, a true democracy requires three "faiths"; faith in our common human nature and the abilities of every individual; faith in the collective intelligence; and faith in citizen initiative to associate and address causes as needed. The tradition of collective problem solving is still evolving but has come a long way. These clues to consensus shed light on the do's and don'ts of effective consensus building based on the consensus experiences in the past few decades.

The central clue is this: Successful decision making takes more than the "right" technique or charismatic facilitator. A similar conclusion emerges from a recent study of shared decision making in school, *Creating a Level Playing Field* (2). According to Bauer, "assembling a larger group or a more diverse group is not sufficient . . . In fact, viewing shared decision making solely in those terms seems unlikely to shift power or equalize voice, a point consistently made by those who argue that restructuring alone is not sufficient to change schools and the districts must take steps to 'reculture'"(3).

The same is true for any community or organization. Lasting decisions require cultural and political will. To achieve such outcomes, consensus decision making efforts need to be wisely positioned and conducted by three key players—*sponsors*, *participants*, and *facilitators*.

- *Sponsors* who link consensus processes to mainstream decision making or operations,
- *Facilitators* who design and deliver a fair, rigorous forum for shaping common will, and
- *Participants* who engineer solutions that will be supported by diverse stakeholders.

Each player is vital to constructive consensus building.

A GUIDE TO THE GUIDE

This book is for those who are considering or committed to sponsoring, facilitating, or participating in consensus-based problem solving. It will give you an insider view of how consensus *actually* happens as opposed to how it *should* happen based on the experience of sponsors, facilitators, and participants in numerous consensus efforts over the past decades. It will pass on many veterans' insights about the rewards, realities, and requirements of making effective decisions collectively. Each chapter is designed to make sense on its own. Please consult the book in the order that meets your needs.

Chapter 1 overviews the consensus basics including definitions, trends, pitfalls, comparisons to other forms of decision making, and reasons it ought to be a preferred option for decision-makers. Chapter 2 features the benefits and results of consensus building. Chapter 3 describes the dynamics of consensus politics. According to past process participants, the informal activity backstage is often more influential than the formal process occurring at the table.

The last three chapters share specific clues for setting up and conducting effective, productive, consensual problem solving. Chapter 5 is a guide for sponsors, the organizations, and leaders that call the process to order. Chapter 4 advises process facilitators on the pressure points of navigating the dialogue. Chapter 7 describes ways that participants can enhance and influence consensus solutions.

MAKING OF THE BOOK

These clues to consensus do not prescribe a new process theory. They offer nuts and bolts advice for structuring group problem solving. The advice derives from four sources of knowledge:

- The collective genius of community leaders, administrators, public officials, and process participants that shared their problem-solving trials, triumphs, and tips
- Formal research in consensus building
- Active professional interchange with other facilitators
- My three decades of experience as a facilitator and educator

The result is a pragmatic blend of formal knowledge and field wisdom. I explain a little more about each of the sources.

Lessons from Local Laboratories

Very *particular* experiences tend to reveal *universal* realities. Hence, the very particular and real experiences of diverse groups are the heart and soul of the book's consensus descriptions and prescriptions. The clues derive from the pioneering, critical thinking, risk taking, and hard work of these consensus builders. The people, examples, and direct quotes in the chapters are from real life laboratories and eyewitness accounts. Fables and folklore are disclosed as such. Specific names, dates, places, and projects are omitted to assure confidentiality. Stories that have been published are cited in the chapter endnotes. Most of the examples take place within the American democratic stage but, with a little translation, should apply to human communities worldwide.

Peer Interchange

This book also conveys the expertise of numerous consensus facilitators. As a founding member of the International Association of Facilitators, I have been the grateful recipient of continuous education at the feet of my peers. The expertise shared through association journals, conferences, and informal exchange has always contributed significantly to my work and writing. The field of facilitation may be new, but consensus practitioners have accumulated decades of valuable on-the-ground knowledge.

Formal Research

The work of selected historical and contemporary process scientists helped crystallize many problem-solving encounters into useful lessons for future consensus builders. Therefore, these clues to consensus build upon time-tested concepts about democratic discourse, mechanisms of civil society, community development, and sociology, political science, and conflict resolution.

My own academic research about the feasibility of genuine collaboration in high-conflict settings is a foundation to the insider view of consensus. I interviewed 35 people that struggled to resolve environmental issues dilemmas in intense multiyear processes. Their candid comments are featured prominently throughout the book. I am grateful to all the people who let me intrude on their lives in the course of my inquiry.

Professional Experience

Many of the observations, findings, conclusions, and recommendations are based on lessons from hundreds of problem-solving meetings I have known and loved. I have specialized in facilitating group decision making, strategic planning, policy consensus building, and community development for 28 years. From small towns in North Dakota to the United States Congress, I have had the privilege of assisting with a variety of issues that could only be solved with the help of multiple organizations, constituencies, and jurisdictions.

I hope the experiments and expertise of numerous process pioneers will convince you to use consensus building as a regular leadership tool for enhancing daily operations and future directions in your community or organization.

NOTES

1. Sorenson, L. D. (1995, February, 10–13). *Site-based management: Avoiding disaster while sharing decision making.* Paper presented at the annual meeting of the American Association of School Administrators, New Orleans, LA.

2. Bauer, S. (1997, March 24–28). *Creating a level playing field: Structuring shared decision making to promote authentic dialogue.* Paper presented at the annual meeting of the American Educational Research Association, Chicago.

3. Fullan, M. (1993). *Change forces: Probing the depths of educational reform.* London: Falmer Press; Elmore, R. (1995). Structural reform in educational practice. *Educational Researcher, 29* (9), 23–26; Wonycott, K. A., & Bogotoch, I. (1997). Restructuring: Assumptions, beliefs, and values underlying processes of restructuring. *Journal of School Leadership, 7* (1), 27–49.

Chapter One

Consensus Basics

The decisions arrived at through consensus or participative decision making are not only better than the initial judgment of the decision-maker but are also frequently more correct than the decisions of any of the members of the group—a phenomenon which may be called "synergy."

—Donald Piper,
"Decision Making: Decisions Made by Individuals vs.
Those Made by Group Consensus or Participation,"
Educational Administration Quarterly, 1974

Consensus building is an unregulated field. Universally recognized codes, procedures, and rulebooks do not exist. Someday we may have consensus equivalent to the Generally Accepted Accounting Principles, Robert's Rules of Order, or precedent law. For now, the first step in any collaboration effort is creating consensus about consensus. I start there as well. This chapter discloses my understanding of the consensus "basics," including the following aspects:

- Definition: What makes consensus consensus?
- Assumptions: How does consensus building differ from other kinds of decision making?
- Trends: What role has it played in the education, private, public, and nonprofit sectors?
- Case for consensus: Why is consensus a sensible first choice for getting things done?
- Pitfalls: What are some major lessons learned about applying consensus to real life?

THE DEFINITION: DEMYSTIFYING CONSENSUS

Much unnecessary energy has been drained over "correct" consensus definitions. Group decision-making efforts define "true consensus" in a wide variety of ways.

Even the repertoire of *published* definitions is endless and ongoing. In one agency planning process it was " an agreement to agree for a period of time." A community-based council defined consensus as "a group decision-making process in which all present must agree unanimously with the action taken." A school district operates shared decision-making practices using "sufficient consensus." The understanding is that "after real dialogue about a particular issues had taken place and everyone had been given legitimate opportunity to state his/her case and be listened to, if a small number of people were not in agreement, such disagreement could not hold up the vast majority taking action." Other sample definitions from school, companies, communities, and organizations are listed in table 1.0.

Table 1.0.   Representative Consensus Definitions

Consensus is being 70 percent comfortable and 100 percent committed.
                                                              —*Anonymous Source*

Consensus is a general agreement or accord, or with the sense of the group. Consensus is often considered unattainable because it is mistakenly seen as complete agreement or unanimity. In fact, consensus is simply an agreement to move in a common direction for a certain period of time.
                                                           —*A State Agency Definition*

Consensus is something we can live with. . . .
        —*A Working Definition of an Environmental Conflict Resolution Process*

Consensus, as I define it, is not the same thing as unanimity. Rather, it is a state of affairs where communications have been sufficiently open and the group climate has been sufficiently supportive to make everyone in the group feel that he has had his fair chance to influence the decision. Someone then tests for the "sense of the meeting," carefully avoiding formal procedures, such as voting.

If there is a clear alternative that most members subscribe to, and if those who oppose it feel they have had their chance to influence the decision, then a consensus exists. Operationally it would be defined by the fact that those members who would not take the majority alternative nevertheless understand it clearly and are prepared to support it. It is a psychological state that might be described as follows:

> I understand what most of you would like to do. I personally would not do that, but I feel that you understand what my alternative would be. I have had sufficient opportunity to sway you to my point of view but clearly have not been able to do so. Therefore, I will gladly go along with what most of you wish to do.

In order to achieve such a condition, time must be allowed by the group for all members to state their opposition and to state it fully enough to get the feeling that others really do understand them. This condition is essential if they are later to free themselves of preoccupation with the idea that they could have gotten their point of view across if others had only understood what they really had in mind. Only by careful listening to the opposition can such feelings be forestalled and effective group decisions reached.

—Edgar Schein, Process Consulting

Consensus means to agree on [whatever] for a specific period of time. It does not require unanimous agreement, but everyone should be able to live with [whatever] even though they are not 100 percent for it.

—A Nonprofit Agency Definition

Consensus is a decision-making process in which all parties involved explicitly agree to the final decision. It does not mean that all are completely satisfied with the final outcome, but that the decision is acceptable to all because no one feels that their vital interests or values are violated by the decisions made.

—A State Agency Definition

Consensus requires unity in the essence of a decision. A consensus decision is something you can support or are willing to let go forward.

—Caroline Estes

Consensus means all concerns are resolved.

—Anonymous Source

Consensus is the convergence of the common sense of the total group.

—Technologies of Participation, ICA

A consensus is an agreement to implement management decisions on the part of all members.

—Richard Wynn and Charles Guditus

Consensus means that everyone agrees with the decision.

—Johnson and Johnson, Joining Together: Group Theory and Group Skills

Consensus is more commonly defined as a collective opinion arrived at by a group of individuals working together under conditions that permit communications to be sufficiently supportive—for everyone in the group to feel that he has had a fair chance to influence the decision. When a decision is made by consensus, all members understand the decision and are prepared to support it.

—Johnson and Johnson, Joining Together: Group Theory and Group Skills

Consensus exists when participants whose support is needed to implement a decision, agree with the decision and express a commitment to support its implementation.

—Harrison and Killion

Sufficient Consensus: "after real dialogue about a particular issues had taken place and everyone had been given legitimate opportunity to state his/her case and be listened to, if a small number of people were not in agreement, such disagreement could not hold up the vast majority taking action."

—Bellevue School District, Bellevue, Washington

"It is easier to find enthusiasts for the consensus method than it is to pin down exactly how it works," according to *Governing* magazine reporter Ehrenhalt (1). This phenomenon is evident in a comparison and critique of collaborative groups in natural resources that the author, Dr. Kenney of the University of Colorado School of Law, entitled "Arguing About Consensus" (2).

According to Webster's dictionary, consensus is "an opinion held by all or most" or "general agreement." Purists point out that only unanimous consent qualifies as authentic consensus. I side with practitioners who follow a looser definition such as the one I have been using:

> Consensus building is a process for making agreements that are supported by all or most of the affected and/or involved members. It takes place in a family, gathering, organization, community, nation, alliance, partnership, or any other group where two or more persons seek common understanding about a given situation and/or mutually beneficial responses to that situation.

Parameters for forming and formalizing consensus must be customized to match the culture, norms, and needs of each group and engagement. Using the lessons learned from interactions in our close relationships, sports teams, project teams, camps, disasters, and other group encounters is a good start to defining consensus game rules. Each of us has gained some knowledge about consensus benefits, costs, and methods from life experience.

For many, collaborative decision making is a commonsense approach to working effectively. For example, Superintendent Jim Fox of Austin, Texas, considers shared decision making inherent to good leadership: "I really don't envision site-based management as being anything other than good management. . . . It's like Coca-Cola. Somebody comes up with a theme, and they pass some legislation, but really, if I hire top-notch principals, I expect them to manage by involving the parents, the students, and the staff (3)."

The universality of the consensus experience is aptly clear in this anecdote from Professor David Ostermeier of the University of Tennessee. He highlighted one person that stood out in his evaluative research sponsored by the Fish and Wildlife Services Department of the United States Forest Service. He was unusually comfortable with the collaborative work. When asked about his ease with consensus building, he beamed as he explained that he was "well trained." He grew up in a home with five sisters and one bathroom.

Always define consensus at the starting line of a process. The task of finding agreement is complex enough without an added battle over what is "true consensus." Once you are outside the jurisdiction of the legal code, parliamentary process, labor relations procedures (or dictatorships), the rules and roles of decision making are what you make them.

I use the term "consensus" interchangeably with other similar concepts such as collaboration, cooperation, group decision making, democratic approach, search for common ground, participation, working together, shared decision making, participative planning, mediation, negotiation, team problem solving, participatory management, and reconciliation. All these concepts share two things—they imply a collaborative mode of interaction and require customized procedures.

In this book, the term "consensus building" applies to any process that produces one or more of the following *results* including:

- Building *shared awareness* among stakeholders regarding situations affecting them.
- Producing *mutually meaningful analysis* to inform decision making.
- Making *mutually satisfying agreements* to resolve issues or work together.
- Initiating *collective action.*
- Developing formal or informal *working alliances.*

THE ASSUMPTIONS: CONTRASTING CONSENSUS WITH OTHER FORMS OF INTERACTION

Consensus is one of many methods for "getting along" together. The Thomas–Kilmann Conflict Mode Model (4) offers an excellent map for comparing consensus-based interaction with various other ways in which humans deal with each other (see figure 1.0). The model has also been used to analyze individual styles related to conflict management. Perhaps you have already encountered this useful tool.

In a nonjudgmental manner, the Thomas matrix sorts every type of human interaction according to the degree of cooperativeness and assertiveness exhibited by interacting players.

Cooperativeness refers to the degree to which a participant actively listens, hears, respects, and considers the contributions of other players.

Assertiveness refers to the degree to which a participant advocates his or her own views and interests.

Avoidance, accommodation, competition, compromise, and collaboration are five major ways to address conflict. The framework implies there is a time and a place for every kind of interaction. To confirm this implication, table 1.1 summarizes 28 chief executive officers' suggestions for when to use each of the five interaction approaches (4).

Here is a brief overview that points out the differences in assumptions and applications between each of the primary modes of interaction—1) avoiding, 2) accommodating, 3) competing, and 4) compromising and collaborating.

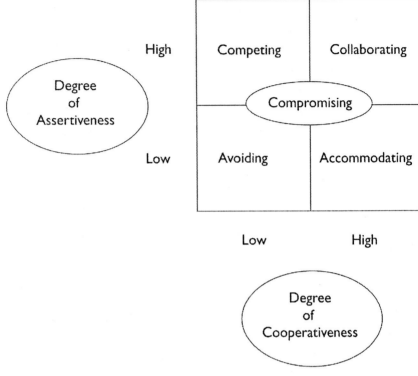

Figure 1.0. The Thomas–Kilmann Conflict Mode Model

Table 1.1. Matching Conflict Handling Modes to Situations

As reported by 28 chief executives

Avoiding

1. When an issue is trivial, or more important issues are pressing
2. When you perceive no chance of satisfying your concerns
3. When potential disruption outweighs the benefits of resolution
4. To let people cool down and regain perspective
5. When gathering information supersedes immediate decision
6. When others can resolve the conflict more effectively
7. When issues seem tangential or symptomatic of other issues

Competing

1. When quick, decisive action is vital (e.g., emergencies)
2. On important issues where unpopular actions need implementing—e.g., cost cutting, enforcing unpopular rules, discipline

3. On issues vital to company welfare when you know you're right
4. Against people who take advantage of noncompetitive behavior

Accommodating

1. When you find you are wrong—to allow a better position to be heard, to learn, and to show your reasonableness
2. When issues are more important to others than to yourself—to satisfy others and maintain cooperation
3. To build social credits for later issues
4. To minimize loss when you are outmatched and losing
5. When harmony and stability are especially important
6. To allow subordinates to develop by learning from mistakes

Compromising

1. When goals are important, but not worth the effort or potential disruption of more assertive modes
2. When opponents with equal power are committed to mutually exclusive goals
3. To achieve temporary settlements to complex issues
4. To arrive at expedient solutions under time pressure
5. As a backup when collaboration or competition is unsuccessful

Collaborating

1. To find an integrative solution when both sets of concerns are too important to be compromised
2. When your objective is to learn
3. To merge insights from people with different perspectives
4. To gain commitment by incorporating concerns into a consensus
5. To work through feelings that have interfered with a relationship

SOURCE: Thomas (1977: 487). © 1977 *Academy of Management Review*. Reprinted with permission of the *Academy of Management Review*.

The Avoidance Approach: Let's Keep Our Truths to Ourselves

The Avoidance Mode is the result of players opting for the least cooperative and least assertive approach. I became very familiar with the "live and let live" avoidance format living in the midwestern area of the U.S.A. It is a culture that is rooted in Scandinavian, Protestant, and/or farm traditions that favor minimal intrusive human interaction. Controversial issues are surfaced sparingly and sensitively. If confrontation does occur, it is so subtle that a nonnative can easily miss an opportunity for healthy conflict. Humorist Howard Mohr's book *How to Talk Minnesotan* (5), warns outsiders to beware when a Minnesotan responds with the phrase "that's interesting." These are fighting words that signal deep disapproval with a situation or opinion.

It is not healthy to deny or escape conflicts on a regular basis, but picking your battles and letting some things go is a valid strategy in some situations. The chief executive officers in the Thomas study (4) reported choosing the avoidance options when an issue is trivial, or more important issues are pressing; when there is little chance of satisfying your concerns; when potential disruption outweighs the benefits of resolution; when it is wise to let people cool down and regain perspective; when gathering information supersedes immediate decision; when others can resolve the conflict more effectively or when issues seem tangential or symptomatic of other issues (see table 1.1) (4). I found the Avoidance Mode to be an essential strategy for raising teenagers. Parents would go insane if they confronted all their children's missteps during their teenage years and other steep learning curves.

Avoidance is no doubt a diminishing alternative on a crowding planet. It is nearly impossible to keep our issues confined to ourselves. In a radio interview, author and *New York Times* journalist Thomas Friedman likened world citizenship to being a member of a large family living in a small home. No matter where in the house you go, you cannot escape the heated conversation going on around the dinner table. The intensifying interrelatedness of our issues and lives make it more and more difficult to practice a laissez faire approach in hopes that issues will just go away.

The Accommodating Approach: Let's Go with Your Truth

The Accommodating Mode involves a high degree of cooperativeness and requires minimal assertiveness on the part of one or all players. It applies to situations where people choose to go along with others' choices and suggestions. Leaders recommended using the accommodating option when "you recognize that you don't have a good answer and it is better to let other voices be heard, when you need to save your social capital for other matters or when unity is critical" (see table 1.1 for details) (4).

Occasional accommodating by group members is useful. A mutually beneficial package of outcomes can be crafted within a reasonable time frame, if everyone exhibits reasonable give and take in deliberations. Picking a fight over every aspect of a complex issue can hinder or even prevent resolution. On the other hand, "selling out" to other interests is never preferred or popular. Individuals or interest groups should not disempower themselves by making a habit of deferring decisions to others.

The Competing Approach: Let's Determine
Whose Truth Is the "Real" Truth

The Competitive Mode entails minimal cooperativeness and high assertiveness on the part of interacting parties. Debates, war, disputes, protests, litigation, grievances, and other adversarial methods of interaction are examples of the competing mode in action. History-long and worldwide, it is the most familiar and institutionalized process for working things out.

In *The Argument Culture*, author Deborah Tannen (6), shows how the Western culture is rooted in the competitive form of conflict interaction. Contemporary society encourages people to approach interaction in an adversarial frame of mind. The assumption is that opposition is the best way to get anything done. There seems to be a subconscious conviction that issues have not received proper attention until we have fought about them. Tannen counters that, saying, "We have to find metaphors other than sports and war . . . [and that] smashing heads does not open minds" (7).

The competing mode involves "turf soldiers" (8). Each side believes they have the correct answer or solution. Various "absolutes" try to establish themselves as "the truth." The goal is to win over another and prevail as the dominant "rightness." If that is not possible, the best alternative is compromise—to get as much of their truth accepted and implemented as possible. Parties are expected to convince, co-opt, control, convert, and even use violence in order to win. Those with the most staying power become the victors. These days the victors are often the financially endowed parties. In fact, veterans of public issues problem solving suggest that the Golden Rule no longer means, "Do unto others as you would like them to do unto you." In light of the current power realities, the operating Golden Rule is "those who have the gold make the rules."

The competing approach is the inevitable alternative when unilateral winning is a stakeholder's sole goal. There will always be those who feel more knowledgeable and wiser than others and have the wherewithal to enforce their will. They consider it their duty to help bring others to the light and have little incentive to respect others' insights and ideas except as clues for customizing further persuasion. The search for consensus solutions becomes extremely labor-intensive if most players prefer the competing approach.

The competitive mode is the best approach when emergencies or crises require fast response. Leaders tend to choose a competing mode of intervention when (table 1.1) including "quick, decisive action is vital" in emergencies or when implementing unpopular actions such as cost cutting, enforcing new rules, or preventing other from taking abusive action (4).

The Compromising Approach: Let's Use Some of Everyone's Truth

In the middle of all the modes is compromise, sometimes known as the "fastest way to get to a result neither side wants." A compromise solution is pieced together by combining elements of several competing alternatives.

A popular compromise tactic is to grant each player a part of his or her wish. The disadvantage of "splitting the difference" or "meeting halfway" is conveyed well by a well-known story about two sisters fighting over the last orange in their pantry. They resolved the conflict using a fair, equitable, and sensible compromise: They cut the orange in half. One sister immediately peeled and ate her half of the orange, savoring the delicious taste and thinking how much better it would have been to eat a full orange. Her sister rushed to the kitchen, carved out the inside of the fruit, grated the rind, and blended it into her cake batter. Both got 50 percent of what they wanted. However, if they had taken some time to share their stakes, hopes, and needs for the orange, both would have secured 100 percent of their wishes. The story could have had a "win-win" ending with each sister scoring all of the inside or outside of the orange.

Another compromise tactic is to find a common interest within a diverse group. This alternative is often known as the quest for the "lowest common denominator." The expediency and dissatisfaction of this approach is illustrated in this story about a youth group planning their Saturday night outing. They chose their activity based on a poll of the teens' top 10 choices. The matching activity was everyone's fourth or fifth choice. So instead of movies, video arcade, and concert and other top candidates, the group opted to go bowling. Saturday night came and nobody showed up.

Compromises have their faults but they are better than continued conflict. Compromising can be a useful default position when other approaches have been tried and failed; when confrontation can no longer be *avoided; collaboration* has been dismissed at the start; *competing* achieved an impasse; and no one volunteered to *accommodate*. Compromise enables short-term truces, ceasefires, remedies, and forward movement when diversity is too deep to bridge. People can go on with their lives leaving the door open for future problem solving.

The Collaborating Approach: Let's Negotiate the Truths That Need to Guide Our Action

A *collaborative mode* is achieved when all players in an interaction are optimally both cooperative and assertive. It is the approach often referred to as the search for "win/win" solutions or discovering "common ground." This collaborative path is simple to understand but not easy to achieve. Organizational executives report using collaborative problem solving when they wish to find an integrative solution; when participating parties' concerns are too important to be compromised; when one's objective is to learn; when there is a need to merge insights from people with different perspectives; when they must gain commitment; or work through feelings that have interfered with a relationship" (table 1.1) (4).

The Collaborative Mode is fundamentally different from the other four modes in two ways: an assumption that diverse "truths" are all right and the decentralized role of the neutral party or "peacekeeper." I explain these in more detail in the following paragraphs.

Assumption of Diverse "Truths"

The presupposition at the heart of collaborative discourse is radically different from the presuppositions of the other four modes. Avoiding, accommodating, competing, and compromising acknowledge and even tolerate others' truths, but the presupposition is that one's own truth is the best or most correct. Collaboration implies an assumption that players respect everyone's truth as equally valid. The goal, therefore, is not to convert others but figure out what collective truths—facts, logic, values, criteria, etc.—need to guide collective action. The underlying questions in collaboration are the following:

- What do we do about an issue or situation when everyone is right?
- Given we all have valid beliefs based on unique life experiences, what do we do together regarding a given dilemma or common need?

Admitting and assuming the " rightness" of everyone's truth becomes progressively more difficult when conflicting parties have fundamentally different core values about a problem as in the cases of developing a districtwide health curriculum or deciding how much logging will be allowed near a community landscape.

Decentralizing the "Peacekeeper" Responsibility

Now let's look at another dimension that distinguishes collaboration from other interactive modes. In avoiding, accommodating, competing, and compromising, opposing players rely heavily on a neutral third party when they are a part of the process. A middle person is primarily responsible for paying attention to the whole situation and forging a settlement between conflicting interests. The participating parties are free to advocate for their position. In collaboration, participants share the role of the middle person. The interacting players are asked to do more than promote their view. Everyone is charged to find ways to address the whole set of interrelated problems. Consensus participants have two jobs—*advocating* for one's position *and* serving as *ambassadors* in the search for mutually accepted solutions. If a facilitator is present, he or she structures and guides the conversation but success depends on participants cooperating as neutral, objective, third party peacekeepers. Chapters three and six relay the actual activities, politics, and challenges participants encounter in performing this dual role.

The power of collaboration derives from adding *new agents* into the problem-solving task. Collaborative problem solving catalyzes more forces to address a problem than the historical two and three agent problem-solving alternatives: War, intimidation, and conquest are usually *two-agent constructs*. Two parties battle each other until one side dies, is humiliated, or concedes.

Conventional conflict resolution processes graduated to a *three-agent construct*: Litigation, arbitration, dispute resolution, negotiation, mediation, and other refereed processes were a major step up from historical alternatives. They involve two adversarial entities and one neutral entity. The role of the adversary is to advocate relentlessly for one position. The role of the neutral party is to find and finesse ways to maximize gains, implement justice, reduce harm, end the fight, and/or allow the adversaries to move on peacefully.

Collaboration is a *multiple-agent formula.* Two or more agents with diverse stakes and desires for resolving the matter at hand work together to identify differences and craft mutually agreeable solutions. The role of a neutral party is to provide a safe forum and technical assistance for a self-directed pursuit of consensus answers.

Collaboration is powerful but difficult to orchestrate. If it were easy, consensus problem solving would have replaced war long ago. In the following excerpt, Superintendent Raymond Poulin describes the "turbulence" to be expected before harvesting the results of shared decision making:

> Moving from top-down management practices to site-based management and shared decision making is disorienting and confusing. Throughout the maturing process, mistakes will be made by all those involved. Tripping over one's own feet will not be unusual. As a result of this confusion, everyone will learn to communicate with each other and hopefully become what Roland Barth calls a "community of learners." This effort to change will test the most dedicated and most supportive. But, by staying the course, those involved, and those being served, will be recipients of the rewards put forth.
>
> One way to help alleviate the confusion and frustration is to have staff members involved in retreats and in workshops that cause them to look at themselves and those around them. This process will create challenging interactions which may lead to better understanding of all those involved. But this will only occur after some turbulence and readjustments. To truly grow into shared decision making, you must find your way up a rocky and creviced slope. Courage, stamina, and determination are a prerequisite to getting where you are going (9).

Despite the challenges of taking the cooperative route, numerous leaders and groups attest to positive results achieved through building and implementing decisions cooperatively. Table 1.2 lists some books that feature success stories about consensual agreements and action in the education, community, public, and private sectors. Here is an account of a school district transformation that reflects the spirits and simplicity of many other similar consensus successes:

In a few districts, site-based management and shared decision making have become a way of life. In some cases, a participatory approach was driven by the vision of a particular administrator. Bjorum documented the experience of such a district in a study entitled *Listening for Voices: A Leader in Action* (10). The superintendent of this 2,420-pupil district in an outer-ring suburb was an entrepreneur by nature who was convinced that "innovation was the only way to accomplish new agendas in public education and

Table 1.2. Some of Many Books Featuring Collaborative Action Success Stories

Education and Public Sector

1. Twelve Roles of Facilitators for School
   Bruce Williams
2. Focused Conversations for Schools
   Jo Nelson
3. Government Works: Profiles of People Making a Difference
   James Troxel
4. Reinventing Government: How the Entrepreneurial Spirit Is Transforming the
   Public Sector, from School House to Statehouse, City Hall to the Pentagon
   David Osborne and Ted Gaebler
5. Managing Change: A Guide to Producing Change from Within
   Sandra Hale and Mary Williams
6. Citizens' Jury: Effective Public Participation
   Jefferson Center for New Democratic Processes

Private Sector

7. Participation Works: Business Cases from Around the World
   James Troxel
8. Reinventing the Corporation: Transforming Your Job and Your Company for the
   New Information Society
   John Naisbitt and Patricia Aburdene
9. In Search of Excellence: Lessons from America's Best Run Companies
   Tom Peters and Robert Waterman
10. The Power of Open Book Management: Releasing the True Potential of People's Minds, Hearts and Hands
    John Schuster, Jill Carpenter, and Patricia Kane

Community/Cross Sector

11. The Quickening of America
    Frances Moore Lappe and Paul Martin DuBois
12. Citizen Wetland Initiatives: Stories from the Great Lakes
    W. Czwiekel
13. Beyond Prince and Merchant: Citizen Participation and the Rise of Civil Society
    John Burbidge
14. Villages
    Richard Critchfield

[this would] heavily rely on teacher improvement, team building, and staff development. For these he needed a culture that expects innovation (10).

In 1983 he sponsored a "well-strategized annual retreat" that was held far from the district, involved 30 percent of the district staff, and was funded as a district-level staff development activity. Here Bjorum describes the superintendent's goals for the first retreat:

> At the retreat, he will charge participants to think big, think long, and think again, resulting in a new program, a new approach, or a new way of delivering an existing program. The retreat must be away from the harried existence and pressures of the district routine, happen just before the school year commences, and be in a place that offers a time for reflection and bold thoughts.
>
> He needs to give those in attendance a future orientation to the problems and potential solutions that form the focus of the retreat, so he invites a futurist and one or two other contributing presenters. The results of the retreat will be taken back to the remainder of the staff to be further refined and implemented as soon as feasible. Hence was born the concept of Gainey [named after the retreat facility].

The annual Gainey retreat tradition is now two decades old and continues to be an anchor for the district's participative management model.

Each year, retreats are attended by a rotating group of 30 to 50 participants representing a microcosm of the school district including teachers selected to represent their buildings, 4 school board members, a curriculum director, support staff representatives, 6 administrators, and the superintendent. Highly qualified futurists and facilitators are retained to lead the retreat. All district personnel participate in preplanning and input to bring to Gainey and participate in implementing the consensus directions developed at each retreat.

Each retreat produces a product, including the following that are described in Bjorum's research (10):

- *Strong communication loops:* The first retreat addressed the need for increased communication and initiated the principal's advisory council that "presents a forum for staff to raise up issues of concern for discussion (10)." In subsequent Gainey retreats, a principal/parent council was added to further enhance district communication.
- *Technology-enhanced curriculum:* Another retreat initiated a business-education partnership with a computer company to demonstrate the effectiveness of integrating technology into instruction for grades 6–8 math and science curriculum. The effort led to innovative district restructuring, individualized courses, and content-stabilized district operating costs. The district's pioneering made business-partnerships common around the state.
- *Delegating instruction budgeting to teachers*: A "unique decentralized teacher empowerment concept" gives teams of teachers authority to decide staffing and budget allocations including outsourcing instructional services.

• *Year-round schooling opportunity:* Students have an option to attend summer school in order to graduate early and teachers can earn up to 25 percent more in salary by teaching during the summer months.

Among the many products, the major one is the process. It has transferred the superintendent's habit of constant innovation, strategic thinking, and rigorous implementation to the entire district staff, school board members, and parents. The Gainey retreat "de-emphasizes traditional school district organizational structure that leads to power along lines of authority." Communication and decision making occur across functions and all levels of participants are given the opportunity to exert leadership and influence.

All district members share a "cultural expectation of change." At the high school, middle school, and elementary levels, everyone is ready to help implement Gainey plans in vertical teams made up of board members, administrators, teachers, and staff. In addition to the direct teamwork on official plans, the Gainey experience has influenced indirect and informal patterns of collaboration. "Some teachers report formations of coalitions as a result of their team building experiences at Gainey." Here is the superintendent's view of what it means to practice shared innovation:

> At first, I was always looking for the grand plan. So, when it comes to my leadership, I have no grand plan, no great expectations. But my vision isn't about product, it's about process. I'm a concept person; I let the teachers manage the detail. But I do have to know and understand ideas long before I bring it to Gainey, and then I let the specialists do the details to accomplish it.

The superintendent is proud of the Gainey accomplishments and always gives credit where credit is due — to the district personnel that create and implement operating innovations. According to Bjorum, the superintendent has a "long view and patience . . . Even before one retreat is over, he is planning for the next one."

Critics have questioned the proliferation of happy endings of consensus stories such as this district culture change. They wonder why case studies in collaboration tend not to discuss failures. Consultant Roger Harrison expressed this sentiment when reviewing the victories cited in Spencer's *Winning Through Participation* (11). He criticized the book as unrealistic and concluded that "writers seem afraid to acknowledge any limitations to their methods. They feel that if they do, they will lose credibility" (12). He argued that readers would be more receptive if consultants shared the darker sides of group dynamics. In his experience, this is not a "world where the clash of selfish interests is overcome by elegant design and skillful facilitation" (12).

Common ground consultant Weisbord responded to Harrison's book review by reporting his own research findings (13). He claimed that collaborative processes are revolutionary departures from the traditional forms of conflict resolution because they force all participants to see their own views in the context of all the other related issues, trends, histories, and options. Weisbord acknowledges the existence of "shadow forces," but explains that they do not dominate in unifying consensus processes:

> I share the general realism about power dynamics and the darker forces in groups. However, these dynamics tend not to dominate conferences structured toward the discovery of common ground . . . Getting people outside themselves somehow brings them together . . . In shifting from problem solving to systems improving, from rehashing past relationships to future focus, there is something new here under the sun . . . It's not that dysfunctional "shadow" dynamics don't exist anymore. People don't magically get better than they already are. Rather—I believe—we tune in on different parts of the collective unconscious. (13)

Consensus building is a joint search for commonality and therefore tends to achieve positive results on a regular basis. Furthermore, collectively developed decisions and solutions add up to more than the sum of diverse suggestions. Consensus approaches often generate undiscovered and wiser solutions due to the synergy achieved by engaging multiple dreams, insights, resolves, resources, and perspectives in dialogue. The "mechanics" of fostering group synergy are a part of the discussion of consensus benefits in chapter 2.

THE TRENDS: A RELUCTANTLY
PRACTICED POPULAR THEORY

How are consensus-based approaches being adopted and utilized in societal discourse? I find that consensus building is a popular theory that is practiced cautiously and even reluctantly. It tends not to be a preferred method of decision making despite the urgings of countless management guides and gurus.

Over a decade ago, former U.S. Labor Secretary, Professor Robert Reich, made a compelling case for what he called "collective entrepreneurship" (14) in his 1987 *Harvard Business Review* article about staying competitive in the global market. He called for a radical shift from valuing and celebrating individual heroes to championing the power of team action. According to Reich, "Most Americans would prefer to think that Lee Iacocca single-handedly saved Chrysler from bankruptcy than to accept the real story—a large team of people with diverse backgrounds and interests joined together to rescue the ailing company."

Collective entrepreneurship has yet to sink in and take root. Yes, we strive for teamwork. Yes, no one objects to cooperation. And yes, groups have been awarded the Nobel Peace Prize including the International Campaign to Ban Land Mines (1997), Doctors Without Borders (1999), various United Nations agencies, the Institute for International Law 1904, the International Committee of the Red Cross

(1963), Amnesty International (1969), the Friends Service Committee (The Quakers) (1947), and the U.S. Soldier. Yes, even Superman, Batman, and other invincible cartoon heroes have teamed as the "Super Heroes" after finding the world too tough to face unilaterally. However, collective entrepreneurship is still minimally celebrated, trusted, or fostered in the day-to-day operations of schools, districts, organizations, communities, and nations.

I explain more about the two consensus trends I declared upfront: 1) theories about consensus-based decision making are in good currency, but 2) application of consensus lags behind.

Consensus Trend 1: Theories have attained the status of mainstream management science

The heightened awareness and acceptance of consensus theory is an important trend. Pieces of literature related to consensus building, participation, teamwork, organization development, and other forms of "win-win" approaches have taken on a life of its own in the past few decades. Consensus practices have been the cornerstone of communities throughout history and around the world including many native cultures, cooperatives, labor unions, and religious groups, such as the Quakers. In the Quakers' way, the natural approach for reaching a decision is discussing it at length until public opinion has settled overwhelmingly in one direction.

More recently, *Getting to Yes,* by Roger Fisher and William Ury (15) popularized the notion of interest-based negotiation and collaborative modes of settling disagreements. It is a standard text in many fields. Since then, many authors and consultants have directed leadership attention to collaborative, systemic, or participative ways that assure customer/employee friendly operations. Others have stressed the need for holistic change management and "win-win" solutions.

The public affairs media have duly noted the blossoming demand for effective, collaborative multiparty decision making. In 1997, *Governing* magazine acknowledged the new "Consensus Industry" (16) and a rapid rise in government's demand for outside experts to "broker hot community disputes" and avoid the biggest danger of "a lowest common denominator decision that leaves major differences unresolved " (16). The following excerpt is a good summary of how a longstanding profession is getting renewed recognition:

A different scenario is playing out these days for quite a few governments fed up with [unmanageable local conflict] situations. They are calling in facilitators. Sometimes known as mediators. Or negotiators. Or consensus builders. The jumble of jargon notwithstanding, a growing number of legislative bodies are seeking outside specialists to sit down with opposing parties and get them to come to some form of agreement on a complex issue . . . The concept of facilitation is not new. It does seem, however, to be newly appreciated. (16)

The acknowledgment and encouragement consensus approaches spread beyond the public sphere. Collaborative methods of management have been packaged and promoted in every field of practice for several decades. I review the representative consensus-related themes, practices, theories, and models in the education, public, nonprofit, and business sectors in the following pages.

The Education Sector

While the education sector is often considered a subset of the public sphere, I give it a separate spotlight. Leading and managing educational enterprises is a cross-sectoral effort. Private organizations began the first schools and continue to be strong players in the continuum of "cradle to tomb" education. State education institutions have to work with the public, private, and civic sectors in order to gain the resources and support for students, programs, and facilities.

As with other sectors, consensus-based tools or programs have been introduced at all levels of the education enterprise—classrooms, boardrooms, playgrounds, staff development forums, community relations, school improvement planning, special issues resolutions, and more. Oversight agencies or certification requirements have prescribed models and programs. Local collaborative efforts have been initiated by teachers, administrators, and school board members as a way to maintain education excellence in times of ever-shrinking resources, weakening family support, increasing diversity of the student backgrounds, economic status, language, needs, etc., and a widening gap in community attention and investment on children.

Site Level Trends: At the school site level, school administrators have been encouraged to involve teachers, school personnel, students, and community in all dimensions of operating the school's mission through approaches such as Site-Based Management, Shared Decision Making, Schools Run with Teams, and Educational Effectiveness Program. The premise has been that educational opportunities for children are most improved when decision making involves those most directly affected by operating decisions. Attention to team management of schools has intensified with the growth of the charter school and now, the small school movements. However, funding has tended to remain centralized, posing significant limits to true autonomy of site-directed management and thus, decreasing the scope of influence in directing local resources.

Raymond Pulin, superintendent of schools in Maine, is a strong advocate of site-based management and consensus decision making as the engine for making the necessary changes to truly educate children for life. Current governance models do not cut it as is evident by the fact that "despite a decade of focus on school reform and calls for organizational restructuring of schools, they have continued, for the most part, to look as they have always looked" (9):

Today's schools are faced with meeting the needs of all students, not just the needs of regular students but all special students everywhere along the spectrum. Twenty-five years ago schools dealt with only a select group of students, yet today we are expected to see the needs of each student. This change in society's expectations of education was not met with a change in how schools operated. Most school systems continue to function as they have for the last fifty to one hundred years.

To meet today's needs educators must begin to work with smaller communities of people as well as larger communities of people. The shaping of our schools will require that the smaller community of people, those within the educational organization, make every effort to work with the larger community of people, those not directly related to the educational system. Everyone must have the opportunity to participate. Direct input into how schools are run must be accepted by those responsible for the education of our youth. The practice of isolating "outsiders" from the school system is no longer a style that will be tolerated.

Many of the original governance structures that were adopted by schools came from those practiced in private business. The "top down" hierarchical format was the means. How could those accustomed to a management position understand the complexities of any operation? Certainly no one outside the organization could possibly understand its inner workings. Given that many schools reflected this attitude, one might better understand why students, parents, and those out in the community were intimidated by teachers and principals.

It is my contention that unless we adopt some of the strategies of site-based management and consensus decision making, we will continue in the downward spiral plaguing many schools in our country. Until we begin modeling our schools after the democratic principles we espouse, our course will be charted in the wrong direction.

Not even a majority of educators use site-based management and shared decision making but when used, collaborative decision making has played a role in helping schools deal with the ever-increasing challenges of delivering quality education: Inter- and intradepartmental teamwork or learning communities have been launched to make comprehensive curriculum changes, integrating and connecting learning outcomes across grade levels and within subjects.

Under the banner of "Outcome-Based Education" or the recent push to steer student achievement using schoolwide date and performance measures, school personnel have used consensus-based planning to analyze, streamline, and integrate efforts to bend negative trends in student achievement.

Leadership training for superintendents, principals, specialists, and others has included many of the private sector models that stress systemic and team-based methods for managing the school enterprise including situational leadership, leading meetings of all types—PTO, site councils, committees, faculty, school board, administrative groups, unions—and facilitating school change. Regular strategic and operational planning involving key school stakeholders has become an ongoing part of many school operations.

Students have become more involved in school governance through direct representation on site councils, staff meetings, or student council. Students have been asked to participate in issues through special focus groups and forums.

The increasing diversity of school populations and issues has called for consensus-based conflict resolution training for all members of the school community—administrators, teachers, human resources personnel, and even students. In many buildings, peer mediation programs are ongoing mechanisms for fostering cooperation in playgrounds, clubs, and sports.

District Level Trends: By choice or necessity, collaborative approaches have become a tool for cooperation on problem solving and resource sharing between buildings and districts. Consensus decision making has been a necessity for school consolidations but in many situations, entities have opted for integrative operations. For example, the High Success Consortium, Inc. is a partnership of 20 suburban/rural school districts dedicated to continuously improving schools to accomplish significant result with kids by sharing staff development, best practices, and other support resources.

Some superintendents credit wholesale district transformation to participative decision making and systemwide teamwork. In New Jersey, Henderson was hired to deal with a district in crisis (17):

> In an affluent district, seven grievance cases were pending and the board of education had rejected the annual school budget for the first time in twenty years. A general culture of contentiousness enveloped the district, fueled by the statewide discontent with public education. A community cabal had formed to watchdog the board meetings and deploy protests, letters-to-the-editor campaigns, etc. to bash the district budget and leaders. At his first school board meeting, the staff staged a demonstration "decrying the superintendent's selection due to its lack of staff involvement . . . a continued manifestation of the board's and district administration's lack of regard for staff input."
>
> After careful climate assessment, the superintendent initiated multiple consensus mechanisms to turn the system around. Twenty-five percent of the district staff attended training in communication and decision making, the Curriculum Advisory Council was steered to its original purpose of curriculum leadership vs. a grievance forum, and a quality circles model was instituted as a base for participative management at all levels. Within two years results were evident: all grievances were settled out of court, other disagreements were settled at frontline levels of the school, much-needed staff interdisciplinary team leader positions were budgeted and staffed, a follow-up culture assessment indicated improved attitudes across the board, and the first-ever, district-wide staff and board picnic was held; other "unprecedented" staff and volunteer recognition programs were established and entrenched, conflicts were addressed, and a new three-year contract between the Board of Education and the district was successfully negotiated (17).

School–Community Trends: Using site-based management, parent-community organizations, and other means, stakeholders in the community are being asked to help educate the emerging generations of citizens. Parents, employers, civic leaders, homeowners, etc., are increasingly involved with new funding referendums or levies, school planning, evaluation and review activities, and ad hoc issues, such as linking early childhood education to schooling, reducing school violence, and even school budget cutting advice. Also, closer partnerships with parents, other educational institutions, human services organizations, community civic groups, employers, and other community resources become essential given the decrease in funds and increases in educational challenges.

Collaboration with the community is no longer an option. With the enormous changes in the economy, population, families, poverty, and other societal trends that affect youth, the physical, intellectual, emotional, psychological, and spiritual needs of students are growing and diversifying every day. Educators are struggling to fulfill nonacademic needs of the students in the midst of tightening accountability for academic performance. If the whole village created the social changes it should all the more help educate its children.

The late Ernest Boyer was a prominent advocate for accelerating collaborative action between education and all other sectors in order to create a true "community of learning." Many schools have tailored their schools based on his model for a "basic school" where the home is considered the child's first and most important classroom. He urged leaders to make education everyone's business:

> We hear a lot of talk these days about how schools have failed. But what's becoming clear is that it's not the school that's failed, it's the partnership that's failed, with schools taking on responsibilities that families and communities and religious institutions once assumed . . . Former Secretary of Education, Terrel Bell summarized the problem this way: "A lot of schools advocate parent involvement, but they don't have a specific program to get it done . . . The message is clear. It is simply impossible to have an island of excellence in a sea of community indifference, and when parents become school partners, the results can be consequential and enduring (18).

Classroom-Level Trends: The push for action or experiential learning has triggered a rise in skill building and methods for interactive learning models. In schools using block scheduling, teachers are looking for ways to engage students for up to two-hour class periods. Lecturing is not an option for the whole time. While these settings do not require consensus decisions, classrooms can benefit from the collaborative methods used to create consensus—focused conversation, brainstorming, group inquiry, cooperative group learning, etc.

Systemwide Trends: As with public sector governance, consensus processes have played a role in developing state, regional, or national education policies and programs.

I have been involved in facilitating departmental restructuring, developing graduation standards, connecting high school graduation standards to college admission requirements, instituting systemwide staff development programs, and forming multicultural education strategies. Lawmakers and educators understand that very little can be decided or implemented without involving all those that have or will have a stake in education decisions and their consequences.

The Public Sector

The public sector is obligated to stay on the edge of the consensus industry. In nations with democracies, government organizations are expected and/or mandated to apply the principles of broad-based citizen participation processes in designing and delivering public policies and services. As social issues and interest groups grow in diversity and complexity, being inclusive and responsive to all citizens is an accelerating challenge.

Many governments have involved employees and constituencies to find creative ways to meet rising demand in the face of diminishing resources. In *Government Works,* James Troxel (19) features national and international case studies about civic engagement in community development and governance. The movement to reassess and reform government operations was popularized by authors Osborne and Gaebler in *Reinventing Government* (20). The book is filled with numerous examples of "transforming the public sector by releasing the entrepreneurial spirit from schoolhouse to statehouse, city hall to the Pentagon" (20). In the 1980s, the state of Minnesota launched a long-term effort to improve the quantity, quality, and cost-effectiveness of state government by using the minds and energy of those inside the system. The lessons were documented in the book, *Managing Change: A Guide to Producing Change from Within* (21).

Facilitating public problem solving among multiple public constituencies and stakeholders is emerging as a core role of public leaders. In recognition of this trend, MIT and Harvard joined forces over 20 years ago in a long-standing program to apply consensus to public issues. At that time, their newsletter, *Consensus: Helping Public Officials Resolve Stubborn Policy Disputes* (22) reached 35,000 federal, state, and municipal officials quarterly. Proactively or reactively, governmental organizations' role as hosts of cross-sector consensus problem solving will increase through the years.

Several states have official consensus councils that support collaborative decision making in the legislative and executive branches. Two organizations have efforts underway to create a U.S. Consensus Council. The National Consensus Initiative and Search for Common Ground are working to submit a bill that would set up a council to "serve Congress in promoting consensus-based solutions to important legislative policy issues by convening diverse stakeholders to address complex issues" (23).

The Not-for-Profit Sector

The not-for-profit, voluntary, community, civil society, or citizen sector has always operated collectively and continues to look for ways to do it better. It is a diverse sector that includes book clubs, philanthropic foundations, neighborhood protests, special interest groups, car pools, political campaigns, formal and informal civic groups, and much more. All these groups are jointly owned and operated by a group of individuals who choose to associate together to promote a common belief, cause, or interest. They cannot survive without the strong consent of their founders, funders, staff, clients, volunteers, members, and support constituencies. Consensus-based decision making and team approaches are standard operating procedure for boards of directors' meetings, fundraising committees, program planning, outreach events, strategic planning, interorganizational partnership development, and many other ongoing dimensions of nonprofit management.

The nongovernmental organizations (NGOs) have grown to be a powerful force in global development. This fast-growing sector is often referred to as the "civil society." Global and local community development agencies, faith-based services, charities, environmental groups, human rights organizations, children's charities, civic organizations, foundations, women's groups, and many other NGOs are collectively watchdogging and influencing the evolution of a peaceful and prosperous existence for world citizens.

I became personally active in the civil society networks at a 1998 international conference sponsored by the Institute of Cultural Affairs International (a worldwide community development organization) titled "The Rise of Civil Society in the 21st Century." According to Goran Hyden, Professor of Political Science at the University of Florida and a consultant to numerous nongovernmental organizations connected to the United Nations, the concept of civil society is not new but has undergone resurgence in the last two decades (24). According to Michael Bratton of Michigan State University, civil society is a sphere of social interaction between the household and the state that is manifested in norms of community cooperation, structures of voluntary association, and networks of public communication. In addition to his definition, I also appreciate and adopt his cautions:

> First we should not romanticize civil society as an arena in which conflicts are always peacefully resolved. The propensity to do this is evident in the writings of many "communitarians." . . . Second, while civil society stands apart from the State, it cannot exist without it . . . . Third, civil society is usually seen as opposing the state, but can also legitimize and support the political status quo (25).

Civil society is not utopia but the growing global excitement about building civil society was evident in the conference and my conference session on "Facilitating Civil Society." The 30 participants represented multiple continents, sectors, cultures, and social roles but shared 2 things—a passion for pursuing "civil society " and an unclear working definition of "civil society." We decided to start by defining the concept. Our answer to the question "what is civil society?" turned out to be a set of five characteristics:

- Active and inclusive participation
- Respect for differences
- Access and opportunity to meet basic needs
- Empowered community and broad-based responsibility and
- Ongoing creative process

We defined civil society as cultural values and practices rather than economic or political structures. Consensus-based philosophies and practices are clearly a pillar of the nonprofit sector. At the heart of the civil society movement is the conviction that the nongovernmental sector needs to lead in the building of participative, respectful, responsible, and communicative communities that meet the basic needs of all.

The Private Sector

In the business world, the pressure for creating market-responsive companies has focused attention on participative management practices. Mergers, acquisitions, and right sizing have called for more effective ways to harness the synergies within and between business units. While many useful consensus models have been introduced in the business sector, substantive investment in collective entrepreneurship has not been deep or widespread. Here is Robert Reich's observation (14) about how the breadth of collaborative management theory contrasts with the depth of adoption:

> You can find inspirational management texts designed to tell top executives how to be kinder to employees, treat them with respect, listen to them, and make them feel appreciated. By reading these books, executives can learn how to search for excellence, create excellence, achieve excellence, or become impassioned about excellence—preferably within one minute. Managers are supposed to walk around, touch employees, get directly involved, effervesce with praise and encouragement, stage celebrations, and indulge in hoopla.
>
> Some of this is sound; some of it is hogwash. But most of it, even the best, is superficial. Lacking any real context, unattached to any larger understanding or why relationships between managers and workers matter, the prescriptions often remain shallow and are treated as such (14).

In some corners, bona fide work force participation has been recognized as the best route to internal alignment, efficiency, quality, and flexibility needed to operate profitably. Such operations understand that incentives founded solely on money and firings usually achieve only partial productivity gains. Several decades ago, the human resources texts alleged people use only about 10 percent of their creativity and abilities at work. I would be surprised if it has changed significantly. Untapped human energy and ingenuity can do wonders for organization effectiveness if leaders invest real trust, time, attention, and resources to enhance workplace-wide consensus and teamwork.

Semco of Brazil is one company that owes its success to a strong participative management foundation. According to President Ricardo Semler, the simple secret is to "treat the eight hundred employees as adults" (26). This means adhering to three company values—democracy, profit sharing, and information—in every aspect of the operation. Most everyone, including factory workers, gets a monthly salary and sets their own working hours, understands the full status of the company, and votes on important company matters. There is a very pragmatic logic behind Semler's enlightened management model. Here he explains why respectful and collegial relationships are the way to sustainable business success:

> Think about it. Outside the factory, workers are men and women who elect governments, serve in the army, lead community projects, raise and educate families, and make decisions every day about the future. Friends solicit their advice. Salespeople court them. Children and grandchildren look up to them for their wisdom and experience. But the moment they walk into the factory, the company transforms them into adolescents. They have to wear badges and name tags, arrive at a certain time, stand in line to punch a clock or eat their lunch, get permission to go to the bathroom, give lengthy explanations every time they are five minutes late, and follow instructions without asking a lot of questions. [Treating employees as adults entails being] very rigorous about the numbers. Because we are so strict about our financial controls we can be lax about everything else. The employees are expected to make the connection between productivity and profit.

Consensus Trend 2: The Reluctant Adoption of Consensus Practices

Consensus alternatives, methods, and theories are broadly espoused but tend not to be preferred or primary approaches in day-to-day management and governance. If they had, facilitators would be as busy as lawyers. In the 1970s, the idea of letting everyone in on important decisions was a novel but minority pursuit among leaders and communities.

At the turn of the millennium, consensus-based decision making has been used more but sporadically. Usually, desperation prompts consensus processes. Facilitators are called in when the best-laid plans for down-sizing, mergers, or reorganization encounter implementation chaos; when community disputes polarize into a debilitating stalemate; when decreasing budgets force people to work smarter; when teams encounter dysfunction; when organizations discover they cannot succeed alone; or when other group breakdowns occur.

Consensus processes are not speedy enough to be a first resort for decision-makers. Those who promote collaborative problem solving and planning must swim against the stream of fast-service, one-stop, quick-return social expectations. Four major forces discourage leaders from investing in consensus-based processes: a) *Short-range* time frames for action accountability; b) comfort with organizational *silos,* c) reacting to *symptoms* versus seeking systemic solutions; and d) a historical tendency to consider *self-interest* disconnected from the good of the whole.

Short Time Frames: Long-Term Solutions Discouraged by Short-Term Performance Evaluation

Every school, organization, or community is under the gun to show results yesterday. Preferred planning horizons for strategic planning are shrinking from 5 to 10 years to 3 to 5 years. Powers-that-be get impatient if planning sessions don't identify 6-month deliverables and 90-day paybacks. Incentive systems do not reward investing in holistic, longer-term solutions that would be lasting and powerful.

Frances Moore Lappe addressed this problem at the 1989 Kyoto Conference on the Environment (27). She used succinct images to convey the dangers of political and economic time being "out of sync" with real-world time and needs:

> We face (but choose not to confront) a profound disjuncture between political time, economic time, and ecological time. The time frame in which our decision-makers must answer to us, the citizenry—political time is out of sync with the real world time it takes to reap the consequences of today's choices:
>
> *Political time* is as short as two to six years between elections. *Economic time* can be much longer. For example, obtaining approval for a new city transit system might be a two-year task in political time. Bringing the system from concept to reality could easily take twenty years.
>
> *Economic time* can be as long as it takes human beings to evolve and contribute to society. The cost of investment in one young person's development could include nutritional support for the infant, preschool education, tutoring and a subsidized summer job for the teenager, and education at a public university. All this comes to about $40,000 in today's [1989] dollars). The invisible net social gain from such an investment is suggested by a negative $40,000 price tag: the cost of keeping one inmate imprisoned for just seventeen months.
>
> *Economic time* can also be much shorter than political time. It can be as short as a company's fiscal quarter to which many executive fates are bound. It could be as brief as the split second it takes a speculator to shift from dollar to yen in international currency markets. Such foreshortened timeframes play havoc with economic planning (27).

The pressure for short-term results permeates our lives. Administrators and teachers are charged to reverse student failure rates among students within several semesters. We expect individuals to lose 40 pounds in a week and organizations to diversify their revenue bases in a year or less. Leaders who want to seek collaborative means to systemic improvements must do so while delivering short-term wins. If not, they can be fired, demoted, replaced, or recalled.

"Silo Operations": Pursuing Holistic Solutions That Compete with the Power of the Parts

Consensus solutions made by multiple groups and organizations usually lead to another collaborative challenge: developing seamless, cross-functional, schoolwide, intraorganizational, and interdepartmental ways of operating. When cross-functional solutions are attempted, many discover that the incredible momentum and power of our operating compartments can exert strong undertows to stifle change.

"Silo" management has become a popular metaphor and usual suspect for causing organizational dysfunction even for those of us who have barely seen the towering grain-storage silos on a farm. At a recent planning session, a colleague with rural roots explained that the difficulty of "breaking down silos" is a very appropriate way to characterize the challenge of uniting strong and comfortable spheres of operation. "You have no idea how hard it is to tear down a grain silo! Once my father, I, and a whole host of neighboring farmers pounded, pulled, ripped, and hacked for days to dismantle one silo. They are tough!"

Breaking down barriers between several bureaucracies, operating systems, cultures, or budgets is as tough as razing real silos. Attitudinal resistance can inhibit cooperation but usually the root challenge is structural. Rewiring longstanding incentives, patterns, expectations, norms, and infrastructure takes enormous creativity and persistence. This challenge is aptly conveyed in a hopeful quip from one Nobel-prize physicist: "We can lick gravity, but the paperwork would be overwhelming."

Working through administrative jungles and paperwork to forge new partnerships may not sound glamorous or heroic, but I believe it is a key leadership competency for contemporary social pioneers. Even the most harmonious of alliances require the changing of habits such as adopting new ways of doing things, accepting extra giving and taking, and plenty of dancing with the devil in the details.

Despite the pitfalls, these interorganizational partnerships are being launched and lived. For example, the staff of a state education agency found ways to remove the "silos" that inhibit real service to school districts. Three hundred education department staff decided that the best way to serve diverse school districts was to reformat the agency into five centers, each dedicated to assist a unique set of schools. Resources and functions were realigned to maximize the ability to customize agency assistance to the needs of diverse districts. Programmatic support personnel from academic, nutrition, social support, special education, and other specialty "silos" were distributed into each center. Some traditional support functions such as fiscal, human resources, and property management were shared. It was tough to connect the new model to the existing federal, state, and local requirements for funding and administration. The bureaucratic hurdles were enough to tempt even the most passionate staff to return to the comfort and controls of segmented service departments.

Symptom Stewardship: The Squeaky Wheel Still Gets the Organizational Grease

Another force that discourages systemic, collaborative solutions is the sheer number of issues that show up on a leadership agenda. The quantity and pace of complex issues increases each year. As social interactions intensify and more special interest groups bring new and old inequities to mainstream attention, the symptoms of systemic difficulties will grow and multiply. When crisis strikes or problem symptoms flare up, action and resources tend to be mobilized to attack the immediate and presenting problem for a brief period of time.

For example, the recent statistics about escalating teen drinking, suicides, and depression have put pressure to treat the symptom by increasing access to rehabilitation programs and mental health care resources. The depression pandemic among our children is one big indicator of deep community deficiencies in loving and caring for our young. Our attention should focus on broad-based community remedies as opposed to simply fixing problematic teenage behaviors.

Traditional forums for dealing with public decisions are overwhelmed if not paralyzed by the massive barrage of symptoms vying for attention. Many decision-makers and decision-making bodies admit being caught in an endless traffic jam. As the issue agenda grows, officials are forced to spend less and less time thinking through each problem. There are simply too many complex matters that require in-depth analysis but aren't getting it. Locally, regionally, nationally, and internationally, we are flying by the seat of our pants because the existing organizational or democratic mechanisms do not allow enough time to think through every issue. From national governments to local governments, elected officials have less and less time to analyze the systemic roots of issues because of the sheer volume of perplexing and intricate agenda items.

At the Bipartisan Congressional Retreat several years ago, members pondered ways to improve the environment within Congress. The central challenge was the lack of time and forums for going beyond presenting problems and surface symptoms to deeply understand and analyze the issues before voting on bills that affect millions of people.

Similarly, state legislatures are swamped with an unending input of issues demanding careful attention. An incredible variety of weighty matters are considered at a legislative floor session or committee agenda on any given day. One morning I tracked the following agenda items before the Minnesota legislature: selling wine in grocery stores, revamping the education finance formula, banning underage tattoos, addressing growing homelessness, and restricting commercial feedlots.

At the local level, city council meetings, legislative sessions, and board meetings are lasting longer and longer into the night and still fall short of the time needed to hear all the stakeholders, understand the issue, analyze options, and make decisions.

The issues overload breeds inaction until a visible symptom causes a public outcry, and the system is forced to rally to create a Band-Aid solution. I have no magic answer for breaking out of this vicious cycle of responding to symptoms and/or addressing issues discretely. However, consensus forums can increase organizational and community capacity to address issues thoughtfully, systemically, and effectively. Immediacies will continue to drive organizational and societal attention until we develop the leadership and/or public patience and will to invest in consensual analysis of systemic dreams and challenges.

Self-Interest Disconnect: Inability to Recognize Individual Interests Bound to the Collective Good

The ageless deterrent to collaboration is self-preservation. Voluntary sharing of power and resources to achieve mutually agreed-to goals goes against historical norms. From bullies on the school playground to geopolitical conquest, individuals and groups throughout history have tended to vie for domination versus collaboration.

Bill Ury, coauthor of *Getting To Yes*, discussed this phenomenon informally at a 1998 Renewing Democracy Conference. His research of historical patterns in human conflict has led him to wonder whether we are trapped in the competitive mode forever. His study raises a sobering question: if the story of human community is a long saga of one group dominating another, is collaboration really possible? Addressing long-standing adversarial relationships such as those between religious groups, races, economic classes, and geographies raises agonizing questions about whether there are limits to peaceful coexistence. Can there ever be a collaborative way out of our famous stalemates, such as those in the Middle East or Ireland? Are we doomed to a debilitating polarization regarding issues such as reproductive rights, racial divides, labor-management schisms, and party politics? Is collaboration a false hope?

I have moments when I wonder if consensus building is worth the effort. The doubt intensifies after a long day of facilitating contentious issues or when a turnover in management wipes out years of investment in cooperative management practices. This sentiment is shared by my colleagues, as was evident in the professional comedy at a facilitator conference 10 years ago. When asked to reflect on their past year using titles of books, movies, or songs they could have written, participants suggested:

Seven Steps to Offensive Facilitation
Getting to Maybe

50 Ways to Undo Consensus
Farewell My Paradigm
The Empire Always Strikes Back

Humor is one way to embrace and maintain hope in the daily struggle to integrate clashing self-interests. Sociologist Alan Wolfe recommends not only accepting but also appreciating the phenomenon of individual difference. He points to the strong forces of *sociological exclusion* that underlie the external rhetoric of *democratic inclusion* in a community (28) and offers a refreshing reminder about the importance of having boundaries separating diverse identities and interests:

> Although they would seem to work to some degree at cross-purposes, both inclusive democracy and exclusive group centeredness are necessary for a rich but just social life. Without particular groups with sharply divided boundaries, life in modern society would be unbearable. We would be constant pawns in power struggles taking place over our heads. Our identity as residents of a particular place would have no currency in the face of national and international needs.
>
> In the absence of social boundaries, in short, we would never belong to anything with texture and character. Yet if the boundaries between particular groups are too rigid, we would have no general obligations . . . We would live together with people exactly like ourselves, unexposed to the challenges of strangers, the lure of cosmopolitanism, and the expansion of moral possibility that comes with responsiveness to the generalized other (28).

Frustrating as it is some days, consensus building is a forum for addressing boundary disputes through discourse rather than force; a place where stakeholders can sort out strategies for meshing individual needs and the common good. The goal of consensus is not sameness and loss of identity, importance, or uniqueness. Former Israeli leader Golda Meir put it this way: "Internationalism does not mean the end of individual nations. Orchestras don't mean the end of violins."

Consensus-building technology has come a long way but the successful use of consensual decision making will forever ebb and flow according to a fluctuating trust, belief, or reliance in collaboration. Collective entrepreneurship (14) doesn't get front-page billing but I believe consensus-based solutions are the secret behind successes that *do* make the headlines.

THE BENEFIT: A CASE FOR CONSENSUS

If consensus tools are not in your leadership tool kit, they should be. I give you three reasons why. The first reason is an ageless argument: 1) It is simply good business to include all relevant stakeholders in decisions that affect them. Choose participation before it chooses you. The second reason is inspired by future trends. 2) The urgency for cooperative solutions will only increase as intersections between people, organizations, and nations intensify. Looking out for the common good is in everyone's best interest. Finally, 3) collective decisions and actions generate new power for tackling old problems. It pays to adopt a consensus habit as early as possible not out of benevolence but because it is a smart alternative.

Reason 1: Choose Participation before It Chooses You

The most pragmatic reason to opt for consensus building is that it is inevitable. One way or another, people will shape the decisions and directions that affect them. If they are not in on the original planning or decision making, they will participate with their feet, money, time, complaints, sabotage, inertia, or rebellion. At some point, leadership time will have to be invested in employee involvement, citizen input, or stakeholder participation. The only choice that leaders make about participation is *when* stakeholders participate. Do you want to spend the time proactively building consensus or reactively fighting fires caused by minimal ownership, misunderstanding, or other unanticipated factors?

Every stakeholder group has some kind of power. Money may be a very potent influence, but everyone has ways to affect decisions. Interest groups have the power to stage disruptive protests, media campaigns, or lawsuits if they disagree with public decisions. Employees can impact directions through strikes, slowdowns, or sickouts. Constituency groups like senior citizens or hunting groups can supply or withhold a decisive voting blocks in elections. Consumers have the power to boycott products.

Sometimes stakeholder feedback is immediate. In other cases it has taken decades for the affected masses to influence the consensus about such things as expanding civil rights, conservation, or public smoking. People will find a way to "vote" in the courts, public bodies, and the marketplace even if they are not formally invited.

Through the school of hard knocks, more and more leaders understand the advantage of involving all stakeholders upfront on any collective ventures. One administrator offered this assessment:

People will get their two cents in one way or the other. What goes around comes around. If they are involved up front, they will do so when you are trying to get things going. I have never seen so many ways that individuals can slow down and even sabotage a project they don't understand or agree with. It is the end of management by memo or decrees. Consensus building is slow but a smart way to go.

Another executive put it bluntly: "In the good old days, a leader could simply decide, announce, and defend decisions. Now, in order to get things implemented, a leader must negotiate, agree, and implement action with groups of affected people."

If the *people*—citizens, "worker bees," parents, special interests, staff, donors, voters, residents, landowners, members, customers, students, constituencies—are instrumental to the end game, it is smart to have them play early in the game.

Throughout history, people have weighed in on decisions whether they were allowed to or not. Given this reality, sociologist Jurgen Habermas (29) encouraged leaders to utilize processes and power of "communicative action" in public forums as a primary strategy for steering social policy and change. Citizen activism is the linchpin for fundamental change. In the early 1980s, Habermas (29) predicted that if those in positions of power did not offer inclusive mechanisms for community decision making, the environmental, human rights, and other disestablishment movements would take the lead in challenging the democratic processes. This prediction is coming true across the world as we speak. The World Trade Organization (WTO) protests exemplify people demanding a voice. The WTO consists of self-appointed business leaders who chose not to include representatives from other economic stakeholders groups sectors around the decision table. Now, the human rights, environmental, and labor advocates have invited themselves to the table by showing up in mass to speak out against the exclusive process for identifying and addressing global economic priorities.

The evolution of America's constitution is a longstanding example of stakeholders participating without invitation. The nation is closer to living the ideals proclaimed in the founding documents due to persistent citizen activism. In the first American presidential election, only 4 percent of the population, the landowners, were eligible to vote. Tireless grassroots efforts expanded voting rights to black men in 1870 and women in 1920; outlawed literacy testing and other discriminatory voting practices in 1965.

These vivid and large-scale illustrations show that people have and will continue to participate through protests, marches, movements, campaigns, Internet action, and other grassroots efforts to shape consensus about social directions.

At the local school, district, organization, or community levels, leaders are acknowledging the power of early and inclusive participation by decision stakeholders. One state legislature has decided that after a long period of suspecting consensus processes to be largely a gimmick, it will use it as a primary way to identify public policy opinion in the initial stages of a policy dispute (1). According to Ehrenhalt of *Governing Magazine*, the current challenge is to "move consensus from being the last resort to being a first resort" (1). How are these consensus efforts different from the task forces, committees, panels, public forums, and commissions that have been appointed through the ages? This was precisely the question raised and answered by Alan Ehrenhalt in a recent *Governing* magazine article about the use of consensus in policy applications:

> At this point you may be wondering what the difference is between invoking a consensus process and appointing a blue-ribbon commission to solve the problem. A few decades ago in this country, we relied on commissions to solve a good many of our most perplexing problems at all levels of government. When schools didn't seem to be working properly, or the military needed reform, or there was too much waste in the bureaucracy, we appointed the best minds available, waited for their report, and then generally followed their advice. It didn't make problems disappear overnight, but most of the time it did some good.
>
> As you may have noticed, the commission approach hasn't worked so well lately. The president appoints a distinguished panel to look into Social Security, or violence, or race relations, or obscenity in the media, and they come out a few months later as bitterly divided as they went in. I think that is largely because the whole structure has changed . . . . It was assumed that prominent leaders "were above the battle and had no agenda other than the [common] interest." Most Americans believed middle-aged men sitting around a table knew what was best for everyone. We don't believe that anymore (1).

Consultant Marvin Weisbord has a similar conclusion. In his book *Discovering Common Ground*, he identifies a trend away from entrusting "experts or benign neutral leaders to solve problems *for* people and toward *everybody,* experts included, improving whole systems" (30). As the planet gets more crowded, we can or should expect more reliance on consensus work groups that come together to sort through diverse public needs and recommend practical ways to fashion public policies, services, or budgets.

Management by consensus is a matter of pragmatism versus altruism. Without the support of all stakeholders, solutions are more vulnerable to being derailed, deterred, or lack the resources for implementation. In the end, binding agreements and agendas developed by consensus are the ones that stick and get done. Broad-based participation in decisions concurs with the Total Quality Management principle advising us to "do it right the first time."

Reason 2: On a Finite Planet, Striving for the Collective Good Is in Everyone's Self-Interest

The second reason to adopt preemptive consensus building is our intensifying interdependence. In schools, organizations, and communities, collaborative and broad-based decision making is an opportunity to stop rearranging deck chairs on the *Titanic* and start investing time into finding systemic solutions.

Our interdependence is a powerful reality and opportunity. Messes of issues affect everyone. The pursuit of the common good is in everyone's best interest. I explain more about these two parts of the interdependence equation in the next several paragraphs.

Messes of Issues Affect Everyone

Most school, district, organization, community, and societal problems involve a "mess of interacting issues" (31). This reality hits home during long-term power outages, strikes by sanitation workers, transit system shutdowns, and major catastrophes. Similarly, our deep interdependence surfaces each time we struggle to increase education resources through levy or referendum, resolve zoning disputes, divert access to water from one river to several states or cities, face health insurance increases to cover emergency care for the uninsured, etc. Complicated, unstructured, and moving targets are becoming the norm. Our private matters are increasingly public business (and vice versa), yet we continue to address issues in silos and by symptom.

Education is a multiplex challenge that we still address harder but no smarter. From national politicians to building administrators, we fight dysfunctions separately and on multiple, parallel tracks. Inadequate school funding, low test scores, education standards, teacher salaries, large class sizes, increasing teachers of color, early childhood support, diversifying needs of urban student populations, students' readiness for K–12, student obesity, special education, student dropout rates, lack of basic skills among college freshmen, bilingual education, and other key issues take turns being the focal point depending on political priority of the day. I once facilitated a statewide meeting regarding graduation standards and discovered that the leaders of K–12 systems and higher education have rarely, if ever, met to discuss how graduation levels and issues mesh with the needs and standards of college entry.

As mentioned in the section on trends, school issues cannot be affected without fundamental changes in other aspects of a student's life. This eliminates very few stakeholders from the hot seat. Parents, relatives, employers, property taxpayers, daycare providers, civic institutions, and many others are needed to answer the bigger question posed by the intersecting issues and symptoms: "How do we prepare the emerging generation for adult life?" Radical changes in family life have forced schools to take on parental roles such as breakfasts, after-school care, homework assistance, psychological treatment, daycare for students with children, and much more. As one *Washington Post* reporter concluded, "It's not that our schools have failed. Our full-service kibbutzes have succeeded." U.S. Senator Sam Nunn observed the huge statistics of teen suicides, juvenile crime, children as a majority of the homeless population, youth runaways, etc., and concluded that human beings may soon be the first species that is unable to care for its young. The next chapter shares specific ways that education leaders are using multiple-stakeholder processes to make visible and systemic improvements in local or regional education and youth development.

An organizational example of a systemic problem that is treated symptomatically is "low productivity" in a workplace. When management is not getting eight hours of work for eight hours of pay (plus or minus an hour for shift changes, meals, and breaks) the problem is identified as employee attitude and the popular response is to tighten surveillance and institute new punitive measures. I've heard this knee-jerk strategy described as the "beatings will continue until morale improves" approach. Employee attitude can be an issue in its own right but more often than not, it is a valid symptom of multiple, interacting operational gaps. A consensus-based strategic planning process in one company revealed those gaps to include a system of outdated, uncoordinated, inadequate, or neglected management practices and organizational habits including the following elements:

• Minimal or even missing job orientation
• Subjective standards and requirements of each job
• Midnight shift scheduling on short notice that wreaks havoc on family life
• Inefficient matching of person power to jobs
• Lack of timely worker access to tools and equipment
• Unsafe and dangerous work practices to keep up with production quotas
• Union peer pressure to minimize effort to contract specifications
• Tradition of hard-hitting frontline supervision that fosters fear
• Workers unclear about the relationship or importance of their jobs to the operation
• Dirty and cold work environments
• Inconsistent standards and disciplinary actions between work sites

Even the most dedicated workers were forced to decrease their pace as they waited for parts, taught themselves their jobs, guessed work standards, or reacted to shortsighted work orders. Some employees did waste time intentionally, but the collective assessment revealed that productivity could be dramatically improved by instituting or upgrading missing management mechanisms, such as an automated work management system that programmed maintenance needs, documenting equipment histories and operation, expediting access to parts, standardizing company work standards through supervisory training, and implementing a month-in-advance shift schedule that would enable employees to plan their family weekends and lives in general.

At the community level, urban sprawl is begging for systemic attention. The haphazard and fast spread of the urban area to rural areas is threatening important air, water, and land resources; taxing municipal infrastructures; compounding traffic problems; and widening the gap between underresourced inner city communities and affluent suburban residential areas. Where do you start making a difference? We need to address the underlying root problems that feed the dilemma in a simultaneous and interactive manner. Some of the issues include minimal public transportation that restricts job and leisure mobility to those without automobiles; the desire and expectations for remote home sites with all the comforts of urban services; weak cooperation between municipalities and inadequate tax bases for developing parks, neighborhood centers, people-friendly urban environments, etc.

Seeing the Link between Collective Well-being and Self-interest

Interdependence is a fact of life around the world, at every level of society, but some communities are much farther along in acknowledging the direct link between self-interest and collective well-being. Here is a comparison of communities with and without a clear understanding of interrelatedness. It will explain why collaborative problem solving is still a tool of last resort in many places.

Small and isolated communities have internalized interdependence for a long time. These include historical pioneer settlements, remote rural villages, poor communities, pockets of ethnic groups in urban areas, island nations, religious groups, and other groups that have a common enemy, share scarce resources and/or engage in a mission that requires tight teamwork. Collaboration is a way of life in cultures that understand individual survival to be integrally linked to collective survival. Everyone and everything need each other.

For example, in Japan, 100 million people live in a small space. They would have only a day's supply of fuel left if an oil tanker does not sail into the harbor every 10 minutes. Tight teamwork, resource conservation, and good international relations are a part of the operating software. They have 3,000-year-old protocols for living together effectively including when and where to speak to guard each other's privacy on crowded trains, small homes, workplaces, and other dense living situations. For example, the underlying code of conduct is to first pay attention to the whole situation and then decide how you fit in or contribute. It is not altruism or naïve obedience. It is smart living and good business. Individuals fare best if each looks out for the good of the whole. Communities that understand the life and death nature of interrelatedness don't simply tolerate others, they cooperate and respect others and the group. I had the privilege of growing up in Japan. This may explain my foundational bias for collaboration.

Some communities and societies have been able to keep up the illusion of independence longer due to abundant resources, space, and open political processes. In these societies the metacode of conduct is reversed. People are encouraged to decide individual goals first and then look for ways to get them accomplished in the whole. For example, the United States was built on the principles of individual life, liberty, and the pursuit of happiness. No one was in charge and everyone was in charge. There was plenty of land and resources to go around. If you did not like what was happening around you, you could move west to the countryside, out to the suburbs, and onto other unsettled territory. These days, however, escaping to new and uncharted territories is getting difficult. There is community everywhere and all the land belongs to someone.

The expand-explore-and-exploit mantra has been a driving force in global development. Communities and nations that have acquired resources and power continue to operate in that paradigm. People who are victims of such development know that infinite growth is impossible on a finite planet. The old frontiers of land and sea are gone. The new frontier is no longer physical but social. The quicker we make the connection between self-interests and the common good, the better off we will be. Pioneering means turning our interdependent fate into meaningful destiny or face the consequences. Collaborative problem solving is a vessel for navigating that frontier. Teaching interdependence was the main reason one parent found a democratically run school for her children; a school where everyone from kindergarteners to school council members make decisions consensually. Learning collaborative life skills was a key to preparing her children for the future:

> For me, the consensual way of life is the most important part of this school. We live in a self-centered society. The preoccupation is with "what do I get out of this" or "what's good for me." This is not a healthy way of life. I want my children to live the benefits and acquire the life skills of looking out for the best interest of the whole community. It starts with learning "how to get everyone to go to a movie together."

Reason 3: Collaborative Action Generates Its Own New Power to Tackle Old Problems

How does a consensus approach to decision making produce long term, inter-silo strategies to address the problems and possibilities beneath the steady barrage of symptoms? A well-constructed collaborative decision-making forum aggregates individual or subgroup energy into collective power for change. The powerful forces of our interdependent self-interests are called to work by involving the expertise, infrastructure, resources, attention, passion, and support of a "whole system" of affected stakeholders, parties, interests, jurisdictions, territories, organizations, service areas, or scopes of responsibility. Author John Gardner alluded to this source of leadership power when he declared the ability to work across organizational and social boundaries as the most important skill for today and tomorrow's leaders (32).

Building consensus through shared awareness, mutually acceptable analysis, joint agreements, supported action, and working alliances releases at least five new bases of power including 1) the power of shared priority; 2) the power of aligned reasoning; 3) the power of common will; 4) the power of pooled resources; and 5) the power of joint ownership:

The Power of Shared Priority

Sometimes planning is referred to as attention management. Declaring something to be a priority is a foundational first step to any forward movement. A consensus process that begins by developing shared awareness of an issue enables a system of stakeholders to understand how a complex of issues affects everyone and what expected benefits or WIIFMs (what's-in-it-for-me) deserve to elevate problem resolution to collective priority status. Focused attention is the gateway to focusing formally disparate energies into a search for solutions.

The Power of Aligned Reasoning

Even after the mutually beneficial reasons to handle issues is established, efforts can be destroyed by one-sided or incomplete solutions based on narrow problem assessment. Therefore, a rigorous forum for analyzing and understanding the issues from everyone's perception of the facts, feelings, meanings, and proposals is the best way to avoid missing important elements and form a collective logic about what is going on with a given issue. As scientist, inventor, and social philosopher Charles F. Kettering reminds us: "A problem well-stated is half solved." Never underestimate the power of developing a collective logic to support needed solutions.

In a study of the accuracy of group decision making, Donald Piper found that a committee may indeed generate better solutions than individuals acting alone. In 1974, the *Educational Administration Quarterly* published the results of Donald Piper's scientific study of group versus individual decision making (33). The goal was to see which produced the more correct decisions—individuals acting alone or decisions made by group discussion and agreement (consensus) or by individuals using information and advice from others (participative decision making).

Eighty-two graduate students in education participated in a simulated decision-making exercise where they played the roles of astronauts who have crash landed on the moon and must rank in order of importance 15 items of equipment they might use to return to the mother ship. The correct rankings were provided for the test by the staff of the National Aeronautics and Space Administration Crew Equipment Research Department. The research participants ranked the items first as individuals and then in groups of three to five persons using consensus or participative decision making.

While the study was not intended to "settle the question of whether decisions should be made by consensus or by a designated decision-maker," (33) Piper does make conclusions that group decisions are most reliable:

> The results of this study do not provide definitive answers as to which model of decision making an organization should choose. However, they do suggest that if arriving at the most correct decisions is the primary goal, the involvement of several persons—whether it be through a consensus or a participative model—will provide better results than the "one-man-deciding-alone" model. Within the context of this study, and for the type of task represented by the "Moonshot" exercise, the following conclusions seem warranted.

Decisions made by a group discussion and agreement (consensus) or those made by individuals using information and advice from others (participative decision making) are more correct than decisions made by the same individuals acting alone. This conclusion applies whether the decision-maker initially has the knowledge to make the best decision or the worst decision of any member of his group.

The decisions arrived at through either of the two models are not only better than the initial judgment of the decision-maker but are also frequently more correct than the decision of *any* of the members of the group—a phenomenon which may be called "synergy."

I illustrate the power of aligned reasoning with a group process where the power was missing—the U.S.-led war on terror. Much has been said about the needs, benefits, and justifications for unilateral versus multilateral action. The United States requested nations to participate in multilateral agreements, actions, and alliances following a worldwide awareness of terrorist threat. Wouldn't the collective awareness of the crisis naturally lead to broad-based support? It didn't. I suspect the weakness of the international response can be attributed to the fact that the United States carried out the analysis step by itself. What would have happened if national representatives had gathered after 9/11 to examine the terrorist threat and jointly analyze the root problems and pressure point issues? Building a collective logic and strategy would have taken some time but I believe that a genuine international battle plan would have emerged. Multilateral endeavors begin with shared awareness and mutually acceptable analysis.

The Power of Common Will

It takes initiative and commitment to do anything. Strong resolve does not guarantee success, but it is a good indicator of good outcomes. Each time we take the time to forge groups from individual desires, we symbolize and demonstrate the profound connection between self-interest and the common good. Collective entrepreneurship benefits from the strong energy that self-interest brings to any endeavor.

Rosann Sidener was deeply impressed with the level of participant buy-in and "emotional investment" produced in the site-based management and shared decision-making (SBM/SDM) processes she studied in Dade County Public Schools (34):

> Respondents strongly identified with the SBM/SDM project at their school. They discovered the process for themselves because they were implementing a new concept and the district provided few guidelines. Many expressed a keen sense of ownership and even those who were not proponents of SBM/SDM had strong feelings about what they perceived to be the positive and negative outcomes. It was evident they had an emotional investment in the successes and failures of their shared decision making project. Participation in shared decision making was a powerful experience that molded the beliefs of those involved. The researcher was struck with the sense of frustration and loss that many respondents expressed over the decline of the program. This leads the researcher to believe that school-based management/shared decision-making has potential to generate lasting change. Participants truly felt accountable for the results of the project (34).

The Power of Pooled Resources

The test of all ideas and promises is in their implementation. This is a refrain throughout the book. Implementation is the process of mobilizing energy and resources to activate plans and decisions. Theodore Leavitt of *Inc.* magazine underscores the power of implementation:

> Creativity is thinking up new things . . . A powerful new idea can kick around unused in a company for years, not because its merits are not recognized, but because nobody has assumed responsibility for converting it from words into action. Ideas are useless unless used. The proof of their value is only in their implementation. (49)

The chances for optimal support are greater in broad-based consensus building than in any other form of decision making. This is a central observation and leadership implication of *Leadership for the Common Good: Tackling Public Problems in a Shared-Power World* (35). John Bryson and Barbara Crosby echo the need for organizations to share their information, ideas, resources, and therefore, their power in order to get things done. This call to share power is not out of charity but the reality that problems are too big for any one entity and can be solved by deploying the expertise and resources of multiple organizations. They describe how traditional and new forums, arenas, and courts must be used wisely to get input, shape recommendations, make agreements, evaluate decisions, and assure successful partnerships.

The Power of Joint Ownership

Consensus building generates a power that is impossible to gain any other way—the long-term and broad-based will to carry through with an initiative. Substantive and sustainable solutions take time and require ongoing nurture. Even the best strategies often come to an abrupt end with a leadership change. We don't have the resources to be constantly shifting direction. But how do we commit to strategies that last beyond one political administration, one leadership change, or one quarter? A collaborative problem-solving approach offers a chance to develop political consensus and broad-based issue ownership that can last years, decades, and even generations. A community in Finland offers a clue and a hope. They have worked for over 10 years to prepare to be a uranium disposal site. The nuclear material requires utmost care for hundreds of years, so the current citizens have developed a consensus about the care of the facility that will be honored by their children and grandchildren.

The link between ownership and long-term implementation of solutions was a focal point discovery in Debra Crump's extensive assessment of the site-based management and shared decision making in the Chicago public schools. The effort was initiated in response to issues of fiscal crisis, poor student performance, underserved minority students, and soaring rates of high school dropout in the 1970s. She found that the reform produced many visible results including 1) the fixing of a number of initial defects; 2) school councils proving their competence; 3) parents and community feeling ownership of their local schools; 4) schools maintaining substantial discretion over their budgets; 5) teachers able to draw on an array of excellent in-service programs; 7) local school councils finding high-quality help and advice; 8) ways of identifying and assisting poorly performing schools is under way; 9) a leaner and stronger central administration; 10) decreasing violence in and around schools, and 11) abundant signs of educational innovation and improved student learning abound, especially in elementary schools.

However, the most hopeful result that Crump noted was a community-wide will to sustain continuous and comprehensive improvement:

> Chicago school reform gained strength and penetrated deeply into the fabric of the city because it originated not as a narrowly targeted attempt to improve schooling, but as a broad-based movement. Its social movement origins spread "ownership" of reform among many groups; it helped define reform as an ongoing process rather than a quick fix. (36)

Since remedies to most complex problems require sustained effort, the ability to stay with an improvement process is perhaps the ultimate source of social power.

The reasons to adopt consensus as a primary leadership strategy seem compelling to me but I let the convictions and experiences of consensus practitioners continue to make the case for consensus in chapter 2. You will hear about additional and specific benefits of each of the consensus steps and/or power bases using illustrations from a variety of sectors and situations.

THE VULNERABILITIES: PROCESS SKEPTICISM AND PITFALLS

Consensus building is a live field for process experimentation. The consensus industry may be on the rise, but because problems are messy and unstructured, expectations and approaches about how to solve them are all over the board. Few familiar or formal processes are readily available for consensual problem solving. Meeting methods vary greatly and are often created by default versus design. Furthermore, despite the increasing complexity of problems, there is a growing demand for shorter meetings and less time available at existing forums.

Be suspicious of anyone who claims they have *the* right way to secure consensus. Attempts are underway to codify the consensus process, but the answers are not due any time soon. For example, the League of Cities and various consensus outreach organizations teamed up in recent years to create a consensus-based version of Robert's Rules (37). The goal is to have a guide to help local town boards, city councils, and other government bodies conduct deliberative forums and build binding public agreements based on consensus. In the early phases the manual was nicknamed "Roberta's Rules of Order." Organizations such as the National Coalition for Dialogue and Deliberation (NCDD), the Deliberative Democracy Consortium, Public Conversations Project, and other nonpartisan groups in the United States are dedicated to providing democratic tools to help people connect across divides, make good decisions, work cooperatively, and engage actively as citizens. Perhaps someday we will settle on universal game rules for consensus building, but for now use consensus manuals to develop rules that fit your decision-making needs.

Many have yet to buy into consensus and for valid reasons. Without a compelling personal experience of consensus rewards, reluctance to use collaborative methods is understandable. Twenty-five years ago, one such leader, the city manager of a northern Minnesota town, impressed upon me the dangers of assuming that consensus efforts would be successful. He listened patiently to my energetic pitch to conduct a grassroots town meeting. After a long, thoughtful silence, he declined the invitation and said quietly, "The last thing we need is one more false hope." This warning has stayed with me ever since. I have no desire to lead people on a wild goose chase. There is a time and a place for collaboration. It should certainly not be used if leaders do not value "committee" thinking, see process as a detriment to substance or believe their role is to be directive and decisive. Also, consensus participants need to be engaged carefully if people have developed a strong distrust of process due to many past efforts that did not go anywhere.

Despite the rise in the need for consensus-based problem solving, there is strong reluctance to use it. In fact, many of you may be ready to close this book saying "been there, done that" or "I'll never sponsor another consensus process if my life depends on it."

I don't blame you. You have probably been involved in one or more misengineered processes. I regularly run into people who have been burned, formed allergies to participatory process, fear creating chaos and false expectations, don't want to take time for games, consider "collective intelligence" an oxymoron, or are waiting to see proof that consensus is cost effective. If you consider yourself a consensus skeptic, this book may help you decide again whether to reconsider adding consensus tools to your leadership arsenal.

This final section of this chapter presents the pitfalls to consensus success. Specifically, I share common reasons for 1) what fuels consensus skepticism and 2) why some consensus processes fail to generate positive results.

Reasons for Consensus Skepticism

Nothing Good Ever Comes Out of a Committee

Many believe that process is a time-consuming way to get to the "lowest common denominator." If the group produces the lowest common denominator, whose is the highest? The implied message is that the speaker or a smaller group could identify better solutions than a large committee. If that is the case, they should go ahead and develop "high denominator" strategies and propose them to the affected parties. If the issue at hand does not need further information, input, or insights from others, there is no need to undertake a costly consensus activity. Nobody appreciates contributing to an effort that is seen as an inferior approach to decision making. If there is a faster formula for generating and implementing excellent solutions for a group dilemma, I recommend going with that route. Condemning the results of a good-faith effort as low-quality solutions reflects a competing mode mindset; that "my truths are superior to anyone else's."

The assumptions of collaboration underscored that consensus process should be used if the sponsors feel that finding and implementing good solutions requires ideas from all affected parties. The corresponding belief is that problem solutions generated by the group represent the "highest common good" because the solutions are the result of everyone's best thinking and a combination of many "ideal" options.

A recent consensus process shed some practical light on the value of group solutions. I was helping a management team of 21 people determine their annual business priorities. The group leader interrupted the goal's brainstorm with an observation that the goal is already clear. He felt further discussion would simply water the goal down. I apologized for not realizing that the destination was already determined and asked him to describe the goal. After recording it on paper, I checked with the group to see if there were any questions and whether they were ready to proceed to the next step of the planning process. Two hands went up. Each participant had a different impression of the existing goal. I wrote those up and three others raised their hand. Many goals later, we had 18 versions of a "highest common denominator" goal. It was clear that the group needed to negotiate the shared goal. Everyone experienced the same thing. Their individual input was great but the most valuable goal was the negotiated goal that would enable them to know which way to direct their attention, energies, and resources.

Process Delays Getting to the Point!

I have worked with a good share of clients who declare up front they are not "process" people. They like to get right to the point. When this substance versus process conviction surfaces in a discussion, my best argument is to compare the situation to the judicial process. If you tell me that "you are not a process person" or ask how a complex decision process can be shortened to a few hours, it is like asking a judge to conduct a trial with the opening and closing arguments, skipping "all the stuff" in between. Whenever I use this analogy, the reaction is the same: "Well you couldn't do that," they say. "How would you assure justice if all sides aren't presented and pondered?" I then rest my case for including ample time for airing all the views and analyzing solutions thoroughly.

Process is the way to secure binding public agreement or action. The task of public consensus building is to ensure "due process," not just process. Pay attention before bringing people together for a meeting. If there is another way to do what you need to do, do it. Every meeting or process makes demands on each participant's time, energy, and resources during and after the problem solving. The quest needs to be worth the investment.

Process determines substance. Also, process influences substance. The way in which you frame the questions and organize the discussion helps shape the answers that emerge. Agreement about how to approach a problem is essential. The insider accounts of actual processes in chapter 3 will show how participants take charge of process because they see its influence on the outcome.

Weakening a Directive Leadership Role

Consensus building can clash with traditional images about decision making and go against long-standing assumptions about how trustworthy decisions are made and executed. We have been trained to expect strong and correct solutions, directions, and answers from people who have position responsibility as leaders and/or major control over implementation resources. This "father knows best" paradigm is alive and well. Many who serve in leadership roles were raised in a time and culture that taught people, especially men, to be strong and rational, and take responsibility for caring for their families, employees, or constituents. A good leader, therefore, has been defined as someone who knows what to do. Therefore, when I or others recommend that a leader use a participatory decision-making process, it can be taken as a sign of leadership failure: The troops had to be called in because the leader could not come up with the right answers on his or her own. Inviting everyone in the department or organization to help determine priority strategies may feel like an indictment of weakness.

Consensus-based decision making does not replace leadership. It is a leadership tool for assuring that the elaborate web of daily, weekly, quarterly, and long-term decisions are based on the best possible information and backed by the awareness, analysis, action, and alliances necessary to execute them. Effective leaders know when, where, and how to produce with people. Also, once the consensus is formed, leaders at all levels must steer the translation of the will into timely, operational action. As Rosabeth Moss Kanter, author of *The Change Masters* (38) reminds us, power is ultimately connected to the ability to mobilize people to achieve great results.

Overcoming the Gap in Public Trust

Participants will join the public discussion with varying degrees of trust in democratic decision making. Earlier I discussed the signs of resurgence in citizen participation. While it is real, it is still a minority phenomenon. The majority of Americans participate passively in their governance and this is often translated into skepticism about any type of collective decision making at the workplace, community, or association. They prefer to leave leadership to their bosses, boards, and government officials for many reasons: Many don't have time. Others don't know where to start. Some others just may not care. Still others have participated and lost faith after their input in hearings or forums seemed to go nowhere. Even those who are very active tend to be suspicious of government or institutions. They are reluctant to participate unless they are assured a neutral space that gives equal time, voice, and power to all interests around the table.

One way or the other, the public has grown distant from government. Democracy has become a lost art and growing profession. Critical theorist Jurgen Habermas (39) wrote extensively about the waning public participation within a democracy and discussed the growing legitimization and motivation crises among citizens. Government grew to protect the rights and livelihoods of citizens from the harmful effects and inequities of capitalism, but in the process, citizens have become alienated from their government because it is too big to access or support. Less than meaningful employee involvement, team building, and other participation experiments have resulted in similar eroding of trust within organizations.

I have encountered many skeptics and recovering skeptics who felt used or demeaned in public process settings. I don't blame them. Too many times, meetings have been called after the decision has already been made. Public input mechanisms were mere facades for selling and implementing the decisions of a few. In one forestry department, staff used firefighting analogies to describe the less-than-sincere efforts of employee involvement: By the time everyone is invited to the table, the attack and suppression phases have already occurred. The people are called in at the mop-up phase.

Even when meetings have a valid purpose, participants can be alienated by confusing or vague processes. Such an experience is described vividly in this excerpt of a newspaper column entitled "Is There a Cure for Meetingitus" (40):

> The most frustrating manifestations of "meetingitus" are the warm-and-fuzzy public gatherings variously called open houses, roundtables, workshops, and task forces. The purpose of these get-togethers—held by agencies that make people angry—is to numb an unruly public into submission.
>
> The process works like this: everyone shows up mad as heck and in great disagreement over an issue. The agency gives them all free coffee and a comfortable chair. Then everyone sits in a semicircle, exchanges pleasant banter, and fills flip charts. People blurt out whatever comes to mind and some agency moll with a smile and a magic marker writes it all down. After an hour of this everyone is either talked out of being tongue-tied. . . . Tossing out old-fashioned democracy (majority rules) in favor of consensus (nobody gets mad) the agency then picks out "solutions" from whatever platitudes elicit no disagreement. "We need more education" inevitably wins. The agency then schedules another meeting to discuss "education strategies." Of course the issue never gets resolved but the bureaucrats keep themselves in free coffee ad infinitum (40).

Each disrespectful exercise in using people's time and creativity erodes a leader's capacity to build the trust and support needed to make things happen in organizations, communities, and society.

Reasons That Consensus Mechanisms Fail

Much process skepticism is the result of badly managed consensus deliberations and minimal trust in consensus solutions. There are no guaranteed steps to success, but there are some sure ways to assure consensus failure. I describe on the following pages the most common reasons collaborative problem solving falls far short of its potential: 1) unclear purpose and roles, 2) process by default, 3) inappropriate application of tools and techniques, 4) canned process, and 5) the magic pill expectation.

Unclear Process Purpose and Roles

It is surprising how many meetings are called without participants knowing exactly why their input is needed, how it will be used, or what the expectations for their involvement are. What difference will their input make? How does it benefit or affect each person? Is the input for ideas, advice, recommendations, or actual decisions? All those purposes are valid, but if the roles are not explained, the process can end up with disillusionment and unfulfilled expectations. People put their hearts into participating only to discover that their input was advice, not recommendations.

Without a clear or necessary mission, a venture is generally wasteful and extremely disrespectful of the people involved. (Good) meetings are a lot like funerals, according to the consultant Roger Mosvick. There are a lot of people sitting around in uncomfortable clothing wishing they were someplace else. The only difference is that usually funerals have a purpose (41). This quote gets a laugh in every group. It is a sad reflection on the fact that there are way too many staff meetings, committee sessions, and other group processes that seem less than relevant to the participants. Gathering people together is an enormous investment of human resources. If you multiply the time it takes to prepare, commute, attend, and execute the obligations acquired at the meeting for every participant, you would think twice, maybe 10 times, before convening another one. In fact, Mosvick described one manager who passed the time in meaningless meetings guessing and adding up the salaries of those present and multiplying them by the meeting-related hours to price the cost of each event. The point here is an obvious reminder.

I am not advocating that everyone be part of every decision. They just need to know the purpose and role of their participation. If it is advice or input, so be it. If it is recommendations for decisions, let people know. If it is informing people on an existing plan, let them know it is an informational forum. If a model exists, don't pretend that the models are yet to be created. Don't call a meeting unless it is necessary.

Once the purpose and roles are clear, provide participants with confirmation that their input will make a difference. What is the follow-up? How will the input translate into "through-put and output?" How does the consensus connect to mainstream decisions? If input continues to disappear into databases and reports, consensus process becomes synonymous with a "useless exercise."

Process by Default Versus Design

Some typical symptoms of unplanned process include all the elements of the previous paragraph plus things such as last-minute agendas, lack of background information, minimal leadership attention, too much to do too fast, no time to air all the issues and ideas, and a room that prevents people from seeing or hearing well.

Constructing group process must be seen in the same light as other public processes we know and love such as a football game, trial, jazz quartet, or a wedding reception. Can you imagine conducting a football game without the rules, and everyone knowing and abiding by them?

Consensus-based engagements require elaborate structure and preparation. The game rules need to be set and understood by all because the outcomes are dictated by how players participate within the agreed-to rules of engagement. In many group processes, we attempt to play the game while each player is trying to make sense of the rules, ends, or purposes. In fact, part of the confusion at many meetings is that we may be playing football, golf, and polo at the same time. Let's say that many processes do not make pleasant music because we have in essence thrown together people and instruments with sketchy directions or agreements about why and how music is to be made.

At a K–6 elementary school that has successfully operated with a high degree of shared decision making, everyone understands that participation cannot be left to chance. Respectful and meaningful sharing of ideas, needs, resources, and power must be carefully cultivated and supported: common principles and procedures are established, taught, refined, and followed by everyone. Protocols are available for managing task forces, leading meetings, building consensus, and operating site teams including the following tools:

- Guidelines for the site team's work; 10 ingredients for a successful team
- Roles, ground rules, grounding activities, and reflections for Site Council meeting
- Considerations for successfully sharing a decision
- Task force tool kit
- Consensus strategies, definitions, characteristics
- The Fist to Five method for indicating level of consensus (see page 172)

These and other shared decision-making procedures are as familiar to school participants as the Robert's Rules of Order are for practitioners of parliamentary process. They are consistently used across all levels, classroom to boardroom (42).

Inappropriate Tool

Another planning error is to use an approach that does not fit the situation or the readiness of the players. Earlier in the chapter we reviewed various strategies for conflict resolution and interaction. Collaborative problem solving is not the universal answer to every mess of issues. Diagnosing a situation is a fundamental first step to good process that reveals whether collaboration, negotiation, mediation, or something else is the best way to create solutions to an organizational or community problem.

For example if two parties were seeking to resolve a dispute but each side was committed to a position, mediation with a strong third party would be the best match for the dilemma. This was the case in a heated dispute between fisherpersons, resort owners, local government officials, and others regarding fishing limits and privileges on their lake. A meeting was called to discuss solutions but succeeded in producing only shouting matches, flared feelings, and a worse stalemate. Not enough research had gone into understanding the situation. The players were too divided to participate in a collaborative meeting. What was needed was shuttle diplomacy. A third party was needed to hold a series of meetings or interviews with each stakeholder group to formulate the key issues and solicit ideas for resolving the conflict. Then, after sharing the results of the other meeting with each group, the next steps to forging solutions could be devised. The state agency ended up serving as the shuttle diplomat, and eventually a consensus process culminated the long route to settling a tough problem

Canned Process

Rarely will one technology work as-is for any situation. Predeveloped methods and techniques such as a particular brand of strategic planning or problem solving can be useful, but only if they are applied carefully and sensitively. The duty of a process consultant or facilitator is to listen to the *ends* that the community is seeking and customize a *means* to get there by combining tools, techniques, and procedures appropriate to the situation. Unfortunately, one-size-fits-all facilitators frequently counsel and service leaders. One frustrated state agency director hired a consultant to help complete their strategic planning process and was advised to start from scratch using the "correct" brand of planning because the department's method was flawed. This meant nullifying over six months of active department-wide efforts. It was not an option for the agency. He looked for another consultant that was willing to build on the work done to date to determine strategic priorities and an annual work plan for the organization.

Prepackaged programming has contributed to the failure of many shared decision-making efforts in school districts, according to Bauer's study "Leveling the Playing Field: Structuring Shared Decision-Making to Promote Authentic Dialogue" (43):

Although researchers emphasize that there is no single recipe for successfully implementing site-based management that works in all districts or schools (44, 45), there are few systematic discussions about the alternative approaches pursued by actors of how these action alternatives are selected. A single model of site-based management dominates the literature, resulting in a bias toward defining the process in terms of whether authority over budget, staffing, and curriculum is devolved to the school level.

The complexity of site-based management practice reduced to a handful of simple factors and site-based management is judged to be adequate in terms of the existence of these attributes. Adoption of shared governance has tended to follow the American tendency to "package, simplify, and sell" (46) or to paraphrase Metz (47); the garment of site-based management comes in "one size fits all."

Bauer corroborates the underlying message of the book by concluding that "emphasis must shift to a focus on site-based management as *process to be designed* (48) rather than as a *program to be implemented.*"

Magic Pill Expectation

Another barrier to finding a meaningful way to solve problems together is to expect a final answer or other miracle by employing a new process or person. For a decade or two, we anticipated the coming of the conflict Messiah—the one method, theory, technique, mediator, consultant, quick fix, silver bullet, or some other tool for achieving instant unity. This has not occurred and common sense has made a triumphant return. Good methods and competent process leaders are one important component in attaining consensus, but no one process or person replaces critical thinking, raw initiative, and hard work. I have yet to find a shortcut to waging consensus.

Complex problems resist quick fixes and simplistic either/or alternatives. They cannot be "solved" with one remedy or permanently. They require a system of solutions that take time to launch and bear fruit. Just think about how difficult it is for one human being to address a physical fitness issue. Just drinking vitamin-packed protein shakes will rarely make a difference. What works is a portfolio of strategies including diet, exercise, new social habits, medical remedies, and many other solutions. Furthermore, success depends on a mundane and disciplined effort to live the required new daily practices. If that is what it takes to change the patterns of one person, a massive arsenal of schemes is surely needed to eliminate homelessness in a community, improve student achievement, or shift the transportation patterns in an urban area.

Implementation requires getting on a path to solutions that build in short-term, incremental victories. Catalyzing fundamental change usually means finding collaborative mechanisms for ongoing, relentless attention to redirecting, revitalizing, rethinking, reinventing, and developing the problem area. The parable of the tortoise and the hare is an apt metaphor. Going slowly and surely may indeed be the fastest way to fundamental change.

Like quick fixes, framing complex problems into polarities is a typical coping mechanism for dealing with major conflicts and controversies. Some popular dualisms include the greens against business, the republican model versus the democratic model, big versus small government, conservative or liberal, the neighbors opposing a halfway house versus those who don't mind, or being for or against voucher-based education. People fall through the cracks when we draw simple lines in the sand and divert attention from examining solving social dilemmas to defending superficial "sides." Time is spent tracking the points and power versus addressing the issues jointly.

The pursuit of consensus methods has made a refreshing return to the basics. The many trials and errors with collaborative approaches in the 1980s and 1990s have minimized illusions about miracle cures. As one strategic planning consultant put it, "For every complex question there is a simple answer, and it is wrong!"

CONCLUSION

To control or collaborate? That is the question at every level of society. The manner in which leaders and citizens of the planet answer that question in the next decade or two will determine the merits of using discourse versus force in mobilizing community directions. The case for consensus seems compelling to some of us, but consensus building is not doomed to success. Everyone needs to decide whether consensus building is a worthy pursuit.

We may not have rules, but the experiments of the past several decades have produced written and unwritten wisdom about structuring and facilitating consensus building. Over the years, process sponsors, meeting leaders, and participants have pooled their expertise and common sense to construct procedures that meet situational mandates. The next chapter relays the benefits and successes of satisfied consensus users.

NOTES

1. Ehrenhalt, A. (2002, February). Meetings of the Minds. *Governing.*

2. Kenney, D. (2000). *Arguing about consensus: Examining the case against western watershed initiatives and other collaborative groups in natural resources management.* Boulder, CO: University of Colorado School of Law.

3. Smith, S. (1998, June). School-by-school; how site-based management is transforming education in Austin. *The American School Board Journal, 22–25.*

4. Thomas, K. W. (1977). Toward multidimensional value in teaching: The example of conflict behaviors. *Academy of Management Review, 12*, 484–490.

5. Mohr, H. (1987). *How to talk Minnesotan: A visitor's guide.* New York: Penguin Books.

6. Tannen, D. (1998a). *The argument culture: Moving from debate to dialogue.* New York: Random House.

7. _____ (1998b, February 27 and March 4–5). How to turn debate into dialogue. *USA Weekend.*

8. Caranicas, P., Management Consultant, Minneapolis, MN.

9. Poulin, R. H. (1992). *Restructuring today and tomorrow, school governance revisited.* U.S. Department of Education, Office of Educational Research and Improvement.

10. Bjorum, W. (1991). *Listening for voices: A leader in action.* St.Paul, MN: University of St.Thomas.

11. Spencer, L. J. (1989). *Winning through participation.* Dubuque, IA: Kendall/Hunt.

12. Harrison, R. (1991, December). [Review of the book *Winning through participation.*] *OD Practitioner,* Winter, 16–18.

13. Weisbord, M. (1992, June). Comments: Reflections on a Harrison book. [Review of Spencer's *Winning through participation*]. *OD Practitioner, X,* 13–15.

14. Reich, R. (1987, May-June). Entrepreneurship reconsidered: The team as a hero. *Harvard Business Review.*

15. Fisher, R., & Ury, W. (1983). *Getting to yes: Negotiating agreement without giving in.* New York: Penguin.

16. Perlman, E. (1997, January). The Consensus Industry. *Governing, 10,* 33–34.

17. Henderson, J. E. (1993, March 25–27). *Quality through involvement: A school-based decision-making success story.* Paper presented at the National Conference on Creating the Quality School, Oklahoma City, OK.

18. Boyer, E. L. (1995). *The basic school: A community of learning.* Princeton, NJ: Carnegie Foundation for the Advancement of Teaching.

19. Troxel, J. (Ed.). (1995). *Government works: Profiles of people making a difference.* Alexandria, VA: Miles River.

20. Osborne, D., & Gaebler, T. (1992). *Reinventing government: How the entrepreneurial spirit is transforming the public sector, from schoolhouse to statehouse, city hall to the pentagon.* Reading, MA: Addison-Wesley.

21. Hale, S., & Williams, M. (Eds.). (1994). *Managing change: A guide to producing change from within.* Washington DC: Urban Institute.

22. Massachusetts Institute of Technology/Harvard Public Disputed Program. (1997, April). Practitioners: "Show us the money!" *Consensus,* 34.

23. National Consensus Initiative/Search for Common Ground, USA. 1601 Connecticut Avenue, NW, Washington DC., www.sfcg.org

24. Burbidge, J. (Ed.). (1997). *Beyond prince and merchant: Citizen participation and the rise of civil society.* New York: Pact.

25. Bratton, M. (1955). *Civil societies and NGOs: Expanding development strategies.* InterAction's Civil Society Initiative. Report of Workshop #1, 1.

26. Semler, R. (1984, September–October). Managing without managers. *Harvard Business Review.*

27. Lappe, F. M. (1989, August 29). Finding a way to make decisions that pass the test of real time. *Minneapolis Star Tribune.*

28. Wolfe, A. (1992). Democracy versus sociology: Boundaries and their political consequences. In M. Lamont & M. Fournier (Eds.), *Cultivating differences* (pp. 309–325). Chicago: The University of Chicago.

29. Habermas, J. (1987). *The theory of communicative action, Volume I: Reason and the rationalization of society.* Boston: Beacon. (Original work published in 1981).

30. Weisbord, M. (Ed.). (1992). *Discovering common ground.* San Francisco, CA: Berrett-Koehler.

31. Ackoff, R. (1998). A quote from Hanson, M., *Facilitating civil society*. In J. Burbidge, *Beyond prince and merchant: Citizen participation and the rise of civil society* (p. 242). New York: Pact Publications.

32. Gardner, J. (1995). *Leading minds: An anatomy of leadership*. New York: BasicBooks.

33. Piper, D. L. (1974, Spring). Decision-making: Decisions made by individuals vs. those made by group consensus or group participation. *Educational Administration Quarterly, 10* (2), 82–95.

34. Sidener, R. P. (1995, April). *Site-based management/shared decision making: A view through the lens of organizational culture*. Paper presented at the annual meting of the American Educational Research Association, San Francisco.

35. Bryson, J. M., & Crosby, B. C. (1992). *Leadership for the common good: Tackling public problems in a shared-power world*. San Francisco: Jossey-Bass.

36. Crump, D. (1999). *Road to school reform: The Chicago model information analyses (070)—opinion papers (120)*. Washington, DC: U.S. Department of Education, Office of Educational Research and Improvement.

37. The Consensus Building Institute. (in press). A short guide to consensus building: An alternative to Robert's rules of order for groups, organizations, and ad hoc assemblies that want to operate by consensus. In Susskind, McKearnan, & Thomas-Larmer, *Consensus building handbook*. Thousand Oaks, CA: Sage.

38. Moss Kanter, R. (1989). Foreword. In L. J. Spencer. *Winning through participation*. Dubuque, IA: Kendall/Hunt.

39. Habermas, J. (1973). *Legitimization crisis*. (T. McCarthy, Trans.) Boston: Beacon.

40. Perich, S. (1996, March 1). Is there a cure for meetingitus? *Outdoor News; Star Tribune.*

41. Hage, D. (1987, April 20). A meeting of the minds on meetings. *Star Tribune.*

42. Valley Crossing Community School. (1997–2003). [Site council materials]. Woodbury, MN.

43. Bauer, S. (1997, March 24–28). Creating a level playing field: Structuring shared decision making to promote authentic dialogue. Paper presented at the annual meeting of the American Educational Research Association, Chicago.

44. Ogawa, R., & White, P. (1994). School-based management: an overview. In S. Mohrman, P. Wohlstetter, & Associates (Eds.), *Designing high performance schools: Strategies for school-based management,* San Francisco: Jossey-Bass.

45. Sharpe, F. (1996). Towards a research paradigm on devolution. *Journal of Educational Administration 34* (1), 4–23.

46. Glickman, C. (1990). Pushing school reform to a new edge: The seven ironies of school empowerment. *Phi Delta Kappan, 72*(1), 68–75.

47. Metz, M. (1990). Hidden assumptions preventing real reform: Some missing elements in the educational reform movement. In S. Bacharach (Ed.), *Education reform: Making sense of it all*. Boston: Allyn and Bacon.

48. Mohrman, S. (1994). High involvement management in the private sector. In S. Mohrman, P. Wohlstetter, & Associates (Eds.), *Designing high performance schools: Strategies for school-based management*. San Francisco: Jossey-Bass.

49. Leavitt, T. Judicial Council of California's "5-step to planning model," retrieved August 4, 2005, from http://www.courtinfo.ca.gov/programs/community/planning/5stepmodel_5.htm.

Chapter Two

Consensus Advantages and Applications

We live in a world where no one is "in charge." No one organization or institution has the legitimacy, power, authority, or intelligence to act alone on important public issues and still make substantial headway against the problems that threaten us all . . . As a result, we live in a "shared-power" world, a world in which organizations and institutions must share objectives, activities, resources, power, or authority in order to achieve collective gains or minimize losses.

—John Bryson and Barbara Crosby
Leadership for the Common Good

What are the major benefits of consensus? What are some real-life examples of solving complex problems collectively? This chapter continues to make a case for consensus as a primary leadership tool by citing lived examples of consensus efforts that are making a difference in the education, public, private, and civic sectors. They are only the tip of the iceberg. Some are success stories, others a work in progress. Hopefully they convey the wide variety of applications for collaborative problem solving.

I discuss the consensus benefits and examples as they relate to the five major results consensus can deliver (see figure 2.0): 1) building shared *awareness* about a situation affecting them; 2) producing mutually meaningful *analysis* to inform decision making; 3) making broadly supported *agreements* to resolve issues or work together; 4) initiating collective *action,* and 5) developing formal or informal working *alliances*. Since sustainable agreements cannot form and perform without collective awareness, analysis, action, and alliances, successful decision-making ventures involve each of the five results to some degree. I have therefore listed the case stories under the consensus result that was the most prominent or instrumental to producing a consensus solution in a given problem.

A. Shared AWARENESS

- Benefit 1: Agree on the current reality
- Benefit 2: Induce a needed crisis

B. Mutually Acceptable ANALYSIS

- Benefit 3: Translate data overload into information
- Benefit 4: Form collective logic
- Benefit 5: Generate innovative solutions

C. Binding AGREEMENTS

- Benefit 6: Resolve conflicts
- Benefit 7: Determine common will

D. Supported ACTION

- Benefit 8: Get ideas implemented
- Benefit 9: Build partnerships

E. Working ALLIES

- Benefit 10: Establish working relationships

Figure 2.0.   10 Benefits of Collaboration

BUILDING SHARED AWARENESS

Assembling all the stakeholders related to an issue is the fastest way to get everyone on the same page and assess the whole situation. As figure 2.1 depicts, the closest thing to the "whole" reality is the meshed perceptions of people from all parts of the system. The awareness step of a consensus-building process delivers the power and benefit of revealing a shared priority for action by 1) quickly developing an understanding of how an individual's issues link into a common urgency and/or 2) "inducing a needed crisis" to reveal how discrete issues are symptoms of a pervasive problem.

Benefit 1: Allows Stakeholders to Quickly Realize How Issues Link into a Common Urgency

A great deal of group conflict and dysfunction stems from a limited view of any given dilemma or situation. When participants see how their burning issue fits with all the related issues in the bigger puzzle, they realize that the resolution of their issue requires addressing the whole system of problems. It is quite remarkable how quickly and quietly this can happen. Without heroic speeches about attacking the future as a team, joint assessment of the situation softens preconceived perceptions. Group tensions tend to drop several notches if people can fully air their issues and/or produce a complete inventory of the interacting problems and possibilities they face. This is not as mysterious or magical as it sounds. It is a testament to the astute nature of human beings.

In almost every debriefing conversation, participants are amazed and appreciative about understanding the totality of circumstances surrounding their personal concerns. One member of a first-ever summit meeting of public and private day care delivery groups observed the magic of finding out that her "enemies were not really enemies":

> "I've been fighting for day care for years. My enemies were in my group. It was amazing to see my issues actually fit with theirs. Before today, I had just never heard it!" (1)

In the same vein, the following are the top four comments participants make regarding the advantages of gaining a shared understanding:

> "I didn't realize how much is involved in the business."
> "I thought I was the only one that was concerned about the issues."
> "It seems we think more alike than differently."
> "I didn't realize the situation was so complex and serious."

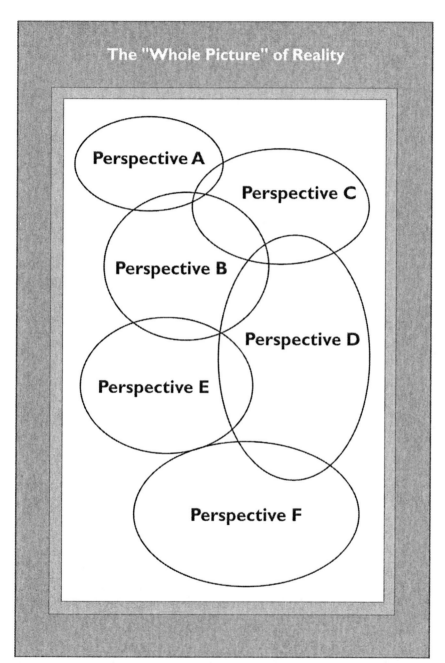

Figure 2.1.   Getting Closest to the "Whole Picture" of Any Situation

Discovering that personal concerns link to a broader set of issues is a simple but powerful first step in generating new directions.

Sharing Police, Fire, and School Services among Communities

Here is an example of how sharing common issues helped historically independent communities pursue consolidation of public services.

Issue: Like many other rural areas, a mining region in the northern U.S. was facing a declining economic base, a decreasing tax base, shrinking employment opportunities, continuing loss of residents, and a struggle to maintain the existing level of public services in each community. Over the years, fear of losing control and identity had made "consolidation" of police, fire, water, waste, and other basic services an undiscussable "C-word." The consolidation of schools had happened several years ago, slowly and painfully. Now the goal was to do the same with public services as quickly and painlessly as possible.

Consensus Response: In order to maintain a quality of life during a challenging time, three rural cities and one large township decided to get together to explore combining community services. Each community contributed funds to retain a facilitator to provide a neutral decision-making forum for the planning work. One elected official, one city staff member, and one citizen representative from each community was appointed to develop recommendations for intercommunity service alliances. Concerns about losing community identity and autonomy were still on everyone's minds as they gathered for the planning.

Results: As each participant shared their perceptions of community challenges, the universality of the economic crisis became obvious. Everyone identified issues that cummulatively revealed sobering trends affecting the future of all participating communities:

- A growing challenge to maintain businesses and employers
- Rising costs and significant loss of government aid
- A decreasing population and political voice in the legislature
- Minimal foresight and preparation for the recent economic downturn

One of the specific economic urgencies was identified as the replacement of fire and emergency equipment: the current operating budgets for fire and emergency services were somewhat feasible. However, a fiscal crisis loomed for each community as soon as insurance requirements demanded the purchase of a new emergency vehicle at the cost of over $250,000.

On the other side of sharing the external challenges, participants identified areas of proactive opportunity:

- Communities can build on existing examples of cooperation
- Communities have duplicative services that can be streamlined
- Over the years, some communities have formed successful joint powers agreements to operate fire, ambulance, and other activities.

Traditional territorial conflicts decreased in importance as community representatives faced the common challenges of all the communities. Active work groups are currently researching best practices and strategies for combining the police, water/sewer, emergency services, health care, and recycling and recreation services of the four communities. An ongoing governance mechanism will be formed for managing, directing, and operating a combined service department.

Benefit 2: Inducing a Needed Crisis That Compels Action

Sometimes getting on the same page helps illuminate a major, systemwide quandary that was not fully visible from any one vantage point. Everyone experiences similar issues but without an exchange of notes, they fail to be recognized as symptoms of a fundamental and pervasive problem that threatens the effectiveness of the whole operation. When the observations of players from multiple functions and levels are combined in a collaborative assessment, problems can be detected and dealt with.

For example, in a large mining operation, the new general manager began his term by conducting a technical evaluation of the physical and human assets of the business operation. For the first time in the history of the company, he brought together over 200 managerial staff to help determine the status of the operation. The group was shocked to discover that both the human and physical systems were in dangerous need of repair after 10 years of ignoring maintenance practices. After the collaborative evaluation, the general manager made this pitch for consensus: Things are too big and complicated for even the most dedicated leaders to keep track of what is going on. The astute way to make decisions is to get everyone around the table. It can be done fairly quickly. You don't get rid of all the fighting, but people see it's in the interest of their jobs and departments to prioritize and cooperate to keep the place profitable.

This conclusion represents the experience of many consensus believers. Consultant Marvin Weisbord, a long-time advocate for the power of collective action, offers this compelling defense of a group's ability to come to terms with its whole reality (2):

> I worry more about responding to the need for dignity and the meaning of work rather than about supplying the right answers . . . There is considerable anxiety and confusion everywhere. I think it is wrong to assume our mutual dilemmas mean sickness, as if the diagnostician is whole and in control . . . on my bookshelf I find more models for fixing

things than there are stars in the galaxy. Yet I am strangely undernourished by this intellectual cornucopia. My objective, I keep reminding myself, is not to diagnose and heal "sickness" but to help people manage their work lives better and to enact productive community.

A consultant's task in the movie is to see confusion and anxiety through to energy for constructive action and learn along with everyone else. The consultant's role is to help people discover a more whole view of what they are doing than any one discipline or perspective can provide.

An effective snapshot portrays the whole system in relation to a worthy purpose. It can only do that accurately when the whole system, to the extent possible, takes it, appears in it, and looks over it together. . . . As soon as people start making a collective self-portrait, it is no longer a snapshot. Voila! It's part of the ongoing movie, as messy as life itself. (2)

New power for the course is generated when energy and passion behind individual concerns and stakes can be agglomerated to fuel a group problem-solving priority. This is the power added when a group assesses the urgency and elements of a situation together. Building shared awareness hatches the incentives for a diverse group to launch a focused search for solutions.

A Call to Arms for Drastic Literacy Improvement

The following example of a successful literacy partnership in a California elementary school illustrates the instrumental role shared awareness building can play in triggering effective and collective problem resolution.

Issue: A 1,400-student elementary school in Oakland, California, experienced very low literacy scores despite being known as a "shining star of the district." It was the largest elementary school in the district where the student body consists of 88 percent that qualify for free or reduced-price lunch, 12 different ethnic backgrounds, and 74 percent that speak only limited English. Official school communications must be written in six languages—Spanish, Vietnamese, Cantonese, Cambodian, English, and Lao.

Consensus Solution: School personnel decided to open the issue for public scrutiny and invite all the stakeholders together. This was not an easy step: They recognized the need to evaluate the reform efforts systematically and to hold themselves accountable for improving student achievement. And, although they could have done an in-house assessment of progress, in keeping with its tradition of inclusiveness, the school opened up its reflection, assessment, and visioning process to all members of the community (3).

Acknowledging publicly that many students were not reading at the levels where their teachers and families wanted them to be was a big step. The admission raised all sorts of issues among faculty members: deeply rooted fears of finger-pointing and talk about student failure, the potential for conflict regarding bilingual education strategies, and concerns about the biases of tests and district pressure to raise test scores (3).

All parents and community members were invited to a "mutual accountability event" called "Parents and Teachers Together: An Honest Look at Reading Scores."

Results: Expecting about 150 participants, teachers and administrators "looked at each other in disbelief" when over 300 people poured into the classrooms. For many parents, it was the first time the sobering statistics were reviewed and possible causes explained. After the opportunity to hear the full situation, jointly analyze root problems, and generate solutions, everyone was ready to help change the trend.

By the end of the evening, when families crowded into the main auditorium for the grand finale of Brazilian martial arts and a turkey raffle, dozens of flipchart sheets papered the classroom walls. The charts were filled with ideas for how the community could work together to increase student literacy (3).

Parents were very vocal about their commitment to action. Reporters Cohn-Vargas and Grose quoted poignant admissions of several participants. One young Latina woman said in her maiden tongue, "I am glad you are explaining the reading scores to us. I feel bad that I haven't done it before, but now I will start finding ways to help my child (3)." Likewise, a Vietnamese father used his own language to sound the wake-up call: "The reading level is too low compared to the benchmark. We are very surprised that it is so low. We need help from parents and teachers" (3).

The event proved once again that their site-based and participative management model continues to work and pay off. It was a continuation of a plan built a decade ago. About 100 members of the school community—including teachers, parents, office staff, administrators, and custodians—held a planning retreat to develop a strong, shared vision and action plan for the school. The focal point was having all children reading by grade three. The literacy "accountability event" is another successful example of what happens when all stakeholders are made aware of a problem that affects them. Getting the issues out honestly and simultaneously tends to jump-start community will to reform and act.

MUTUALLY MEANINGFUL ANALYSIS

Once participants are aware and attentive to the full scope and pieces of a problem, the floodgates open and a stream of possible facts, history, statistics, explanations, scientific evidence, perceptions, assumptions, and other background knowledge flows in for consideration in making collective choices about the future. This is a challenge for all decision makers and situations—individual or a group, policy level or ground level, matters with or without controversy.

"Due diligence" can indeed be entrusted to well-structured consensus forums on policy issues, budget choices, problem-solving recommendations, or program priorities.

Consensus-based analysis is a little used but powerful tool for leveraging the intelligence of many to analyze, assess, and ponder the problem in a way that makes sense to all stakeholders. Specifically, consensus building offers the benefits of 1) translating data overload into meaningful information to support decisions, 2) formulating a collective logic for justifying decisions, or 3) generating innovative solutions.

Benefit 3: Translate the Data Overload into Meaningful Decision Information

Every issue comes with volumes of background information to digest and understand. At the highest levels of policymaking, members of congress and state legislators struggle to keep up on numerous issues by adding more and more staff to track each issue area. Each office has become a veritable government in miniature. However, even with the help of more and more staff, most issues could use several days or weeks to fully understand and debate. The increased capacity is used up responding to hundreds and thousands of letters and e-mail messages that pour into their offices regularly.

Similarly, the overabundance of background material is a challenge when tackling complex problems as a group. Chapters 3 and 7 will describe how consensus participants responded individually and collectively to their information intake task.

A combination of good method and diverse participants is the formula for converting an overload of inputs into information. The human mind is the core technology. Filtering data through the multiple minds and belief systems of issue stakeholders generates the power of shared logic to justify collective choices. In hours, days, or few weeks, mountains of inputs can be analyzed, weighed up, prioritized, and negotiated into the data points, findings, and conclusions that everyone considers relevant in making joint decisions. Some common tools for strategic analysis include trends assessments, multiple scenario analysis, cost benefit analysis, force field analysis, and problem mapping.

Digesting Two Years of Development Desires into a Land Design Focus

The following story about a local land design dilemma shows how a well-structured group problem-solving process can translate an overabundance of input into meaningful analysis using the power of collective reasoning.

Issue: Several rural communities were interested in launching a joint effort to diversify the economy of the mining-dependent region. Over the years, each community had developed formal and informal plans, held community meetings, and even hired a business developer to plan recreational attractions and business parks as well as other options for growing jobs and commercial vitality. The discussion records, project ideas, feasibility assessments, and possible plans accumulated. However, for decades, decisions and follow-up action did not materialize.

Consensus Solution: When the communities learned about a land design planning workshop available to them, one community invited others to gather for a two-hour town meeting to discuss the purpose, scope, and process for conducting a community landscape design workshop to develop economic and land use options.

Results: At the first facilitated meeting over 50 people representing diverse groups from many towns reviewed existing plans, received official data about relevant geographic constraints, and shared dreams and desires for future development. By the end of the meeting, the group identified several focal points for further land design planning. During the debriefing, a participant summed up the victory: "We got more done in two hours than we have in two years on this issue. This cooperation is a big deal!"

Subsequently, a landscape design workshop was conducted. Teams of landscape architects worked side by side with community members and produced three different visual options for developing the commercial, recreational, natural, and residential areas within a limited amount of land. Work is underway to determine how to select, fund, phase, and implement the best plans that will benefit the most people.

Benefit 4: Formulate a Collective Logic for Justifying Decisions

Consensus decision making acknowledges that beliefs drive data. There is no such thing as objective data or science. Every stakeholder comes into a process with a position that is backed by some body of knowledge or convictions. The consensus forum is a vehicle for sorting through the underlying assumptions, worldviews, facts, explanations, and other evidence that drive each individual's analysis and agree on the joint values and criteria for determining which facts and truths should influence decisions and actions.

A Community School Makes a Habit of Effective Group Problem Solving

The benefits of formulating collective logic for decisions are evident in the successful results of an issue resolution process at a Minnesota community school (4). A task force–driven issue resolution process is the lifeblood of school innovation. "Issue task forces" are powerful, ongoing mechanisms for analyzing problems and developing solutions in a consensus-based manner. It works like this:

Issues: All current and emerging school issues qualify for the process. The following is a list of subjects that came up before the site council during one month:

Inconsistent and numerous middle school rules among teachers
Drop in math score following the introduction of a new math series
Custodian concerns with students consistently leaving a mess in the lunchroom

Increased 6th grade discipline problems on the playground
Staff desire to change the grade configuration to a multi-level age grouping

The wide range of incoming issues makes this model a vivid example of nuts and bolts democracy in action.

Consensus Solution: Anyone can bring new issues to the site council by submitting a one-page "issue sheet" 48 hours prior to any meeting. As stated at the top of the sheet, "new issues are the first order of business at each meeting." To be considered, participants need to identify the issue and its significance:

- What is the issue?
- How does this affect students and learning?
- What are the possible causes of this issue?
- What has been done in the past to resolve this issue?

The council decides what action needs to be taken and which stakeholder groups need to be involved, and usually designates a task force to steer the problem-solving process. Cornerstone steps for any task force are to seek diverse input and discussion and conduct research on best practices. Every decision must consider all stakeholder perspectives and access state-of-the-art lessons and models related to the issue.

Results: The successful resolution of sticky issues is an ongoing accomplishment. Here are highlights from recent products, starting with a controversial venture that staff described as a "test of the consensus process"—developing a schoolwide health curriculum acceptable to parents, community, and school stakeholders.

The health education curriculum: Entering into a dialogue about the extremely value-laden and controversial topics of personal health practices, body systems, family living, and human sexuality was a daunting task. The issue task force designed and implemented numerous forums for airing the diverse interests within the community, parents, staff, and students. They brought in models from other districts. It took over two years to agree on the values, content, and methods for teaching. According to one parent, the journey was painful at times, but the payoffs were rewarding:

> Many ideological conflicts occurred along the way—even the ground rules were a big discussion. The big victory was that hardly anyone showed up for the informational meetings before the program began. Once curriculum was approved and rolled out, everyone accepted the product. Everyone had been heard and all views considered. It was no longer an issue. They had had their say and trusted the results.

A fair lunch/prep scheduling process: This process demonstrated the benefits of decision making by those most affected. The current schedule wasted enormous teacher time "switching-out" materials between subjects. Changing to larger teaching blocks released more time for lunch and lesson preparation.

The homework policy: After hearing the needs, preferences, and ideas from students, parents, and teachers, consensus emerged on a homework policy based on the real world. For example, no homework is now issued on Wednesday nights because the input revealed it to be a heavy activity night for a majority of families. Also, consequences were adjusted to not punish kids for an occasional "no good night."

The holiday celebration policy: A task force was charged to look at the divergent assumptions and concerns about holiday celebration practices. After several meetings, a consensus recommendation emerged for celebration symbols, music, calendar, exemptions, and a complaints process that would allow observance of holidays, emphasize nonviolent aspects, be nondiscriminatory, tie into curriculum as appropriate, and continue to address concerns of those who choose not to participate.

Getting Beyond Positions and Analyzing Real Needs of Children and Families

Engaging in rigorous joint analysis can be the bridge out of polarized debates. This was the case in a consensus-based conference that was able to move beyond the pro-choice/pro-life debate to address the real needs of families and children (5).

Issues: In the early 1980s, the White House sponsored a series of conferences across the U.S. to identify the status of community life and identify ways that public organizations can best support strong families and children in the coming decades (4).

Consensus Response: Midsized cities were chosen as host locations and various organizations retained to design and lead the large gatherings. They drew sometimes over 1,000 people from the region. The dialogue in the first 10 of 11 was brisk but polarized into a shouting match between the pro-choice and pro-life interest groups. The unaligned majority of community citizens were left on the sidelines.

Results: Only one conference was carefully constructed to enable the massive audience to work in cross-sectional groups of 15 to 20 people, each led by a trained community facilitator at the helm. The conference resulted in hundreds of recommendations that were then merged into five to seven major areas of need and action. The experience proved that well-planned consensus forums can get past underlying controversies and produce comprehensive and realistic analysis about multidimensional problems.

Benefit 5: Generating Innovative Solutions

Another benefit of multiple-stakeholder analysis is generating new insights and uncharted courses of action. The likelihood of birthing "out of box" ideas is greater when ideas are shared, merged, pushed, and pulled in team settings versus solitary sittings. The ingenuity of ordinary people was constantly confirmed during my work with local town meetings in the 1970s and 1980s. Two innovation stories have become classics within the oral tradition of the Institute of Cultural Affairs, a worldwide village and community development organization:

In a remote village of India, community income was tripled and basic services such as clean water and food became available to all residents in the span of one to three years. A major achievement was collaboration between people of diverse social, political, and economic classes known as castes. This was a miracle in a culture that strictly forbids intercaste contact among certain groups. The planning session identified full-village participation in anything as an underlying challenge. Several local people had a solution: Start with a village preschool that provides children of all social castes a full meal once a day. Three women from different castes suggested the risky step of cooking the meals. Each family would have the option of following tradition or assuring their child a much-needed nutritional base. When the school opened, children from almost all households joined the program. It was a first step to intercaste cooperation on many fronts.

In another Korean village, rampant chronic illness and lack of medical care was affecting many people throughout the year, particularly in the winter. For years, villagers struggled to gain access to basic emergency and health care services. During the community-wide planning process, villagers discovered the root cause: Minimal availability of warm water discouraged regular bathing during the numerous cold months. The innovative problem-formulation resulted in a break-loose solution to build a community bath house. The investment was a fraction of what it would have cost to access and build medical infrastructure. The rate of diseases shrank dramatically. Regular cleansing prevented small cuts from infecting into major health problems and contagious illnesses spread much less readily.

Most consensus innovations may not be as colorful but equally dramatic. They involve numerous and novel details in mundane areas. For example, when 120 union and management representatives from all of Miami's city departments came together in a truly collaborative Labor Management Committee, they found a package of synergistic solutions to increase city services, cut costs, and assure supportive working conditions for all employees. Some of the tangible results of implementing the joint initiatives included decreasing employee grievances by 12 percent, civil service appeals by 75 percent, and legal actions by 38 percent. Absenteeism was reduced by 72 percent due to an effective sick leave policy that saved over $750,000 in sick time (6).

Sometimes the exercise reveals what one client called "BGOs (Blinding Glimpses of the Obvious)": long-standing and/ or commonsense ideas whose time has come. The group analysis reconfirms the utility of a good-old solution and raises its priority. For example, an interagency consensus group tackling long-term health care and welfare issues reconfirmed the need to pursue the existing goal of assuring "dollars follow clients." They proceeded to recommend ways to refocus agency attention and resources to serve clients, not bureaucracies.

Community Ideas Inject New Energy into School Dilemmas

A recent article in the *American School Board Journal* reported on the ways site-based management is transforming Texas school districts. Many stories highlight innovative ideas gained by involving all school stakeholders in the improvement dialogue (7).

Issue and Consensus Solution: The Texas legislature mandated site-based management in 1991 to respond to national and citizen demands for education reform. Bit by bit and drop by drop, school districts have experienced the benefits of collective action and the increased capacity to generate innovative ideas. For example, in the constant battle to improve math competency, the campus advisory council got more than 200 parents to take the math portion of the statewide standardized test. This improved the parents' understanding and ability to help their children at home.

In another district, a fresh idea from community participants turned around the dismal rate of parent involvement. For years, this urban district of mostly low-income households struggled to involve any parents. However, everything changed after a grassroots community organization was invited to join problem solving and suggested applying techniques of neighborhood organizing to schools. The key was to begin where the parents were, physically and consciously.

Scores of "house meetings" of 8 to 15 people were held in the neighborhood surrounding a school. Participants started talking about their dream school and moved on to specific school agendas. According to the lead organizer, "That agenda may not focus on academics at the start." Here is one example of how small first steps led to substantive parent involvement:

> At one elementary school parents learned that rats were eating the paper supplies every night and had caused a terrible odor in the teacher's lounge. Getting rid of rodents was at the top of the agenda. At one point, twenty-three parents turned out for a 7:30 a.m. meeting with the head of maintenance for the school district. Crews showed up before the meeting ended to seal up rat holes and remove old ventilators where rats were nesting. After the success, the parents have turned to academics (7).

Over a dozen elementary schools now have active community and parent support.

Saving National Electric Power from Being Unplugged

Another example of generating innovation is a national-level consensus process that developed a model for saving the electrical infrastructure of an entire country.

Issue: In the mid-1980s, the Colombian government needed a way to save the national production and distribution of electricity from falling into a devastating debt as a result of worldwide recession, devaluation of the local currency, and a lower-than-expected rate of demand. The World Bank offered assistance if an organization was created to build greater physical interconnection and coordination between all the stakeholders in the electrical delivery process (8).

Consensus Response: A Future Search Conference, a specific method of collaborative inquiry and problem solving developed by consultant Marvin Weisbord and others, was used as a policy and service development forum involving 60 participants representing three levels of the power sector: the core entities of electrical utilities; the support tier of suppliers, engineering contractors, customers, ministry of mines and energy, coal and oil companies; and three international aid agencies. The third level of stakeholders was the government and academic agencies and research resources. The intense process developed recommendations for aligning and interconnecting the operations of each stakeholder systems in order to redirect the nation's power supply, distribution, and ongoing coordination.

Results: In general, the parties understood and appreciated the need for joint influence and control. They innovated a horizontal flow of power between stakeholders to replace the constraining vertical flow between the government and each enterprise. One of the government participants became the next prime minister of the country, partly because he was regarded as the only minister with a plan. The collaborative process solved the problem it was charged to address and set up a solid ongoing approach to improving the national power operations (8).

Consensus groups augment the capacity of an organization or democracy to hear, analyze, and formulate public policies, laws, statutes, ordinances, and public services. They are an invaluable way to dedicate time not only to ponder issues but also to decipher the consensus will of constituencies. When a group of staff or citizens can choose the best possible information and insights to back up recommended courses of action, there is a strong likelihood that the reasons for a new direction will not be discredited. Instead, the jointly-constructed bases for action will continue to reinforce the implementation of the solution. The power of common reasoning will pay big dividends throughout the ups and downs of putting agreements to action.

CREATING BINDING AGREEMENTS

Collaborative efforts are a slower but steadfast way to develop solutions and strategies that have the consent of those who can make or break their implementation. This section will feature stories about achieving binding public agreement. As you will see, the secret to success has been covered already: Consensus agreements tend to emerge quite naturally if thorough work has been put into building a shared awareness of the subject and conducting mutually acceptable analysis of the issues, considerations, and options. The specific benefits or shared agreement include 1) moving out of debilitating conflict and 2) determining the common will among diverse players.

Benefit 6: Moving out of Debilitating Conflict

Consensus building is the labor-intensive, commonsense route for moving out of conflicts or longstanding stalemates. Sometimes it is a first choice remedy, but more often it is a fallback resort after other approaches have failed. After years of attempting to "handle issues" by fighting it out, constituencies are reeling with the costs of conflict and are willing to look into the possible payoffs of cooperation. Groups may show up at the table more out of desperation than inspiration. They have tried and failed to resolve problems using old methods such as benevolent dictatorship, persuasive diplomacy, aggressive salesmanship, intimidation, and economic leverage. They return to dialogue a little more lucid and humble about the challenge of catalyzing cooperation. Granted, consensus building is not a sure path to mutually acceptable agreements, but it beats war. This was the case in a long-term dispute over the water, forest, and other natural resources of a watershed area in the northwestern part of the United States. One of the community leaders agrees that sheer exhaustion with fighting and stalemates brought warring parties to the consensus table: It really is easier to do war, but I think people were just tired of fighting. We desperately needed to come together for the sake of our forests and our communities.

A growing area of deep conflict is disputes over air, water, land, and other finite natural resources. These tend to be triggered by the lawsuits, petitions, protests, or activities of one or more constituencies that object to public or private actions. The path to harmony is not obvious. When an issue affects *my* land, *my* backyard air quality, or *my* pocketbook, the issue brings out deep diversity in deeply held beliefs. A consensus-based process for addressing these issues is viable only as long as it is a better alternative to continued protests, more lawsuits, or other shows of nonviolent force.

Value-laden conflicts can and do occur anywhere. Here are three examples of working through disputes using consensus — a statewide childcare system conflict, a labor-management dilemma, and a quest for a statewide forest policy acceptable to a multitude of clashing interest groups:

From Infighting to a Working Children's Agenda into the State Day Care System (1)

Issue: A state in the northwestern United States was struggling to respond to the ever-increasing need for early childhood care and education due to rising economic pressures on existing families and a sharp rise in teenage pregnancies. The incoming governor pledged to address the challenges of raising future generations and leave "successful child stewardship" as his legacy. The current system of day care and early childhood programs had failed to find answers to service gaps. One underlying issue was that no entity had stood up to take "the lead." The other problem was the so-called " debate over sponsorships." The child advocate network was mired in constant disputes over funds distribution and control of service budgets.

Consensus Response: Other governors had made similar promises, but this one was followed with successful action. Upon taking office he launched a state tour to "invite, cajole, coerce, and demand" that all stakeholders—parents, social workers, businesses, youth, politicians, government staff, foundations, and others—come to the table to improve the lives of the state's children.

The Child Care Issues summit in the early 1990s became a turning point for the state. Over 200 representatives from the state's 36 counties and all stakeholder groups met to launch a community-based plan for early childhood and day care services. The well-structured summit work sessions enabled people to address the "trilemma" of issues that needed systemic and simultaneous solutions—consistency of care quality, provider compensation, and affordable access to services statewide. The summit participants developed integrated local plans to assure early childhood education and care in every part of the state.

Results: The summit kicked off an ongoing partnership among public and private organizations. Childcare providers, parents, community representatives, and advocates are formally and informally linked, and the state is making significant strides in the level and scope of care of its very youngest children (1).

The Big Shift to Cooperative Municipal Labor–Management Relations

Issue: Most private businesses and public institutions continue to suffer the consequences of debilitating labor wars that have lasted well over a century. Distrust is institutionalized and joint efforts to strengthen services or production are weakened by an ongoing stream of work life issues that are resolved through grievances, arbitration, civil service proceedings, strikes, and work stoppages. When the response time for public emergency rescue far exceeded the acceptable timeframes for assuring patient survival, the city manager of a major municipality in southern United States decided it was time to rally the public troops (6).

Consensus Response: The city manager activated the city's Labor Management Committees (LMCs) as forums for improving the emergency services. The workers came through. A novel solution based on redesigning position and fast-track training was devised to increase frontline personnel and release monies to upgrade equipment. The citizens of the city's west side began to receive emergency help well under the required four minutes.

The successful pilot in cooperation triggered broader collaborative effort to change worker–manager relationships. The city manager raised the question, "What if labor and management sat down together to deal with shared issues regularly, not just when it is time to renegotiate a contract?" About 120 union representatives and heads of all the city departments gathered for an intensive "Shared Visions Conference" to use the LMCs as a base for changing the way the city made its operating decisions about the quality of work life, productivity, procedures, service, communication, and interpersonal relationships.

Results: The city departments have used the participative approach to decision making for over a decade. Developing solutions and agreements has not always been a cakewalk, but the many successes have proved the process viable and demonstrate what can happen when unused human resources are added to operations. Some sample initiatives and changes include significant reductions in overtime, absenteeism, and injuries in the solid waste department; new union-management procedures to negotiate equipment purchase with vendors; a "swap program" between departments to enable less busy areas to cover those that need extra help; and many other internal improvements that improve the quality, quantity, and cost-effectiveness of city services (6).

Statewide Example: Forest Strategies that Satisfy Adversaries

Issue: Citizens of a midwestern state had become increasingly concerned about the continued expansion of logging in state forests. Over several decades, many environmental groups and individuals actively pressured the resource agencies and the legislature to develop policies for balancing the consumption and protection of forested lands. A major study was conducted to see what was truly happening to the state's forested lands, their ecosystems, and related natural resources. Following that assessment, diverse and conflicting parties were assembled to determine consensus about how to implement the recommendations of the study (9).

Consensus Response: Over a seven-month period, 25 people representing diverse forest interests met in 19 daylong working sessions to build consensus for a comprehensive strategy for sustaining the state's forest resources. The group included representatives of environmental organizations, outdoor sportspersons' associations, conservation groups, the forest products industry, commercial logging contractors, the resort and tourism industry, research or higher education institutions, nonindustrial forest landowners, agricultural woodlot owners, state or federal natural resources agencies, county land departments, and labor unions of forest product companies.

Results: Their recommendations became the basis of enabling legislation—the Sustainable Forest Resource Act—requiring the state to adopt multiple interest/ stakeholder mechanisms for managing forest resource concerns at the landscape and site levels, including an ongoing forest resources council with statutory responsibilities to facilitate problem solving and policy recommendations. Other mechanisms were built to assure a broad-based citizen input for coordinating land management activities, monitoring forest status, conducting necessary research, and educating landowners, forestry professionals, and the public on forest stewardship guidelines and practices (9).

Benefit 7: Finding a Common Will Amidst Diverse Preferences

Collaborative discourse is the surest way to identify "public will." As I stated early in the preface, one of my core convictions is that there really is nothing new under the sun when it comes to getting things done as a group. The adage, "where there is a will, there is a way" is still the basic formula to cooperation and solutions. The challenge is determining the common will. This is where collaborative problem solving fills a big need. A well-structured process helps a group share individual preferences and negotiate a group preference or common will about what needs attention, what is mutually worth pursuing, and how resources could be used to address common problems.

Any consensus process is an example of the trials or triumphs of forming common will including all the stories in this chapter. In this section, I highlight a process called "Citizen Jury " developed by the Jefferson Center in Minnesota. It is a process used by many school districts and communities for identifying the public will on issues ranging from school funding to feedlot regulation.

The Citizen Jury Method for Identifying "Public Will"

Issue: National health care reform, budget priorities, environmental issues, and local school district facility needs are among the issues that have been addressed across the United States since 1997 by the Citizen Jury (10) process, a method pioneered by the Jefferson Center in Minnesota.

Consensus Response: The Jefferson Center has conducted over 30 Citizen Jury projects to tackle a number of topics by instituting a randomly selected and demographically representative panel of citizens to carefully examine significant public issues and develop recommendations that reflect the "will of the people." The jury of about 18 citizens serves as a microcosm of the stakeholder community. For four to five days they hear from a variety of expert witnesses, deliberate together on the issue, and develop consensual resolutions with the help of a moderator.

Results: The Citizen Jury process has many satisfied customers among public officials who want to hear the "people's authentic voice" on ways to address critical community issues. Some examples of issues successfully solved by citizen juries include the following:

- Decisions about facility development and funding in a rural school district
- State tax reform recommendations to develop citizen-driven state policies
- Tough choices for transportation/transit and open spaces in county land planning
- Decision about countywide regulation of hog feedlots
- Priorities for allocating the budget of a large urban county

Consensus fosters buy-in. Many consider this benefit as the most important advantage of consensus building. Participation is the only way to exchange perceptions, preferences, ideas, convictions, and power and amass authentic support for joint directions, priorities, projects, and decisions. Taking the time to construct decisions from the bottom up generates the power of "buy-in." There are no short cuts to identifying public or common will. It may be slow in coming, but is the most reliable way to real change and action implementation.

LAUNCHING SUPPORTED ACTION

Once a consensus agreement is made, collaborative problem solving naturally leads to implementing the agreement. Key benefits of collaborative decision making are: 1) Getting ideas activated on the ground and 2) building action partnerships. Consensus generates the power of pooled resources—connecting activities and resources of multiple organizations to achieve things that are impossible for one group to do.

Benefit 8: Getting Ideas Implemented!!!!

The ultimate proof of shared agreement is getting everyone to march forward to implement the decision together. The time invested in the previous steps yields the buy-in to make wishes come true—connect grand policies, models, and decisions to real results; create plans that don't end up on the shelf; identify solutions that are used; initiate reforms that are executed; talk that is walked; and conflict resolutions that are honored and supported.

The Department of Neighborhoods in Seattle has discovered how the impact of seed resources can be multiplied manifold through a collaborative approach (11). The city has instituted an ongoing matching grant program which provides funds to its 200 neighborhoods if local groups put up half of the resources in funds or in-kind labor. As a result, communities have been activated to conduct surveys and town meetings, and work cooperatively to identify needed projects and get them implemented. The quantity and diversity of new services and programs are far beyond anything the government could have developed on its own. The partnership has spawned such projects as after-school homework programs, ravine reforestations, playgrounds, parks, and initiatives addressing youth crime, murals, and many other important actions to enhance quality of life in residential neighborhoods.

Of course, even collaborative approaches are not a panacea. Negotiating realistic plans or aligning bureaucracies, programs, or resources of diverse entities is not a cakewalk. Consensus produces good outcomes, but they tend not to look like the ideal of any one stakeholder. In order to encourage public leaders, consultant Kathleen Osta passed on this encouraging advice about implementing projects in the public sphere: "The pressure to walk the talk or be all things to all people is tremendous. Let us not beat ourselves up if the results of collaboration don't go by some book or standard. The world is so confusing and complicated that it is a genuine miracle if we can just stumble the mumble!"

Implementing School Block Scheduling

In a study entitled *The Invisible Path to Shared Decision-Making* (12), David Webb follows two principals who implemented the same mandated program in their buildings, one using a consensual process and the other, a more directive approach. The findings and conclusions make an excellent example for the action benefit of shared decision making.

Issue: Introducing new mandates and requirements into a school system has been and always will be one of the major challenges of any administrator. As Machiavelli noted, there is nothing more difficult to carry out, nor more doubtful of success, nor more dangerous to handle, than to initiate a new order of things. In recent years, shifting to block scheduling has been one such change.

Consensus Response and Results: The paybacks of steering by the will of a diverse public is dramatized in a study of how two principals went about introducing block scheduling in their schools. They both held the requisite constituency meetings but conducted them very differently. The first principal "sold" the concept and failed to gain acceptance. The second principal successfully implemented the new scheduling system due to a bottom-up approach for getting broad-based understanding and buy-in (11).

Principal A created an informational strategy based on his own successful experience with the approach at his previous assignment and was a believer. He appointed a committee of three teachers to study the new scheduling option and conducted several information sessions and site visits to let the school and community personnel learn about the new approaches from satisfied users from other districts. After the staff development meetings, he asked for a staff vote on adopting block scheduling. The "yes" vote did not meet the 75 percent requirement he set. A year later, he reintroduced the concept and held additional presentations regarding the block-scheduling system. The staff acceptance seemed strong enough to go to the school board for approval. After the presentation, many stood up to oppose the system during the comment period. The principal was advised to put it off for another year.

Principal B involved the faculty, parents, students, and other administrators in a series of interactive meetings that enabled joint assessment, agreement, planning, and implementation of the new concept. Each step included education, reflection, addressing of concerns, and generating conclusions or next steps. The block-schedule system was predictably approved and implemented by all the stakeholders because they had built the system based on their common hopes, concerns, and will.

Benefit 9: Forming Interorganizational Action Partnerships

The advantage to collaborative problem solving is instant partnerships. Rather than costly agency mergers, consensus decision making has allowed multiple organizations to spend their precious resources and energy on better service delivery rather than bureaucratic transition. For example, when one state realized that a parent of a disabled child must go to 14 different agencies to get her child's daily needs met, the affected organizations got together in a few weeks of work sessions to develop a one-stop approach to service access.

Collaborative problem solving is the fastest way to develop service links between unlikely and likely players. If the representatives around the table have formal assignments to represent their organizations, consensus discussions and deliberations can devise workable ways to understand and work through challenging institutional systems to better achieve the missions of several organizations. I share two examples of interorganizational partnerships that were launched through consensus planning processes. The first is a research partnership that links university experts to agency managers. The other is an intersector alliance to serve people who have multiple health issues and experience chronic homelessness.

Linking Federal Agency Needs with University Resources

Issue: The academic community possesses and generates research products and services that managers urgently need to help with daily problem solving. For example, regions across the United States and the world are experiencing an escalating need to address complex environmental issues that transcend political, geographic, and social boundaries. Unfortunately, the scarce access to rigorous science and technical assistance limits the knowledge resource managers can bring to bear in addressing local and regional pollution management crises.

Consensus Response: To respond to the science gap in regional problem solving, research, education, and outreach partnerships have been established between major universities and federal agencies in multistate regions that share one large ecosystem, such as the Southern Appalachian Mountain Region, the Chesapeake Bay Watershed Region, and the Great Lakes Northern Forest Region. A team of representatives from 20 to 30 universities, land management agencies, and environmental nonprofit groups engineered a virtual organization that links resource managers on the ground with high-quality scientific research, technical assistance, and education from multiple sources of expertise.

Results: Every region of the United States now has an active ecosystem study partnership in various stages of development. The longest standing regions report progress identifying, conducting, and funding interdisciplinary research targets that can improve adaptive management approaches that would not have been possible without a collective effort (13).

Serving Homeless That Are the "Hardest to Serve"

Partnerships between public, private, and nonprofit organizations are challenging to develop, but collaborative service partnerships like this one may be the only way to address society's complex issues.

Issue: An urban area in the Midwest identified a population of persons experiencing chronic homelessness who were falling through all social safety nets: They were individuals and families with severe and persistent mental illness, HIV/AIDS, and/or chemical dependency diagnoses who have been homeless or were at high risk of losing their homes.

Consensus Response: A not-for-profit supportive housing organization stepped up to the plate to do something about the problem. They convened and funded a planning effort involving over 20 representatives of counties, state agencies, nonprofit service providers, consumers, consumer advocacy groups, managed care companies, and affordable housing organizations. The goal was to innovate a public/private, interorganizational, and consumer-centered service network to provide those "hardest to serve" with housing, health care, and support services.

Results: The work group secured the commitment of most organizations, devised meticulous but workable mechanisms for financing and administration that satisfied the protocols of their respective organizations and began serving clients in March 2001. An urban and rural pilot are operating today as concrete demonstrations of successful interorganizational problem solving (14).

According to Rosabeth Moss Kanter, the ultimate power is the ability to mobilize people (15). If so, consensus approaches are a leader's power tools for launching committed and supported action. When solutions draw on collective passion, power, and resources, two plus two can equal six.

DEVELOPING WORKING ALLIES

In addition to the pragmatic benefits of participative consensus decision making, the intangible outcomes are perhaps the most cogent. Face-to-face and heart-to-heart discourse dialogue builds human resolve and relationships. Policies and plans are worth very little without people who commit to the trial-and-error process of changing community—make the calls, run the committee meetings, write the grants, coordinate the budget cycles, lobby the authorities, gather over lunch to build strategies, set up the meetings, carry out the mutual favors, and execute details that convert ideas into lived realities.

Collective decision making generates the political and social capital necessary to execute agreements and actions. In the East, this understanding is embedded in practice. Joint ventures are initiated after trust and relationships are built over time and tea. The Western approach seeks to seal a deal and create trust and relationships as the engagement progresses (16). The task-trust-relationship sequence may be different, but both acknowledge that all three elements are essential to getting things done together.

Benefit 10: Creating Collegial Working Relationships

Consensus processes tend to achieve results because they generate mandates and motivations at the same time. Consensus methods encourage participants to engage as three-dimensional beings and use all their experiences, emotions, and intelligence to solve problems. Human energy, spirit, determination, and esprit de corps grow as stakeholders see their concerns, aspirations, frustrations, insights, and ideas merge into a contract for joint action. In the same way that a frown takes more muscles than a smile, consensual ventures can catalyze more action with less stress.

As individuals engage in formal and informal conversations with others at the table, they don't necessarily become fast friends, but they get to know real human beings connected to faceless departments, functions, organizations, positions, and propaganda. More often than not, participants in dialogue find even their alleged "worst enemies" to be credible people. The working relationships developed during the consensus experience are instrumental not only in carrying out the joint solutions but instigating cooperation on future projects.

I assume you have experienced the difference that passion can make in getting things done and would confirm that Maslow was right: human beings are at their best when they have a strong sense of safety, belonging, and significance. Quality of life and coexistence in a community of practice capacity translates to quality services and products. An anonymous sage observed history and put it this way: "Nothing great was ever achieved without enthusiasm." Once you have experienced the pleasure and power of collaborative activity, it is difficult to go back to stiffer, adversarial, and controlling ways of doing things

More and more, formal knowledge recognizes the critical link between spirit and productivity. In fact, the management literature at the turn of the millennium suggests that adding fun and even spirituality to work life maximizes organizational effectiveness. For example, you may have seen or encountered the *Fish* books and videos promoting play in offices or received invitations to numerous workplace and spirituality conferences. This is corroborated by recent brain research: the part of the brain that regulates emotions is the gatekeeper for all the intelligence functions. If a person is happy, the brain functions at maximum capacity. It may indeed be true that the much-ridiculed "touchy-feely" or "soft management" aspects of collaborative work are the hard cornerstones to making things happen.

Frances Moore Lappe observed how the democratic governance in a school upgraded the performance and life quality in an inner city high school (10). The long-standing tradition of student-driven school operations creates visible energy: "There's a spirit in the air; vibrant kids learning vibrantly—there's excitement instead of the usual metal detectors and 'depressed kids in a depressed environment' found in other similar schools. These students are exercising ownership over their own education." They are active in learning teams, where they make decisions about the course of their education. The contrast between this school and another one close by is dramatic: Instead of a 40 percent graduation rate and near-zero college attendance, they have a 90 percent graduation rate and 80 percent college attendance.

Nixed Education Department Reorganization Produces Lasting Staff Cohesion

Collegial commitment and passion to a direction formed through consensus can often outlast the formal program it created. This was the case in the reorganization of a state department of education (17).

Issue: One state department of education attempted to redesign service delivery using a consensus-based staff involvement process. The change was prompted by a 20 percent cut in staff and loud citizen calls to "fix" the system.

Consensus Response: The department took a major leap to build an agency structure to meet the unique and real needs of school districts and communities without administrative excess. All 300 staff were involved in a thorough review of customer needs and generating the best option to implement the agency mission of "ensuring the success of every learner."

The agency decided to launch a service structure that reduced the administrative hierarchy from 55 managers to 25 service team leaders. These close-to-the-ground frontline team were charged to develop customized service delivery to clusters of districts with similar needs. For example, one team focused on the two largest cities while others served distinct regions in the state or groups of smaller cities. Specialized expertise areas such as school financing, special education, and curriculum support would be made available as needed to districts and communities.

Results: The staff was excited about the change but the results were too slow for the governor. Midway through implementing the new structure, a new commissioner was appointed, resulting in a transition within a transition. Despite the disappointing turn of events, staff pointed out the solid bright side. The broad-based participation in the process increased the unity and solidarity of belief among the staff as reflected in this testimony by a long-time department employee:

> Even though the change process has slowed, as an organization we are never going to be the same again. While the organization design plan has changed and looks more "traditional," a new pattern of teamwork and interchange has been established. I believe this new pattern is governed by a shared set of beliefs and goals across the department developed during the planning process (17).

Joint Planning Proposals Activated Bit by Bit through New Relationships

Issue: I recently heard from a city manager that was part of a land design consensus process—called a design charrette—to find ways to please the multiple development desires for the same piece of geography. Four rural cities were landlocked by the adjoining mining properties and existing highways. The group came out with several strong land use options but from the perspective of outside observers like myself, the implementation seemed slow in coming.

Consensus Response and Results: At a recent project meeting, the city manager interrupted the progress evaluation with an enthusiastic testimonial endorsing the value of working relationships. He listed several spin-off planning projects currently underway simply because the charrette experience opened up an ongoing channel of communication and cooperation between the leaders of cities, agencies, and companies that he knew only by name and association for years.

Forming human alliances to activate plans may be the most important benefit of consensus building. Momentum is self-propelling when it is not dependent on a single individual, organization, term of office, or generation. Catalyzing cadres of change agents is a powerful leadership legacy.

CONCLUSION

Satisfied customers of consensus cite life-changing stories about how their work group, city block, community, department, company, region, or other group were able to accomplish things that were not possible for single individuals or entities. From organizing family reunions to operating the United Nations peacekeeping force, consensus dialogue ignites nontraditional routes to address nontraditional problems. For those who are sold on the power of teamwork, consensus building is a primary and daily leadership strategy.

Consensus unlocks the human capacity to resolve its own issues by leveraging and uniting the ideas, resources, and power of multiple entities. Like laser beams that concentrate multiple light rays into a powerful sword of light, they bring in the energy and ingenuity of citizens to help analyze and address controversial issues that are not being handled by our overloaded legislatures, councils, boards, agencies, and other existing forums and arenas. They bring organizations and sectors together to form new service alliances.

Every time we build consensus across boundaries we are pioneering contemporary ways to practice democratic decision making. Collaborative problem solving is perhaps a new type of "jury duty" and power tool for empowering processes of democratic governance. It is a badly needed "system upgrade" to our democratic technology. In the same way that children must shift their shoe size to fit their growing feet, it probably is time to reinvent the rules and venues of representative democracy to fit contemporary society. Collaborative problem solving continues the democratic experiment in pursuit of ways to practice government of the people, by the people, and for the people.

Many miracles have happened though consensus. I believe we have seen only a fraction of what collective entrepreneurship can do. Hopefully more leaders in schools, communities, corporations, and governments will join the consensus practitioners in demonstrating the power of consensus and add to the growing list of successes and benefits.

The final chapters are a minicourse in the design and delivery of effective consensus processes. Chapter 3 describes political dynamics at and around the consensus table. Chapters 4, 5, and 6 identify consensus-enhancing clues for sponsors, facilitators, and participants.

NOTES

1. True, S., & Elliot, J. (1995). Do it for the kids: Advocating for the children's agenda. In J. Troxel (Ed.), *Government works: Profiles of people making a difference.* Alexandria, VA: Miles River.

2. Weisbord, M. R. (1987). *Productive workplaces: Organizing and managing for dignity, meaning and community.* San Francisco: Jossey-Bass.

3. Cohn-Vargas, B., & Grose, K. A. (1998, May). A partnership for literacy. *Educational Leadership, 55* (8), 45–48.

4. Valley Crossing Community School. (2002). [Site council materials]. Woodbury, MN.

5. Institute of Cultural Affairs. (1980). *Report of the White House Conference on families and children*, Madison, WI.

6. Haydock, E. (1995). Labor management partnerships: Municipal union committees, Miami. In J. Troxel (Ed.). *Government works: Profiles of people making a difference.* Alexandria, VA: Miles River.

7. Smith, S. (1998, June). School-by-school: How site-based management is transforming education in Austin. *American School Board Journal, 22–25.*

8. Smith, W. E. (1992). Planning for the electricity sector in Colombia. In M. Weisbord (Ed.), *Discovering common ground* (p. 180). San Francisco: Berrett-Koehler.

9. Hanson, M. (2001). *Constructing sustainability policy through collaboration: A multi-site case study of decision-making processes that seek sustainable solutions for statewide forests or local watershed development.* St.Paul, MN: University of St. Thomas.

10. Jefferson Center. (1997). *Citizens Jury: Effective public participation.* [Also, a list of citizen jury projects]. Minneapolis, MN: Jefferson Center Board of Directors.

11. Lappe, F. M., & Dubois, P. M. (1994, Fall–Winter). Bringing democracy to life: What works and why—An informal dialogue. *National Civic Review,* 413–429.

12. Webb, D. (2001). *The invisible path to shared decision-making: A comparative case study of two schools attempts to overcome barriers to change.* St. Paul, MN: University of St. Thomas.

13. Cooperative Ecosystem Study Unit. (2002). *Annual report 2002: Cooperative ecosystems studies units network.* Washington DC: U.S. Department of the Interior.

14. The National Center on Family Homelessness. (2004). *The Minnesota supportive housing and managed care pilot: Qualitative evaluation; year two. Hearth Connection Project.* Minneapolis, MN: Author.

15. Moss Kanter, R. (1989). Foreword. In L. J. Spencer, *Winning through participation.* Dubuque, IA: Kendall/Hunt.

16. Meridian Resources. [Cross-cultural business training materials]. San Francisco: Meridian Consulting Firm.

17. Hanson, M., & Laxdal, S. (1995). Building a habit of transformation in the state of Minnesota. In J. Troxel (Ed.), *Government works: Profiles of people making a difference.* Alexandria, VA: Miles River

Chapter Three

Consensus Politics: What Really Happens in the Process?

If one wishes to realize the distance which may lie between "facts" and the meaning of facts, let one go to the field of social discussion. . . . Many persons seem to suppose that facts carry their meaning along with themselves on their face. Accumulate enough of them and their interpretation stares at you. The development of physical science is thought to confirm the idea. But the power of physical facts to coerce belief does not reside in the bare phenomena. It proceeds from method. . . . Only when the facts are allowed free play for the suggestion of new points of view is any significant conversion of conviction as to meaning possible.

—John Dewey,
The Public and Its Problems, 1927

What does consensus building really look and feel like from the perspective of those who have been participants in various processes? "People are the key!" claim guidebooks, manuals, gurus, and ground rules, but more information exists about how "good participants" *should* behave than what consensus collaborators *really* do.

Curiosity about the insider experience led me to study the consensus process from the participant's point of view (1). In 2000, I interviewed 35 people from across the United States who participated in four separate collaborative processes addressing high-conflict environmental issues. The testimonials, stories, and insights of these process insiders uncovered the formal and informal activities involved when diverse stakeholders tackle complex issues in pursuit of shared agreements.

This chapter describes the inner workings and political dynamics of a consensus-building process as experienced and expressed by consensus participants. It offers clues to understanding the political dynamics of any consensus process even though some elements may apply only to extremely controversial situations.

CONSENSUS DOES NOT MAKE POLITICS GO AWAY

Collaborative problem solving is a new wrinkle in the ancient art of politics. Like any other type of problem solving or decision making, collaboration is a dynamic process of exchanging information, perspectives, positions, and proposals, and making group judgments about how to distribute limited resources among competing needs. It is the process of transforming diverse wills into common political will.

Politics is the essence of making history through discourse rather than force. Unfortunately, "politics" has become a much-reviled concept in our day. In disgust, I hear people say, "it all came down to politics"; "can't we take the politics out of the debate?" or confessing to be "tired of playing company politics." Management scientist Gareth Morgan agrees that the negative connotation of political activity is a detriment to living together effectively (2):

> Politics, in short, is seen as a dirty word. This is unfortunate because it prevents us from recognizing that politics and politicking may be an essential aspect of organizational life and not necessarily an optional or dysfunctional extra. In this regard, it is useful to remember that in its original meaning the idea of politics stems from the view that, where interests are divergent, society should provide a means of allowing individuals to reconcile their differences through consultation and negotiation . . . Aristotle advocated politics . . . a means for creating order out of diversity while avoiding forms of totalitarian rule. (2)

The phenomenon of "hackers" has suffered the same fate. Originally a "hacker" was someone that used and navigated the computer world proactively and creatively. Now it has come to mean those who abuse and manipulate systems for criminal intents.

I believe the widespread aversion to politics reflects disgust with the *tendencies* for money or other powerful, narrow motives to dominate the discourse. When people blame "politics" for a certain outcome in elections, legislation, hiring, priority setting, committee selection, etc., they are usually bemoaning the fact that elite minorities with financial, relational, constituency, or other power influenced the decision process to work in their favor. I agree with those who believe democratic processes are in need of some fundamental rebalancing, but that is the subject of another conversation or book. Collaborative forums are not a miracle cure for eliminating selfish motives or power imbalances from the political process. However, well-constructed consensus problem solving can contribute greatly to leveling the political playing field and restore respectability and passion for politics.

Politics involves forming group judgments. Even for individuals, making judgments is the most subjective, idiosyncratic, organic, and human step in decision making. Here is a scientific description of the judgment process according to Professor Gerald Smith:

> Because of its importance to decision making, judgment has been the subject of extensive research. Despite this, the process is not well understood. . . . Judgment involves a high degree of subjectivity. . . . Human judgment is seen as subject to various failings and biases. Though judgment and reasoning are often intertwined, the two are distinct

cognitive processes. . . . A judgmental conclusion can be justified in terms of the factors that are considered, but it cannot be explained by giving reasons. (3)

Reasoning, assessment, and analysis should be a part of good decision making but at some point, one or more human beings makes a judgment about the matter at hand.

In a consensus process as in democracy, people exchange ideas, urgencies, power, resources, convictions, opinions, and solutions and then make decisions about collective priorities using their best judgment. This is true in annual business planning, college course scheduling, legislative action, developing operating budgets, allocating grants, or forming a jury verdict. People interact with the content, process, each other, and whatever else in order to make judgments within a delimited amount of time.

THREE POLITICAL PILLARS IN CONSENSUS BUILDING: SPONSORS, FACILITATORS, PARTICIPANTS

As mentioned early in the preface, the main clue about consensus building is that successful consensus politics requires more than the "right" method or facilitator. Effective outcomes are the result of hands-on involvement by three key players—sponsors, facilitators, and participants—who play crucial political roles for assuring that the consensus process produces mutually beneficial judgments.

Management scientist James Brian Quinn (4) studied the dynamics governing how and why innovations survive, thrive, or die: Like babies, innovations require proactive, flexible, and attentive care of three agents—parent, guardian, and pediatrician. Venture teams composed of dispassionate experts were not effective. Because innovations are as unpredictable and vulnerable as babies, they succeeded only through customized attention, judgment, and maintenance. Quinn concluded that growing ideas into innovations required three key elements:

- A *parent* that loved the project irrationally
- A *guardian* that protected the project with resources and authorization, and
- A *pediatrician* that contributed advice and technical assistance about child-raising

The organic political process of consensus building also requires the multiple caretaker roles of a sponsor (as guardian), facilitator (as pediatrician), and participants (as parents) (see figure 3.0):

- The project *sponsors* are the *guardians* that position a meaningful project. They authorize the consensus group and support it with resources.

Process Sponsors
provide meaningful positioning:
They structure...

- Compelling **Reasons**
- Clear **Roles**
- Engagement **Rules**
- Support **Resources**

A.
Sponsors:
**Meaningful
POSITIONING**

B.
Facilitators:
**Unifying
PROCESS**

C.
Participants:
**Dedicated
PEOPLE**

"The Pediatricians"

Process Facilitators
provide unifying process:
They lead...

- **Plan** Group Process
- **Preside** at Meetings
- Assure **Public Recording**

"The Parents"

Process Participants
provide problem solving:
They serve as...

- **Advocates** for diverse views
- **Ambassadors** for solutions

Figure 3.0.   Key Roles in Collaborative Problem Solving

- The *facilitators* are the *pediatricians*: They do not have a stake in the consensus outcome but know about consensus building in general. They are dedicated to providing state-of-the-art advice and leadership in developing and delivering a unifying process and assuring consensus is reached.
- The consensus *participants* serve as the *parents*. Without their engagement and passion, problems cannot be transformed into solutions that make sense in the real world and which everyone is willing to support.

How does consensus of participants, facilitators, and sponsors inhibit or enhance the effective exchange ideas, urgencies, power, resources, convictions, opinions, and solutions for the sake of determining collective priorities? The rest of the chapter takes a candid look at how consensus processes work as a political judgment process.

THE PARTICIPANTS: THE POLITICS
OF DELIBERATING CONSENSUS

The consensus participants I interviewed had wide discretion in the way they fulfilled the job of representing stakeholder interests in consensus building. Everyone seemed to agree with one key point. The visible actions at the table are just the tip of the political iceberg. In the same way that the majority of an iceberg rests hidden under water, strong influence is exerted and mobilized backstage. The process of collaboration relies heavily on intense and unofficial acts of individual leadership. The front stages are public or official interactions with external parties to connect, influence, give, and take. The backstages are places to "let one's hair down," strategize privately, brief, debrief, caucus, and prepare for the front stage action at the table.

There was no limit to the amount of work a representative could do to help move the consensus mission. The successful or unsuccessful outcome to the collaborative process was heavily influenced by the degree to which individuals engaged their private passion and energy to enact their public role.

The Front Stage Activity

The front stages were times when representatives participated in business meetings or other official activities. Every meeting hour was packed with activity in order to optimize the limited time available for the task at hand. According to the interviews, the representatives found front stage work extremely intense and challenging. After one exhausting day, one member remarked, "In these participation processes, the power really belongs to the guys that can stay alert and aggressive all day and then have enough energy to explain everything to the folks back home." In assessing the participants' experiences, the front stage duty included three main functions: 1) Absorbing background information, 2) participating in consensus deliberations, and 3) holding formal feedback meetings with their constituencies. Chapter 6 shares specific insights and clues about fulfilling these duties.

The Backstage Activity

Almost all of the interviewed representatives reported that their duty involved far more than the activities on main stage. Only one person explicitly limited his service to meeting attendance, explaining, "All I can do is commit to being at the table and do my best to support the right courses of action." When I asked participants to describe the informal "backstage" aspects of serving as a representative (actions not directly connected to on-site meeting participation), the list of backstage duties outnumbered those performed front stage.

Backstage activities were critical to success. Formal meetings tended to reveal, report, exchange, and formalize ideas and resolves that emerged informally. As one person put it, "If you wait until the meetings, you've missed the most important places to affect what is going to end up happening." Like this participant, most were very matter-of-fact about the role of backstage activity:

> You have to work the issue between the meetings. I don't think it's wrong to meet between sessions. I think you have to recognize that it's going to happen. It's a matter of getting in there and mixing it up with everybody else who's going to be doing it. And you can't assume naively that you can just wait until the meeting and then count votes because it just doesn't work that way. (1)

What exactly was involved with "working the issue between meetings"? The specific behind-the-scenes activities fell into four major areas of engagement: 1) Preparing for consensus deliberations, 2) developing participant relationships, 3) advocating position proposals, and 4) promoting collaborative solutions. Chapter 6 follows up with more details and clues about fulfilling these duties.

More Than One Way to Serve as Advocates and Ambassadors

As the consensus process progressed, some interesting differences emerged in the way consensus participants advocated for their positions and acted as consensus ambassadors. As I have observed and listened to the trials and triumphs of the collaboration delegates, I discovered that in the beginning everyone participated in a very similar fashion. However, participation of some representatives intensified as the judgment phase drew closer.

Varying Degrees of Backstage Action

In Phase I, a majority of the representatives engaged mainly through the front stage roles and those backstage activities that were directly connected to on-site meetings such as reading background materials and conversing informally with peers. However, a few members began their proactive stage activities immediately—communicating with the meeting leaders, caucusing with peers in their ideological community to influence the process, and preparing meeting inputs offstage.

The early backstage actions often prompted initial turning points in the deliberation. These turning points focused issues, increased controversies, or influenced the process for arriving at final judgments. After significant turning points, more representatives shifted their engagement into higher gear. The difference in level of engagement was apparent to peer participants as indicated in this excerpt:

> One of the things that amazed me was that some of the stakeholders had more "stakes" than others. Some seemed to put more energy into this than other groups did. It was obvious that [some] groups really networked back within their organizations; other groups just showed up at the meetings. They really didn't do much. (1)

As the quote indicates, many perceived there to be two levels of engagement—those who engaged deeply and those who "didn't do much." However, according to representatives' own accounts, even those who did not look engaged were actually quite active.

In the initial phases of a process, two representation style became evident—those who asserted themselves mainly at the front stage sessions and those who asserted their influence on and off stage. Those with higher personal and professional stakes in the issue participated more aggressively.

Various Interpretations for Being "Collaborative"

As the scheduled ending came closer and many realized the need to produce results, another division emerged in the representation styles. Some representatives began to advocate harder for their party line. Others decided to put more energy into engineering cooperative solutions that could garner general support. One representative referred to these styles as "glitter and grease" (1):

> In these settings you can be glitter or you can be grease. Some stand out in my mind as very constructive and impressive persons who provided some grease in the gears on occasion.

I believe the representative was referring to "glitter" as those who promoted their own interests and "grease" the ones who helped grease the wheels of consensus.

Another representative had a more elaborate analysis of the same phenomenon. She used a Greek philosopher's metaphor about "foxes and hedgehogs" to describe those who were open-minded cooperatives and those who were single-minded advocates for their own interest:

> There were two types of members at the table, foxes and hedgehogs. According to Greek poet Archilochus, "the fox knows many things, but the hedgehog knows one big thing." Author Isaiah Berlin (5) used that metaphor for looking at people and philosophies. . . . For example, Karl Marx was a hedgehog. John Locke was a fox because he was willing to look at different ways of doing things and not hooked into one way of getting at something. One of the reasons that the collaborative process turned out the way it did is that there were a lot of hedgehogs and not enough foxes. Some were half-fox and half-hedgehog . . . and that meant they were a loose cannon at times. That bothered those in their interest group. (1)

In these observations, participants noted that representatives differed in their degree of cooperativeness.

Win/win agreements don't appear magically just because participants are responsible for advocacy and ambassadorship, but a group is more likely to develop consensus if it is the declared objective. The "willingness of the heart" has everything to do with finding solutions, according to a Dyak proverb from Borneo:

> Where the heart is willing it will find a thousand ways
> Where the heart is unwilling it will find a thousand excuses

If participating groups and individuals are not ready to play the dual roles of advocate and ambassador, consensus building may not be the appropriate process for interaction or conflict resolution. Mediation, litigation, or other formats are better suited for parties that wish solely to advocate for their positions.

Four Ways to Participate as Issue Advocates and Consensus Ambassadors

Participants in consensus processes agreed to adopt the collaborative mode of interaction. They were chosen by their constituencies because they were deemed to be effective advocates, good communicators, and committed to help find mutually beneficial and agreeable solutions. In following the actions and experiences of those who served in the collaborator mode, differences emerged in how people interpreted "collaborative" participation. All participants believed they put in a "good-faith effort" to collaborate at the consensus table. However, each participant adopted a unique mix of *assertiveness* for a particular interest and *cooperativeness* to find common ground.

The variance in collaborative styles revealed an interesting pattern: The four quadrants of the Thomas–Kilmann Conflict Mode Model (figure 3.1) (6)—competing, avoiding, accommodating, and collaborating—are mirrored *within* the collaborative mode. As shown in figure 3.1, consensus builders demonstrated at least four genuine ways to participate as a collaborative problem solver.

- The Boundary Guards engaged assertively but not very cooperatively. They were *competitive collaborators* who were very aggressive in promoting their interests and less cooperative in searching for common ground.
- The Team Players were cautiously cooperative and assertive. They chose to reserve their judgments and *avoided* taking stands until they had good reason to side with either the big team—the collective opinion, or any particular smaller team— a special interest caucus that was making sense at the time.
- The Boundary Spanners believed in *accommodating* as much as possible to find common ground. They tended to have broad or neutral interests, therefore, were less assertive in fronting their interests and very cooperative in looking for shared agreements.
- The Solution Brokers were both aggressive and cooperative. They stayed very faithful to their own interests while searching for common ground aggressively. These were *collaborative collaborators*.

One style of collaborating is not better or more righteous than another. They are simply different ways to engage as a consensus builder.

The style of collaboration is not a new way to categorize personality traits or psychological types. It indicates choices participants make about how they implement their role in the consensus dialogue. Participants did not exhibit just one style. Some shifted their style several times in response to the way the discourse evolved and intensified.

Many things contribute to the quantity and quality of consensus participants' style of political engagement including their personal or professional stake in the issue, familiarity with the subject matter, experience with group process, relationships with other members, and availability of time and resources as well as individual characteristics such as personal traits, temperament, and interaction preferences. Ideologies were only one of many factors participants considered as they made choices about how to perform their representational duty. Participants of all persuasions chose all the styles.

Before I discuss the various modes of collaboration, I want to review my reasons for bringing attention to them. First, even though I was not looking for categories in my practice or my studies, they emerged. Second, the identification of consensus builder styles enabled me to appreciate every role as valid and necessary. Third, the framework provides a useful way to understand and appreciate the central role of individuals in

Roles participants choose in the politics of deliberating consensus

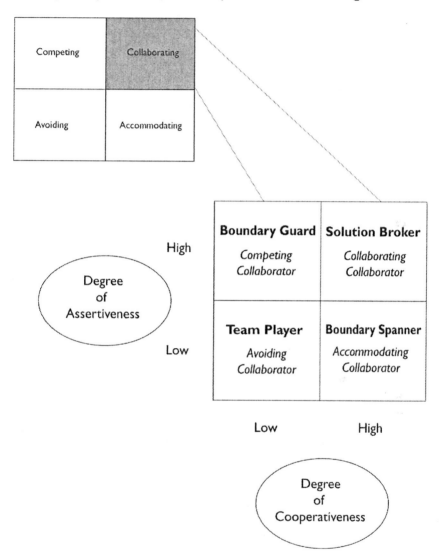

* (Adapted from the Thomas–Kilmann Conflict Mode Model)

Figure 3.1.   Four Different Styles of Consensus Builders

Even among consensus builders, there are differences
in their interpretation of collaboration.

Style Features	Less Cooperative in being consensus ambassadors	More Cooperative in being consensus ambassadors
More Aggressive in advocating their interests	The **BOUNDARY GUARDS** Those who seek collaborative solutions that expand the boundaries of their influence and avoid/minimize losing the ground they have previously gained	The **SOLUTION BROKERS** Those who use every formal and informal channel to engineer meaningful, win-win agreements that satisfy their interests and those of all the other stakeholders
Less Aggressive in advocating their interests	The **TEAM PLAYERS** The "undecided voters" who side with their interest group "team" or the multiple stakeholder "team" based on the issues or merit of argument	The **BOUNDARY SPANNERS** The "big picture" participants who support and promote any approaches that favor harmony, closure, or boundary bridging

Figure 3.2.   Consensus Builder Profiles

consensus success. In the next four sections, I describe the way in which the Boundary Guards, Team Players, Boundary Spanners, and Solution Brokers each tackle the quest for "win-win" solutions (see figure 3.2).

The Boundary Guards

Boundary Guards adopted a style of collaborative representation that was highly assertive and minimally cooperative. In their view of the world, an effective collaborative process was like a contract negotiation. Therefore, they felt that the best way to ensure sustainable development was for each party to negotiate as effectively as possible for its stake or position. For the Boundary Guards, "negotiating in good faith" meant that collaboration would be achieved if all parties bargained aggressively for their positions. They assumed a leadership role in guarding or even expanding their influence on the given issue. They did not want to lose ground in fronting their interest. They were willing to consider solutions that did not cross sacred boundaries in their sense of right and wrong. As one participant summarized the style: "I was careful not to give anything up." Other participants described Boundary Guards as "soldiers of fortune," "confrontational and impatient," "Darth Vaders," "extremists," or "people that were interested more in protecting their turf than finding solutions." At each turning point in the debate, the Boundary Guards intensified their level of assertiveness and commitment.

They aimed to win big, but at the least, they hoped to come through with specific and tangible gains that would expand their domains. According to one observer, "many of us wanted results a slice at a time, but [the most extreme Boundary Guards] wanted the whole loaf, to blow up the ovens, and burn the wheat fields. We just can't deal with that. We can deal with evolution but not revolution." Collaboration meant persuading others to have it your way.

Until the end, the Boundary Guards behaved like missionaries, hoping to convince or convert others to their truths. The imperative to win more political territory and expand their constituent boundaries is evident in this advice about serving as an effective representative:

> I think you can't be naïve about what other people's perceptions are. You have to realize they don't think the way you do. And your number one objective is to get them to think more in your light. And I think that's exactly what I tried to do. But you have to be more forceful than I was at first, back when I didn't understand this process. I was a little naïve in thinking that the right would win. It doesn't win out. You've got to get it in there and fight for your right. You have to be influential and that is tough. (1)

In some sense, the end justified the means for the Boundary Guards. They were skillful communicators that used all of the allotted airtime and available tactics to make their case, keep the debate moving, and ensure a substantive decision-making process. Here, a member explains the aggressive style of participation of many Boundary Guards (1).

> When I walk into a collaborative process, part of my intent, and I'm sure you recognized it at the time, was to intentionally throw in a hand grenade, and part of the reason for doing that was to flush these issues on the table. I know it makes the job tough for facilitators, but we can have a love fest and accomplish nothing, or we can put the issues on the table and try to deal with them.

Because the Boundary Guards treated the collaborative process as a contract negotiation, they were very aware of authority, accountability, and power issues. They were explicitly not interested in promises and intents. They wanted fair and binding agreements and public mechanisms to enforce them. The Boundary Guards were always conscious of the power bases on either side of the boundary. In this comment, a participant describes the essential ingredients of a fair negotiation process (1):

> When you look at mediations, in some contexts that I've worked in, this power issue is real important. I think mediation can work out real well if there is reasonable balance between the parties. But if one party has a real handicap of power (and I include knowledge as being power), there may be a result that will settle the matter, but it won't necessarily have achieved the public policy or the goal that was behind the conflict to begin with.
>
> I would say that before even agreeing to participate, you've got to find another source of power. If there's a credible threat of litigation for example, file a case, and then put it on hold. But make sure there is some other counter valuing power out there, because without that sense of power, it doesn't become an honest problem solving effort, it becomes a way of.orienting a process to help delay the actual changes that are going to happen someday.

As the account reiterates, the Boundary Guards' focused on "honest problem solving." They were constantly guarding the power balance and watching how the various sides were influencing the decisions.

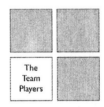

The Team Players

The Team Players adopted a watch and see representational style that was minimally assertive and minimally cooperative. For them, the collaborative process was like a high-level committee, jury duty, or a board meeting. The issues were important to them but not a major priority to their lives or livelihood. As one person stated upfront, "This was not a life or death issue for me." Nevertheless, they felt duty-bound to make the right decisions and were extremely thoughtful in coming to judgments.

They played on two teams in performing their consensus duty. They switched allegiances based on the substantive merits of the discussion. They made their choices about when to agree, sign, support, or oppose by looking for cues from two places: Sometimes they resonated with the arguments of their home team—the stakeholder interests or ideology they represented. However, sometimes they aligned closely with the new paradigms of the collaboration team. Team Players waited until all the evidence was in or the time was up to make up their minds. In the following statement, one member provides a glimpse into the Team Player thought process: Give the discussion the benefit of the doubt and try hard to support whatever seems to be the best truths:

> I don't know if there was any common ground at the beginning. There might have been a common ally. The goal setting gave us some special words that we agreed on and that made me say, "OK. These people are OK. They're not dumb." And once we agreed on those and the process of hanging little tags here and tags there and seeing what those people's comments were and how they were relating into my comments and my vocabulary and my commitment to safe, ethical, and responsible hunting, fishing, trapping, and shooting sports, I could see. I could start picking the connections out. It built my confidence, and then I was ready to work. . . . It was approximately at this time that I remember really starting to put my energies into it, helping come to consensus and working with people. (1)

The major turning points in the deliberation did not have a significant effect on their level of participation. They felt that the way to conduct a fair, collaborative process and to fulfill their duty was to participate wholeheartedly in front stage activities. As these participants put it, "All I can do is commit to being at the table and do my best to support the right courses of action" or "I represented my constituency the best I could. I solicited and received little input." They typically attended all consensus-building meetings and those of their constituency group. They shared reports back and forth. They did their best to advocate for the interest positions of their groups while listening to other sides and participating in group discussions about common ground. They did the best they could to add value to the discussion. One Team Player said, "Most people were respectful of others' opinions, but some were closed minded. I tried to make personal contact to bridge." However, if specifically invited by a member of the home team (stakeholder or ideological group) or full team (consensus-building body), they would participate in needed backstage activities for one team or the other, depending on what teams were aligned with a given Team Player's convictions.

They were active but often perceived by others as "nonplayers" in the ultimate brokering of resolutions and agreements. In the interviews, participants referred to Team Players as "hand raisers" or "freelancers." In talking to the Team Players, it is clear that their silence and or deliberativeness did not mean a lack of participation. As confirmed by this account, they did not consider themselves mere followers (1):

> The amount of time spent speaking is not necessarily indicative of effective participation. I was able to offer some practical solutions as I saw them from a policy perspective and practitioner's perspective.

The few Team Players that represented middle-of-the-road constituencies tended to play mainly on the consensus builders team. They had a clear and simple stance on the proper way to participate, as is evident in this account (1):

> I guess from my standpoint, I try to avoid any advocacy role. That's probably why I was among the one-third on the lower end of being quiet. But that was because I really wasn't trying to push any agenda, just provide knowledge and some perspective and value if nothing else. That's my own personal feeling on that. I felt that was the role I should play.

Team Players were often those that were new to the dialogue and not as familiar with all the ins and outs of the issues being discussed. Therefore, they expected the public agencies and institutionalized interest groups to provide leadership in the debate. In the interviews, many of them wondered why so much of the policy dialogue was left up to an ad hoc committee like the panel or roundtable. This sentiment is aptly expressed in these excerpts that question the value of seeking advice from non-mainstream participants (1):

> Well, I struggled all the time with feeling that I was in over my head on the basis of actually knowing enough about this subject. And more than once I would think, there are people in the agencies that know much more about this than me. Why do they have to call in poor little me? Of course I've got my opinions, but these other people have studied this subject for years. Some of them have studied this in college, they have degrees in it, and they know what really needs to be done. Then why are they putting a person like me up against professional people that are long term paid representatives of an interest group? I felt that I didn't know everything that I should know to adequately understand and discuss the issues.
>
> I don't really know that there were brokers that are able to communicate across boundaries. . . . If those people exist, that's what you have to have; someone who can take an extreme position, absorb it, work on it, communicate it and then bring it back to the table for everyone's consideration. We need the typical mediator type who goes through one party to another party carrying messages. I think frankly that the agencies could have handled this whole process on their own, without this group at all.

Team Players were extremely good listeners and self-conscious learners. One talked about how the process was an "opportunity for me to develop some of my inner skills and that was listening. And that's really helped me now with my career, partnerships, being able to listen to the clients; listen to people." In the interviews, many Team Players identified the educational aspects of the process as one of the key benefits or successes of the collaboration experience. Here are several testimonials to the learning value of the process (1):

- I learned a lot about the perspectives of constituents in the discussion—I preferred to be a listener, especially because I was somewhat well-versed on the topics.

- I learned a lot about other people's views and why they feel that way. After such a long time spent with people you become more familiar and more comfortable dealing with them. You can understand them better.
- My understanding of the diverse values in this topic increased very much because issues were introduced with points that had never crossed my mind. . . . The more you know about others' ideas, the better you are able to interact or counteract. There are real differences in understanding and appreciation.

The Team Player base of power was their mystery. They were, so to speak, the undecided voters that could decide the outcome of the election. They followed the advice of an anonymous sage who said, "A good hunter changes his way as often as he needs to."

The Boundary Spanners

The Boundary Spanners were ready to do anything for unity. They wanted to deal with whole systems. They believed that cohesion is better than competition. They felt both sides of the boundary were necessary to achieve a fair and balanced outcome. They tend to have a broad life context that is persistently biased toward proposals that favor unity and alignment. They take to heart the 1970 message from the biologists of six countries meeting in Menton, France, May 1970:

> To our 3.5 billion neighbors: Earth, which has seemed so large, must now be seen in its smallness. We live in a closed system, absolutely dependent on Earth and each other for our lives and those of the succeeding generations. The many things that divide us are therefore of infinitely less importance than the interdependence and danger that unites us. (16)

The Boundary Spanners were extremely cooperative and minimally assertive on behalf of a particular interest. Their special interest was the good of the whole. Because of their liberal arts orientation, experience in the public or civic sector, etc., they were dedicated spokespersons of bridge building across ideological, geographic, jurisdictional, or other boundaries. If they did represent a narrower interest, they felt that the interest of their stakeholder group would be best served by reaching as much common ground as possible. As illustrated in the next account, many Boundary Spanners felt that consensus success needs some who specialize in "keeping the group together" (1):

> You've got to have people whose bottom line is in representing their interests but you've also got to have people whose heart, soul, and bottom line is keeping the group together.

Anybody who thinks that the latter is not important, that the process should just include a bunch of interests, should take a look at some of the other unsuccessful examples of collaboration. I believe they fell apart because they did not have a mix of participants.

Other participants nicknamed the Boundary Spanners as "big picture leaders," "free agents," or "moderating influences."

This style of consensus participation came naturally for the Boundary Spanners because they did not represent a narrow interest. They tended not to have direct, personal, and/or professional stakes in the outcome of the consensus. They felt it "came with their territory" as is evident in the comment of a Boundary Spanner who said: "I considered myself a public servant—everyone's constituents were my constituents." However, those who had specific interests to represent felt that the long-term interests of their constituencies would best be served if there were systemic progress on the issue being addressed.

The Boundary Spanners were faithful ambassadors for the collective product. Like the Team Players, their primary stage of action was the meetings. They approached the consensus building activity like a policy think tank or a planning retreat. The group could count on them to help identify synthesis points and make compelling cases for bridge-building solutions. Given this type of commitment to minimizing boundaries, the Boundary Spanners were always ready to find and support the emerging areas of common ground. Their role was appreciated by other consensus builders as illustrated in this statement by an activist Boundary Guard (1):

> For most members, there was a willingness to listen, show differences, and respect others' views. We also gained from the presence of some skillful synthesizers' . . . members with a 'big picture' attitude.

As with the Team Players, the major turning points did not influence their level of engagement. They considered themselves active front stage participants from the start. However, if requested by members of the collaboration group, these "big picture" players were ready to lobby offstage if it helped the common cause. They would be willing to call a member that needed persuasion or help testify regarding a bill at the legislature. In this excerpt, one Boundary Spanner "pleads guilty" to going above and beyond the front stage duties to fight for solidarity (1):

> I tried to play a constructive, supportive role. I thought this was a good thing. I do remember that when we got down to the wire, I will plead guilty to making a phone call or two myself. I called one person once because I knew he was wrestling with whether to support the consensus product or not. As a matter of conscience I thought it was a good thing for as many people as possible to support it. We'd done a lot of hard work. So I called him and said, "I know you're struggling with this, and I'm not trying to twist your arm, but if there's anything that I could possibly do to help you be more comfortable about this, I'd like to let you know I'm available." Hopefully, I helped make him a bit more comfortable.

The Solution Brokers

The Solution Brokers were proactive architects, contractors, and dealmakers of collaborative solutions. For them, the collaborative process was like the legislative session—a forum where one could use any means possible to influence individual judgments. They were Boundary Spanners and Guards. They advocated aggressively in both directions: They lobbied for their own interests but listened intently in order to find clues to substantive agreements and/or innovative ways to ensure that some forward movement was achieved in the collaborative process. This role was extremely difficult and labor intensive but as is obvious here, some took it on as proven by this account (1):

> I wanted the process to work, and I was willing to reach out beyond my faction. I tried to find common ground and worked hard at wordsmithing to bring others along.

At the table or away from the table, they worked overtime to serve as evangelists for their interest groups as well as the collaborative cause.

The Solution Brokers intensified their rally after each turning point. Like the Boundary Guards, they had a lot at stake and used every means possible to make sure that the process would produce results that made a temporary or lasting difference in the long-term quest for sustainability. They were described by others in the process as people who were "skillful synthesizers," "extremely constructive about trying to find a middle ground," "trying to figure out ways of solving the problems," "really putting their hearts into it thinking it will make a difference," and "most interested in seeking agreement." One participant described their role as "negotiators" (1):

> There were some friendly and unfriendly elements, but we were pretty civilized most of the time. . . . Also, in any group like that, there were a few people that rise to the top and use their voices to help unify things. And my role was that of a negotiator. . . . When things got tough and it looked like we were going to fracture in the consensus group, a few of us would work out the negotiation. It's not quite that overt in some processes, but there are always the voices with more experience that are willing to engage for the good of the whole.

Most Solution Brokers were veteran players in public life and knew that virtuous principles must be applied in an imperfect and ambiguous world. Like the Boundary Guards they paid close attention to complex power dynamics and realities. They

knew the challenges of enacting policy or making systemic change in any social issue. In the volatile world of public affairs, nothing comes easily. Advocating for anything requires constant negotiation, patience, and persistence. They have also
learned that multiple-stakeholder lobbying and entrepreneurship has more power to
affect history than each interest working alone. Thus, they want to leverage the influence of every consensus-building opportunity. As one Solution Broker put it, "As
one manager in one organization, you are limited as to the impact you can have on
statewide issues. This type of consensus-building process allows you to have a
greater impact." Another had a similar comment (1):

> We worked actively to remind the whole group that keeping the collaboration process
> community together was the key to having policymakers pay attention to the product.
> Also, the key was to know when to stop working toward more detail and recognize the
> points of agreement.

They were pragmatists as they went about their brokering work.

What exactly was involved in the brokering process? In explaining how specific
agreements were crafted, one Solution Broker discussed the importance of not burning any bridges that would hamper future effectiveness (1):

> We were not going to do something that would really set off any key organization. We
> wanted to play nice with them because we were going to have to work with them once
> we got to implement the consensus recommendations.

Solution Brokers took the long view. Then they pursued two major missions in the
consensus-building process. Early in the second phase of consensus building, Solution Brokers engaged in two pursuits. They 1) identified the degree of surmountable
and unsurmountable differences, analyzing the battles at hand and choosing which
were best to fight now versus later. Then, 2) they began to navigate a search for the
best possible agreements between positional boundaries and ideological territories.

Strategy 1: Picking the battles. As soon as the consensus process began, Solution
Brokers were actively gauging how close or far apart stakeholders were in getting to
acceptable solutions. In the rush to find common ground, there is a temptation to
gloss over rather than acknowledge the differences. Naiveté about the disagreements
was one obstacle to successfully achieving even a few agreements. Beliefs are
deeply rooted. Converting the other camp to buy into one side's "religion" was out
of the question. As echoed in the wisdom of many 12-step programs, the starting step
is to admit there is a problem. The Solution Brokers admitted to the deep cracks in
the terrain. As one participant observed, "You can get people that think alike together. That's easy, but that's not what we are talking about. What we are talking
about is bringing people that don't think alike together." Another Solution Broker
was even more blunt about the reality of difference (1):

I don't think that there's a common ground. I don't think that you can find this "balance" of middle footing. This is an evolving dialogue, and the outcome is not clear. Because there aren't any power levers, some parties go to lawsuits. That's the only way some people will appreciate the need for change.

Strategy 2: Navigating a search for the best possible agreements. After conceding (in their hearts) that the consensus process would probably not result in any revolution, they began to pursue a constructive evolution toward solutions. They used their assessment of stakeholders' belief systems to identify overlaps, leeway, or leverage points for putting together a package of solutions that "everyone could live with." Solution Brokers emerged from all sides of various boundaries. They searched for consensus solutions that respected differences, as witnessed by this Boundary Spanner involved in a sustainable development project (1):

> I remember some people who were extremely constructive about trying to find a middle ground. There were people who make their living cutting trees that seemed to me like they were working hard to try to find something that we could all live with. One person in the environmental group could be tough as nails on some things, but generally, that member was trying to find a way to make this work.

Usually the work was done in backstage settings, but they brokered more overtly as shown in this story (1):

> We were in a room without any windows. The room and the debate got really oppressive. It was clear we were butting heads. A break was called and people started to scurry off, but I walked over and starting talking to one person on the opposing side. Then another roundtable member came over and then one other person. We actually met in the middle; we walked to the space at the center of the tables and said, "OK, what about this?" We started putting something together. I think we ended up with something close to what we got to at the end of the process. . . . The key was that there were always people that were willing to think new thoughts and try new ideas.

The search for best possible arguments involved three major tactics: a) searching for the obvious matches, b) targeting the right level of detail, and c) engineering trade-offs.

- Tactic (a) *Search for obvious matches*: First find the remedies that everyone supports. Unfortunately these are not abundant in deep controversies. Typical solutions in this category include agreements about developing accurate or unbiased data gathering and analysis, additional research, public education, and mechanisms to monitor the issue.
- Tactic (b) *Target the right level of detail*: One member talked about the importance of "making agreements at a higher level if we got bogged down on the 'tough issues.'" Another commented that, "the categories seemed very broad and lacking

substance when we worked on them. But in the end, most felt the broad categories were appropriate." They were appropriate and accepted if stakeholders could see that all the issues would eventually be addressed. Boundary Guards or Team Players often criticized high-level agreements as attempts to avoid tackling hard decisions. Solution Brokers expect such complaints but do not agree with them. They don't see agreements of principle as cop-outs. They believe it is foolish to think that one consensus-building effort will cure all ills. Lasting change requires constant, ongoing, and relentless attention and action. Solution brokers understand the power of setting up official mechanisms for continued dialogue and problem solving on the issue at hand.

- Tactic (c): *Engineer trade-offs*: Sometimes consensus requires a system of solutions that equitably please and hurt various sides of the debate. This is the age-old strategy of give and take or mutual back scratching. This may sound impure and distasteful, but it happens. If a package of recommendations represents real solutions that have broad-based support, does it not make sense to allow for specific elements sacred to some "sides" if they don't destroy the overall momentum of the consensus?

In their approach, the Solution Brokers agreed with philosopher Bertrand Russell's view. He claims that most savage controversies are about matters that do not have good evidence either way. Therefore, they welcome all problem-solving processes and believe that officials and grassroots leaders must continue to forge consensus as a part of their regular duties. They believe the devil is in the detail. They understand that those who keep searching for incremental successes and relentless improvement make history.

General Patterns of Collaborator Styles in High versus Low Conflict Situations

In every consensus-building process, people will adopt various styles in different numbers. The more Solution Brokers and Boundary Spanners emerge, the more likely the chances of speedy and/or successful consensus resolutions. Common ground will be harder to find if most collaborators decide to engage as Boundary Guards or Team Players.

Partnership development processes proceed smoother and faster because the mission assumes that all the players have decided to engage in something together. Thus, the consensus group is likely to be composed of mostly Boundary Spanners and Solution Brokers. On the other hand, high conflict settings will include participants that adopt all roles. The distribution of styles in high and low conflict settings is shown in figure 3.3.

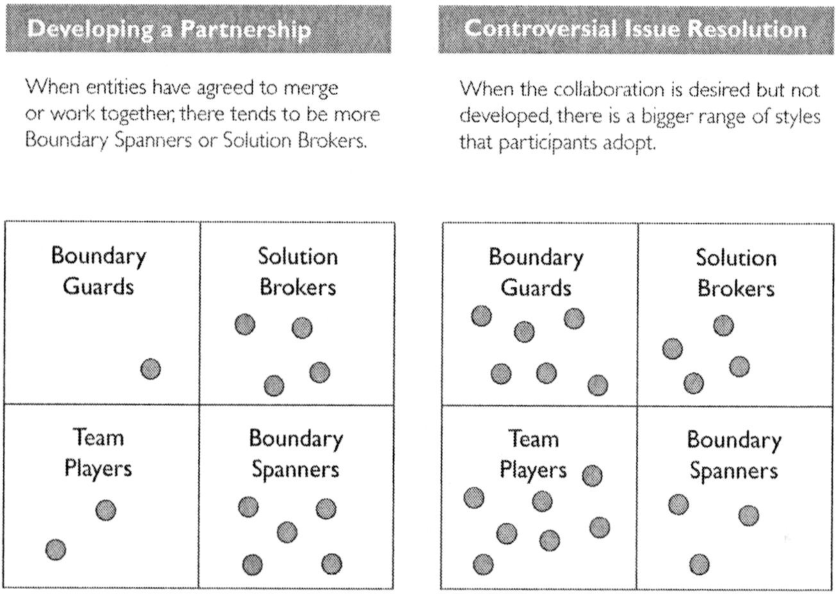
Developing a Partnership
When entities have agreed to merge or work together, there tends to be more Boundary Spanners or Solution Brokers.
Controversial Issue Resolution
When the collaboration is desired but not developed, there is a bigger range of styles that participants adopt.
Boundary Guards
Solution Brokers
Team Players
Boundary Spanners
Boundary Guards
Solution Brokers
Team Players
Boundary Spanners

Figure 3.3. Consensus Builder Distribution in High and Low Conflict Settings

There is no question that process politics—the way participants choose to engage in the deliberation—is a make-or-break variable in achieving consensus. The participants are the human magic behind consensus success. The collective product is as good as the individual participant's level of engagement—their commitment, effort, knowledge, and imagination.

Being an agent of collaboration was not like any professional or volunteer duty that participants had experienced before. Often the costs were high, and rewards very long range; yet no one defected. Despite the obstacles, representatives carry on because they care about the issue at hand. Not all collaborative problem-solving experiences are as long or intense as those in my study, but to some degree, success in any consensus-building process depends on what participants do on or off the table.

Participants chose various styles of aggressiveness or cooperativeness, but one thing was clear and common: Participants in collaborative decision making have two jobs. They serve as both advocates and ambassadors. In other words, each participant is to be a potent advocate for their position as well as a dedicated ambassador for constructing mutually beneficial solutions. As mentioned in chapter 1, collaboration requires 100 percent assertiveness and 100 percent cooperativeness in order to achieve the best results for all. The mission is to produce agreements that everyone will support. Not something for everyone but everyone for something. Consensus players may keep their private scoreboards about who is gaining or losing, but everyone shares the public scoreboard of tracking consensus agreements.

The implication for process sponsors is obvious. Selecting the people to sit at the consensus table is perhaps the most important decision in positioning a consensus-based problem-solving process. Identifying those who will represent the "whole problem system" is critical because the voices at the extremes of the debate never speak for the whole population affected by the issue. The challenge is to find people who are willing and able to serve as strong advocates and ambassadors for the moderate members of the "whole population" affected by a given issue.

THE FACILITATOR: THE POLITICS
OF MANAGING A FAIR FORUM

How do consensus facilitators inhibit or enhance an effective exchange of ideas, urgencies, power, resources, convictions, opinions, and solutions for the sake of determining collective priorities? The facilitator exerts political influence by enabling participants to do their consensus work in a fair, meaningful, and timely way.

The most visible aspect of a facilitator's job is in front of the room, directing the discussion of a group of people. However, here too, much of the work takes place offstage. A facilitator is charged with 1) careful *planning* of the overall process, 2) *presiding* over the formal meetings, and 3) creating a *public record* of the discourse. Planning is the most time-consuming and influential of these three duties. In this section, I discuss how facilitators participate in consensus politics in the course of fulfilling these three duties. Chapter 5 details specific clues for understanding and fulfilling the consensus facilitation role.

The Politics of *Planning* a Meaningful and Timely Process

The outcome of any decision making depends greatly on the process used to make it. What activity or policy will the decision influence? Who is responsible, consulted, or informed in making the decision? What data or evidence will be used? How will a final decision be made? Answering these questions is the joint political task of process sponsors and facilitators. The sponsor determines the basic reasons, roles, rules, and resources of a consensus engagement and facilitators translate the sponsor's "specs" into a fair, meaningful, and timely political forum. More on this shared political role is described in the final section of this chapter, "The politics of sponsoring a consensus process."

Facilitators customize a method for enabling a diverse group to assess, analyze, decide, and translate issues into action. Constructing effective consensus process and assuring a fair field of play includes 1) determining the best methods and techniques; 2) making sure the process is easy to understand; 3) clarifying and enforcing the steps for achieving consensus agreement; and 4) managing science and data proactively. It also means empowering the players by 5) making the process truly participant-friendly and 6) building in the time for the consensus builders' political work. Chapter 5 offers clues for handling each of these planning elements.

The Politics of *Presiding*: Refereeing the Intersection between Diverse Agendas

Once the basic process plan is constructed, a facilitator's key political role is presiding over the forum and knowing when process changes must be made along the way. Even with the best-laid plans, presiding over the exchange of views, ideas, powers, resources, etc., is a full contact sport. When the consensus builders gather and wills converge, a facilitator manages the political forum while simultaneously tracking all levels and aspects of the discourse including the issue content, opinions, emotions, time, meeting space, participant comfort, informal input, and much more.

A facilitator is a nonvoting member but influences the outcome by maintaining a fair and relevant political forum. Since consensus building has no codified rules and regulations, the content and process are both variable elements. The fairness and relevance of a process is constantly under evaluation by participants, sponsors, facilitator, and any other stakeholder that chooses to weigh in. The two major challenges in the politics of presiding fairly are 1) assuring all diverse voices are heard and 2) knowing when to play by the rules or change them.

Assuring Diverse Voices Are Heard

The multiplicity of voices, views, beliefs, capacities, powers, understandings, lives, and needs is the reason we have politics. It is a wonderful alternative to decisions by force. Airing, acknowledging, respecting, debating, negotiating, and integrating the diverse voices of a community into collective solutions is the essence of consensus building.

When a whole system enters a room, the diversity is always surprising. To say that "yes, we do have some differences of opinion" is a serious act of understatement. Any group of humans is *diverse* in *diverse* dimensions. One dimension is our 1) basic diversity in *human characteristics*—personality, preferences, temperaments, and other individual styles. Also, each participant comes to the table with 2) a diverse base of *knowledge* regarding the subject at hand and 3) diverse views about the *process*. Everyone has multiple notions about what makes a good meeting, process, or consensus and has varying expectations about what the engagement should and could achieve. Finally, participants have 4) diverse *worldviews*—strong personal and group beliefs about what is going right and wrong with a given subject. Since diversity is the raw material of consensus building, I discuss these four dimensions of diversity in a little more depth.

Diversity in individual characteristics. The technologies for identifying and describing the myriad of personal traits that affect human interaction are a field unto their own. For this reason I encourage you to refer to a rich world of guides, texts, instruments, and training programs that show how personal temperaments, preferences, and other individual tendencies influence human interactions.

Diversity in knowledge about the subject. Commensurate with the abundance of information connected with any given issue, stakeholders' knowledge of the subject will be all over the board. The huge variance in the knowledge base creates a participant hierarchy based on information.

Interview participants confirmed that minimal information and knowledge about an issue blocked many representatives' ability to be a strong force in the dialogue. All types of information are necessary, but sponsors and facilitators should not assume participants have the same familiarity with an issue. Those with more expertise or a staff of technical people have the upper hand in influencing the group's consensus about what was happening in the problem area. They are extremely familiar with the formal history, unwritten background, science, jargon, and other aspects important to understanding an issue. On the other end are the people who have experiential or anecdotal wisdom about how the symptoms of the problem play out in the real world but may not be versed in the technical or macro-level aspects of the problem. In chapter 6, participants of past processes describe how they took the initiative to educate themselves by private research or talking to other members of the consensus process informally. Despite the conscientiousness of participants, consensus processes need formal ways to provide everyone with a good working knowledge of the subject at hand—minicourses about a knowledge domain, reading materials, jargon dictionaries, access to people who are happy to answer "dumb questions," etc. This will minimize putting people at a disadvantage in contributing to the fast-paced conversation.

Diverse perspectives about group process. The good news is that everyone has experienced some form of meetings and group decision making. The difficulty, therefore, is that participants come with diverse views about what makes good meeting or process. They judge the merits of the dialogue using standards of meetings that are most familiar to them. For example, if a participant is familiar with corporate board meetings, they may wonder why things can't move along a lot quicker and more smoothly. If they are accustomed to labor negotiations, they might criticize the meeting leader for being too loose with the process. People participating in think tanks and retreats are uncomfortable with the excessive structure and fast pace. If they are used to legislative proceedings, they are irritated with the generous time spent in a public hearing mode rather than in debate over the language of specific proposals.

The first step in effective collaboration is to unify the expectations and procedures for the collective decision-making process. Everyone has an image of good
and bad process. Taking time to clarify the assumptions, intents, and game rules of
the collaborative process can relieve some basic frustrations about working together. Conducting the process without such clarification results in a ball game in
which each player thinks he or she playing a different game—basketball, soccer,
dodgeball, golf, etc.

Diversity in worldviews. The deepest and most influential diversity is in core beliefs and ways of looking at the world. Every issue involves multiple belief systems,
no matter how small or large the scope is. The consensus process is a crossroads for
as many fully developed views of the world as there are people around the table. It
is never just two sides. It is never skin deep.

The biggest political mistake for facilitators, sponsors, and participants is to pre-
sume you know or can predict other's stakes and perspectives. Refraining from the
tendency to claim we know what others are needing or believing is the most important new habit we need to cultivate. Here are some vivid examples of our constant
and common propensity to construct what others are perceiving, feeling, thinking, or
intending:

- Sponsors of a first-time homebuyer education program for low-income people
  were frustrated with the lack of participation by the fast-growing Asian immigrant
  community. After all, the curriculum was designed for homebuyers of all cultures
  and backgrounds. In a focus group, a realtor from the Asian community clarified
  the issue. In many Asian countries, mainstream citizens operate on a cash basis,
  and only criminals use debt. The Asian participants were scared away after the first
  session because the topic was building an effective credit history. Something more
  was needed to educate new Americans about acceptance of credit as a normal part
  of the American way of life
- A teenage defendant in a robbery case walked into the courtroom with a brand new
  cartoon-adorned T-shirt. Most people commented on his unfortunate choice of
  clothing at such an important event in the boy's life. Later they learned that this
  was the fanciest piece of clothing in his meager wardrobe. He came wearing his
  "Sunday best."
- In a service improvement seminar, hospitality managers were asked what they
  think conference participants' most important needs were for break times. According to the food, beverage, and event managers, high-quality coffee served in
  elegant urns and ceramic cups were the crucial break elements. When actual conference participants were asked what is important to them, the quality and presentation of the coffee was never mentioned. Their main desires were to get through
  the refreshment line quickly, be close to the restrooms, and have easy access to
  telephones or Internet lines (7).

Professionally and personally I have worked hard to not show prejudice. Yet, even after 30 years of practicing openness, I still find myself falling into the trap of predicting another person's life based on where they stand or what they look like. Here is my confession:

> Just recently, I was dining with my family at a rural Wisconsin diner. As my husband, our adopted African American and East Indian children, and I feasted on home cooked burgers and fries, a thin, elderly man in bib overalls and baseball cap looked up from his bowl of chicken noodle soup and asked me if the boys were our children. After one glance at the man, I decided I could tell his story: A local retired farmer who has lived in the area for a lifetime and never traveled farther than the county seat. I put my arm around one of my boys and replied that they were our children.
>
> He went on to report that he, too, had two adopted grandchildren living in another part of the country. He did not see them much because his wife runs a major health care agency in the nearby major city. Furthermore, since they recently returned from a multi-year teaching assignment in the United Arab Emirates, they had not been able to be a part of the exciting adoption processes. I was deeply impressed with the scope of his life and profoundly embarrassed by my inadvertent tendency to label people.

Have you been there? When have you been amazed and even stunned by the reactions, attitudes, views, or values that were normal and commonplace for another person? This business of being open to others, hearing people out, and allowing people to construct who they are takes relentless effort and practice. As leaders or participants of consensus building, acknowledging and respecting diverse and unique life experience and perspectives is critical. Finding common ground in social disputes begins with a genuine respect of stakeholders' plurality.

One author has devoted an entire book to describing the underbelly of value conflict in contemporary America. In the book, *A House Divided* (8), consultant and writer Mark Gerzon portrays an America that is divided not into geographic states, but into "divided states of belief" (2) regarding what is good in this country. His motivation for writing the book was to support a great nation of the free and the brave but shed the illusion that unity could be achieved by identifying one correct and/or dominant belief system. He advocates for honestly acknowledging our diverse moral codes and suggests we "stop pretending that we can convince other Americans to adopt our particular beliefs. . . . The first thing we can do is to put aside our own opinions temporarily and just listen to other people's views" (8). Following a description of the divided states of belief, Gerzon calls for constructing a new patriotism that honors America's diversity and cautions that "a house divided against itself cannot stand" (8).

Certain issues, such as the pro-choice/pro-life debate and environmental problems have been acknowledged as "value-laden" conflicts or deep philosophical schisms. The escalation of overt religious conflict in the world has demonstrated the dangerous power and consequences of belief-based conflict. These are the famous belief conflicts, but, in my experience, every matter is value-laden. Whether you call them paradigms, perceptions, worldviews, or belief systems, individuals have deeply held notions about what is right and wrong about any and every subject—moving an office, adopting school uniforms, defining the purpose of faculty meetings, etc. For example a simple thing, such as whether to leave the dirty dishes in the sink, relates to a fundamental principle of living life effectively. Washing them before bedtime helps symbolize the notion that each day is the first day of the rest of your life.

Consensus would be simple if the task was to find the obvious right view or truth from among many wrong ones. What makes consensus building difficult is the reality that there are multiple and equal truths. Diverse life experiences result in very different "right" ways to understand and act in the world.

To get a glimpse into the dynamics of negotiating truths, I take you to a statewide forest policy forum triggered by a massive citizen protest over the expansion of logging and other perceived harmful forest practices in state forests. The group included representatives of environmental organizations, outdoor sportspersons' associations, conservation groups, the forest products industry, commercial logging contractors, the resort and tourism industry, research or higher education institutions, non-industrial forest landowners, agricultural woodlot owners, state or federal natural resources agencies, county land departments, and labor unions of forest product. Over an 11-month period, 35 people met in daylong working sessions to build consensus for a comprehensive strategy for sustaining the state's forest resources.

At the fourth meeting, the depth and variety of deeply held "truths" took front stage. The group ranked the top nine issues in statewide forest management and "unpacked" the various perspectives surrounding each one. With each conversation, participants discovered the breadth and depth of each person's views and values. Many were rooted in religious ideals. For example, many landowners who are typically accused of selfishly opposing government regulation of forest management, revealed their religious convictions about land stewardship responsibility:

> I believe that land is a divine gift from God and I have been entrusted to be its caretaker. Stewardship goes with the privilege given by the Creator. I would be shunning my commitment to God if I allowed the government, special interests, and others to dictate how to best take care of the land. That's why sovereignty of private land is the most important issue for me. (1)

Similarly, the environmental activists had faiths based on planetary unity and consciousness, which translated into advocacy for uniform laws that protect large forest landscapes.

At one point in the dialogue, the group explicitly realized that everyone had a right to their beliefs because they were the result of a unique journey of life experiences. The group came away from the dialogue with several conclusions: Each stakeholder perspective made sense. Each perspective was valid and no one was especially privileged with the truth. There are no obvious heroes or villains in an ethical dispute. Fighting over whose values were the more "right" values was a useless quest. The group needed to focus on things the stakeholders can *do* and pursue together as people of many faiths.

Here is the sequence of comments made at the moment when participants discovered the futility of converting others to our world view:

- I detect fears about losing our democratic tradition to socialistic attitudes
- It's the first time I have been referred to as a socialist pagan!
- There are definite philosophical differences in our foundations
- Some of us are rooted in Judeo-Christian beliefs and others in more new age faiths
- We all seem to have abiding respect for protecting the environment but disagreement on how to do it
- The strength of the constitution is its adaptability. We need to adapt somehow to maintain individual and community values
- We need to give each other credit for having valid values and do our best to find mutually acceptable ways to practice stewardship

Each human being builds a unique worldview based on a lifetime of encounters and experiences. They bring these to the meeting table. Acknowledging the existence of many "normal" views is an essential first step to acquiring the patience and humility needed to succeed in a joint search for satisfying solutions. An anonymous adage describes this challenge as *freedom*. It claims "*freedom* means picking your way painfully through a veritable jungle of alternatives, a few of which are satisfactory, none of which is perfect." I believe this is the essence of successful sensemaking at the consensus table. A facilitator's role is to assist consensus builders in navigating through a diversity of "correct" convictions and expectations to forge shared agreements.

Knowing When to Play by the Rules to Change Them

The successful outcome of the collaboration is influenced by how stakeholders buy into the process of decision making. The path taken to reach the destination influences the content and acceptance of that destination. Method is not a mere technicality. Power belongs to those who set the decision rules. That is why campaign-financing reform is an important focal point in the American democratic process. As mentioned in chapter 1, opposition to process is also at the heart of the World Trade Organization (WTO) demonstrations. Human rights, labor, and environmental advocates are calling the WTO process into question—the elitist appointment of members to a global group that makes economic decisions on behalf of over 6 billion world citizens.

Keep the Process Relevant

Facilitators influence the politics of consensus building by maintaining participant consensus about the viability of the process. A strong process plan is a good start. However, sustaining trust in the process depends on knowing when to shift the game rules. Over the years, there have been very few group facilitation sessions that have proceeded completely according to plan.

Take Process Cues from Participants

I am not advocating that game rules be open to constant amendment, but I strongly advise facilitators to welcome process questions and consider modifications in order to deliver robust results. People accept the rulings and verdicts of arbitration and litigation because they trust the process. People will accept the outcomes of consensus building if they feel the process was fair and trustworthy. The only way to maintain trust in an uncodified, uninstitutionalized process is to keep it relevant for the stakeholders. The facilitator's political prowess is enhanced by their ability to keep the collective inquiry process logical and meaningful for all the collaborators.

In the early days I was frustrated by steps taking longer than anticipated or by being questioned about the planned procedures. When I realized that participants will choose their path whether I allow them to or not, I had a change of heart. I now invite participants to be active watchdogs of the process as they engage in the content. Participant "uprisings" feel disruptive but are extremely constructive. The interventions can range from requesting a shorter lunch break, suggesting an amendment to the process, wanting to take more time on an important matter, walking out, etc.

If individuals or subgroups care enough to offer phone, e-mail, or memo feedback, it is a sign that participants take the consensus process seriously. Also, the offline inputs help surface and expedite the brewing issues that would eventually emerge on-line at subsequent meetings. Political unity is enhanced rather than undermined when feedback is in the open versus under the table.

Phases of Consensus Making

What does it look like to really apply the principles of "adaptive management" to a consensus process containing so many dynamic variables, personalities, relationships, revelations, and circumstances? How do you enable consensus builders to influence their decision process? To answer these questions, I share my observations about patterns of forging consensus by providing examples of how participants influence their own political process.

Like a play, consensus processes seem to have three major "acts" (shown in figure 3.4): 1) scoping the multiple dimensions of the consensus "plot"; 2) shifting to heavy

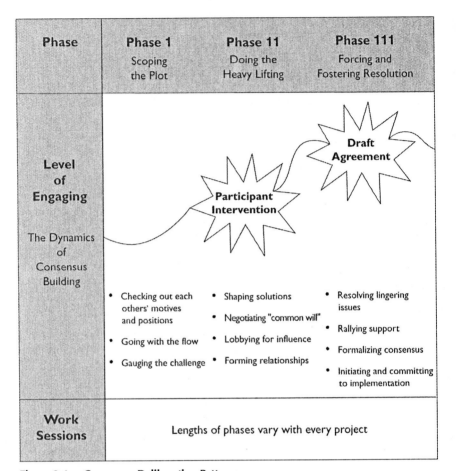

Phase	Phase 1 Scoping the Plot	Phase 11 Doing the Heavy Lifting	Phase 111 Forcing and Fostering Resolution
Level of Engaging The Dynamics of Consensus Building	• Checking out each others' motives and positions • Going with the flow • Gauging the challenge	• Shaping solutions • Negotiating "common will" • Lobbying for influence • Forming relationships	• Resolving lingering issues • Rallying support • Formalizing consensus • Initiating and committing to implementation
Work Sessions	Lengths of phases vary with every project		

Figure 3.4.   Consensus-Deliberation Patterns

lifting in consensus politics; and 3) forcing and fostering resolution. Each "act" is initiated by a turning point that tends to increase and intensify participant engagement on and off the table.

Phase I: Scoping the Plot

The public activity of the initial phase includes introductions of the purpose, process, and participant; briefings about the subject matter at hand; and consensus building about expectations, goals, and the situation. This part of the journey is fairly harmonious. It is a "wait and see" period in which the participants and the process are given the benefit of the doubt.

There are many reasons for this harmony. First, agreements about broad goals come together with relative ease because they are general and conceptual targets.

Second, participants are overwhelmed trying to get on top of the abundance of data. The third reason is that some participants are not accustomed to consensus building. They prefer to sit back, observe, understand who is involved, and learn more about the real game rules for participation. The following represents one of the more honest assessments about this learning mode of participation (1):

> I'm really outspoken, but the beginning of the process was probably one of the first times I ever got really reserved. . . . It was my first experience with collaborative groups and with extremists; by that I mean the extreme right and left people. I felt that I was somewhere in between that. . . . I came in very hesitant, extremely hesitant, wondering, "Who in the hell are these devious people. . . . I was kind of scared that some of those people were planted in there. I was a little skeptical of the department and agencies coming in. . . . I had no clue what they were or what their background was. I was just a little country boy coming in. Here are these seemingly important people with name tags showing who they represent. As I look around I'm thinking," Oh boy! Am I in trouble!" I was not too willing to participate in those initial sessions. I was scared. I was checking it out. . . . I was very skeptical; extremely skeptical . . . I wanted to see how it all goes. At about the fifth or sixth meeting, I could see the direction.

In the first phase, the backstage and informal activity builds gradually as potential issues are previewed in the initial discussions. Stakeholders are busy scoping out the state of the issue, the size of the task, the background or motives of other participants, the requirements of the process, and the game rules. As the phase proceeds, participants assess the initial feasibility to find common ground and chances of achieving a beneficial result. Two participants I interviewed from different problem-solving processes described the hopeful but cautious first meetings. One emphasizes the caution, and the other, the hope (1):

> *The cautionary view:* I remember that the integration meeting tried to get people mingling. The barbecue was good, but everybody tended to sit in his or her own "camps." We might as well have put little labels on the tables, saying, "This is the green table; this is the brown table; and this is the not-sure table."
> *The hopeful view:* This was the first time . . . all of the stakeholders were present and the first time many of them met each other. There was a tremendous amount of excitement in the room. . . . We were thinking, "Boy, it is awesome what we're going to try to do in a period of twelve months. . . . If we could do even a little bit of what we intend, it would be well worth the time." . . . Yes, there were still a few doubting Thomases and impatient folk who were saying, "Oh this will never work; how many meetings are we going to have?"

Whatever their level of doubt or hope, participants tend to share one creeping conclusion after the scoping phase: The task is more complex than initially understood. Simple answers may not be in the cards. One consultant summed it up this way:

"For every complex problem, there is an answer that is simple, clear, and wrong."
And it is wrong (17).

Phase II: Shifting to Heavy Lifting

The second phase begins when the discussion moves from assessing the problem to
deeper analysis and generation of solutions. This phase calls for an active role on the
part of the decision-makers. As the engagement in the subject matter intensifies, real
issues are surfaced and areas of commonality identified. The angles and tangles of a
problem multiply and/or areas of difference are underscored. As participants gain a
deeper understanding of the plot, they become more conscious about having a fair
and thoughtful process. Conditions are ripe for participant involvement in process
adjustments.

The facilitation initiates some turning points. These changes are equivalent to a
quarterback calling an audible from the line of scrimmage. The most common modifications are to manage time differently in order to focus on pressure point issues or
to change techniques for group inquiry.

Then, there are the turning points catalyzed by participants questioning and processing suggestions. In this excerpt, a staff member of a year-long consensus process
attests to how participant input on process became standard operating procedure (1):

> Even though monthly meetings were carefully planned, members often altered them in
> midstream. The chair insisted that all members be heard and their concerns be ad-
> dressed. Evaluation surveys were given to members after each meeting to continually
> improve the process. The results consistently contained opposing viewpoints: some felt
> the process was proceeding too fast, others too slow. When evaluations from the first
> four meetings showed members were anxious to move into addressing "the real issues,"
> the facilitator accommodated that need.

Process turning points indicate that participants are taking responsibility for the
decision outcomes. Their questioning and proposing indicates seriousness about the
success of the collective effort. It is a preferred alternative to input by sabotage. Sabotage is when participants file their complaints at the end and discount the consensus effort.

Participant feedback on the game rules usually happens when consensus building
moves into agreement about the details of future actions and investments. Consensus builders see the clock ticking and wonder if the decision process will address the
important issues and interests they brought to the table. If they feel that issues are
not going to be handled to their satisfaction, they often come forward with proposals for changing the process. Requested changes can vary between friendly amend-
ments to radical changes in the steps of group decision making.

Here are a few live examples of how participants weighed in on the decision process and triggered constructive turning points.

Turning Point Example 1: Adding Missing Voices   The most common challenge relates to insufficient consideration of all the facts or perspectives related to the matter in question. A few years ago, in a large rural school district, stakeholders held consensus-building sessions to define what they meant by a "world class school system." After a daylong work session a mixed group of community leaders and education personnel produced a consensus definition of the "world class school concept." They also realized that the student voice had been very underrepresented. Consequently, participants demanded a process change.

Another forum was held for 80 high school and middle school students. Using the same bottom-up process used by the adults, they constructed their view of a "world class school system." (It was the first time I had been to a session where the meeting mints disappeared by 9:45 a.m.!) Figure 3.5 depicts the two views of a "world class school." As might be expected, the adults and youth came up with different concepts. While they are not dissimilar or incompatible, they identified dissimilar features and definitions of a world-class school. The adult view described a series of care systems including school climate, tools, partnerships, operations, and accountability. The youth view described a series of experiences such as personal comfort, caring teachers, study and relaxation time, quality food, and more class options.

Turning Point Example 2: Including More Perspectives   Another example of redirecting process to include missing voices occurred in a planning effort to improve residential care for mentally ill adults. The group heard input from distressed clients and family members, social workers, and various policy experts. Many of the problems and implied changes fell on the service providers. The managers of the care facilities insisted that they needed a forum to present their side of the story.

Turning Point Example 3: The "Tough Issues" Revolt   In another yearlong consensus project, the process challenge did not occur until the 10th meeting in a series of 14 sessions. It came in response to the fact that a growing list of miscellaneous issues had been tabled as the group moved through previous meetings and various "implementation themes."

The tabled "parking lot" issues were noted in the minutes as they came up. However, each of the representatives that raised a tabled issue did not forget about the unfinished business. The front and backstage frustration about not addressing these underlying issues came to a head at the Meeting 10.

During the general opening conversation, several members demanded that time be allocated to discuss the tabled issues. The suggestion ignited a show of support from a majority of representatives. The message was clear. It was time to address their issues directly. During the break, the designated meeting plan was thrown out and replaced with a discussion of the list of "tough issues." The groups agreed to a specific

As viewed by
students

A. Student Life

> Expanded arts and sports extracurricular activities
> Student personal comfort
> Variety and quality of food options and services
> Study and relaxation space and time

B. Quality Classes

> More realistic and hands-on curriculum and teaching
> Caring teachers and a positive general atmosphere
> More class options

C. Great Facility

> More updated technology
> Comfortable and adequate indoor and outdoor facilities
> Adequate money distribution for all needs

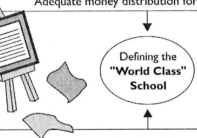

Defining the
"World Class"
School

As viewed by
teachers, parents, administrators, and community

A. Graduates attaining potential

> Maximized education excellence including high expectation
> and world class skills
> Positive education climate

B. Quality Community of learners

> State of art education tools
> User-friendly education system
> Active teaching and learning partnership

C. District credibility and responsiveness

> Integrated and responsive operations
> Student-driven accountability

The actual results of two consensus discussions with the same question but different audiences.

Figure 3.5.   Diverse Views of a "World Class" School

schedule for addressing the issues in the balance of the process. Two meetings were added and meeting agendas were modified to renew participant trust in the process. The formal and informal debate and diplomacy intensified as participants reengaged in consensus building. Here are two firsthand recollections about the airing and addressing of the tabled issues (1):

> I was one of the not-so-loud people supporting discussion on "tough issues." I felt like the vulture in the cartoon where two vultures are hanging out on a tree limb saying, "Let's go out and kill something." I remember how frustrating it was to sit through a lot of the background stuff. I realized then that others felt the same. Without really knowing it, agreements were building in a certain way during the background work. In hindsight, however, I believe we didn't address problems directly because the process leaders were afraid to deal with the hard issues head on. Perhaps they felt it might make the whole process fall apart.

> One meeting I remember well is the one where we had a number of tough issues on the table that we had kept adding over many meetings. Listing them made us behind our time.

This account hints at an underlying reason why participant rebellions occur in consensus building. There is a natural propensity to avoid direct debate of controversial matters in such a forum. Chris Argyris of Harvard talks about the "undiscussable" issues that are present in any human community. Even the discussability of the undiscussables is undiscussable (9). As a result, elaborate and costly schemes are designed to go around the problem rather than addressing them head on. If collaboration representatives take their task seriously, they will force an encounter with issues they perceive to be at the heart of the controversy. It is not wise for dialogue leaders to provoke premature rancor over such issues as they emerge. They must remain open to "hard" discussions when the time is right.

Turning Point Example 4: The "Science Uprising"   Many process turning points were triggered by the use of scientific data, including this example from another sustainable development process. The environmental protection advocates triggered the intervention. When goal setting got underway, they became concerned with the limited time devoted to a "scientific" assessment of how current processes were affecting forest resources. The "science uprising" began backstage, shortly after the second meeting. Several members e-mailed their concerns to the chair, including the following message about the need for "more facts [to be] available" and more time to "deepen understandings about sustainability" (1):

> When I drove the long trip home after our last meeting—alone, having to face myself— I was sick over the memories of the past day and a half. I challenged my internal integrity that I didn't take issue with the "position statements" that were delivered during the time which I thought was meant to deepen our understanding of sustainability, albeit

each group's definition. I believe we must have more facts available so that we may have
the opportunity to expand our positions. The health of our forests and the meaningful-
ness of this process depend on evolving old ways of thinking and doing business.

At a subsequent meeting, the chair and staff responded to the request for more science by proposing a series of field trips and presentations. The group members were
not happy about the suggested itinerary. They did not approve of the choices due to
the lack of balance in showcasing good and bad forest practices in the state. The full
group became interested in the matter because they did not want one faction to define a "balanced roster" of field trips and presentations. The following participant
memos to process leaders point out the key issues that triggered the "science uprising" (1):

> I've been reflecting on the process and want to share a few things with you. Although we
> did get through the whole agenda, I feel that many valuable conversations between oppos-
> ing members were cut off in order to keep the process rolling. I believe that the elephant
> called "philosophical differences" is the largest and noisiest we have to contend with.
>
>   Also, I want to reiterate that we don't have any solid "science-based" information from
> which to make decisions. I still felt pretty good and energized until you got up and handed
> out the agenda for the rest of the meetings. At that point, my good feelings dropped sev-
> eral notches. I felt, once again, we were presented an agenda that was "carved in stone."
> There seemed to be some unwillingness to discuss options—perhaps it was just fatigue. I
> believe the field trips are an important part of our joint discovery, however, I did not get
> the feeling that the list was very balanced—please correct me if I am wrong.

As a result of the concerns the process was modified substantively. A half-day was
scheduled to list, rank, and build consensus about the "science-base" for decision
making, and several additional meetings were added to include new presentations
and field trips. In addition to more information, meeting time was added to identify
and "unpack" the most controversial topics. This meant letting people reveal the
deep "baggage" for each controversial issue. Participants and staff were exhausted
but pleased with the noticeable increase in group members' level of interest in the
deliberation. The logistics of the changes were daunting, but at the staff debriefing
everyone welcomed the fact that the group now had a healthier buy-in on the consensus process.

Turning Point Example 5: Demanding an Alternate Script   Sometimes participants do more than express their complaints about process. They offer an alternative
model for the consensus process. I experienced such a proposal after we were several meetings into the work of developing a fair and equitable public input process
for white pine management. The planned approach was to review the existing
agency flowchart for white pine management and insert the citizen participation
components. This was not acceptable to one member. She stated that the group was

assembled at great expense because public involvement was a gaping hole. It required more than tweaking the status quo process. Her recommendation was to start with an empty slate, identify current problems with public input, and design a process that would make sense from the constituents' point of view. There were no objections from the rest of the work group. We took a break and prepared to implement her mode.

Turning Point Example 6: An Honest to Goodness "Aha!" Experience   Pure, unadulterated innovation can also occasion a turning point. Maybe this is what we always hope for: a break in thinking that boosts faith in the collective problem solving. Unfortunately it is rare. The tensions of controversy, deep distrust, and constraints of time tend not to foster the much touted "out of box thinking." Exercises for encouraging innovative thinking are often dismissed as needless games that waste precious time. However, when innovative thinking does occur, it blesses the consensus process with an enlivening success.

One such example happened in an agricultural valley in the Midwest. A work group of local county officials, state agency representatives, soil and water conservation district leaders, and environmental advocates were assembled to address a longstanding flooding problem. The work group was charged with creating flood control strategies that protect farmfields from frequent and destructive flood waters of a nearby river without destroying wildlife habitat.

Like many such issues, the serious disagreements about science were at the heart of the controversy. Whose "science" about the status and needs of the natural resource should drive the decision making? The process designers came up with an innovative approach for the scientific dialogue.

A technical and scientific advisory committee (TSAC) was commissioned at the point of inception of the work group. The TSAC was to shadow the work group and provide consensus recommendations regarding scientific assessments and strategies. Each member of the work group was invited to appoint their "technical representative" to the TSAC.

The TSAC team of diverse scientists and technicians made a big difference in constructing shared "truths" at the controversial intersection between various sciences of flood control and wetlands protection. The TSAC scientists were assigned to work on major issues regarding sustainable flood and watershed management. Here, a member of TSAC describes the successful and surprisingly informal approach that the science team used to execute their charge (1):

> We weren't that formally organized. We didn't have a facilitator in there, so we just did our own thing. I don't recall ever getting a list as such [from the work group] or making a list ourselves. We knew we had enough things that we disagreed on. I don't recall that we ever made a list. We just started working on a number of issues. We just started to deliberate. . . . First we just started talking. It happened fairly quickly. . . .

There was a little bit of arguing or posturing in the first meeting, but at the end of the day we all went out and drank beer and ate pizza . . . It helped people open up and let their guard down a little bit. It worked, so we did it. I don't recommend that people necessarily take up drinking to accomplish this task. But it worked for us, and it broke down a lot of barriers.

As is clear in this account, the members of the science team were not preoccupied with being the universal model for environmental deliberation. They did what they deemed necessary to "open up" and get on with the challenging task at hand. Establishing human connections was one necessary method. TSAC contributed steadily to the work group's consensus building. At one juncture, they were responsible for a major turning point in the deliberations.

One of the first agenda items for the TSAC was the most controversial "bounce" issue. "Bounce" refers to the water level of wetlands, reservoirs, or lakes that are used as temporary storage for floodwaters in order to protect agricultural and residential lands. For the agricultural and community interests, the bounce needs to be high enough to absorb all the excess water. For the environmental interests, the bounce should be low enough to protect the wildlife and habitat. For example, the over-water-nesting waterfowl's nest is a half foot above water. If the water bounces over a foot, the birds will be harmed. According to one TSAC member, "A lot of people. . . . including people in our [science and technical] group, had almost come to the conclusion that you can't do multiple purpose flood control and environmental projects. They are simply at odds. You do one and you're doing it at the exclusion of the other.

The "bounce" issue was assigned to the scientist designated by the environmental interests. Based on the environmental scientist's draft, the TSAC members came to a fairly rapid consensus about the reasonable limits of the bounce level. Their agreement became a linchpin that built the momentum to overall work group agreements. The results of the deliberation confirm that if an interdisciplinary group of scientists are given the opportunity to develop shared "scientific" positions, they can. TSAC members pioneered an effective way for scientific knowledge to enter the theater of political decision making.

Phase III: Forcing and Fostering Resolution

The final phase of the consensus process is the most memorable and labor-intensive. It occurs after emerging consensus areas are identified and before they are officially approved as binding agreements. As a facilitator in long, multiple-session processes, I have not been privy to the real work of Phase III because the primary activity occurs offstage. However, I was generously introduced to the informal politics of the final phases of consensus building through my interviews with participants in long-term consensus processes.

During the evenings and breaks members discussed which recommendations to support and reject. Here one representative recalled the rapid pace and heightened politics of the final "act" of decision making (1):

> The importance of the final voting was not as clear to me as it should have been. When we realized what was going on, we realized the importance of working together. In a very short period of time, there was a lot of wheeling and dealing. It would have been better to know early on about the winning and losing aspects of the process.

Caucusing in like-minded groups seemed to be a predominant activity.

However, there were those who were influenced by persuasion activities of peers in the process. Several representatives used the backstage to make sure that even the passive players were contacted and encouraged to act in favor of a consensus agreement. Some representatives worked hard to get the entire group to "work together." The following excerpt depicts the lobbying efforts of those who served as unifying forces (1):

> I've worn the public relations hat for many years in many settings. I know it is important to do stuff before the group gets together . . . I worked hard to develop relationships with people on the [other side] in off-line conversations. I tried to meet with as many people as possible prior to the last meeting to work out the "wording" of recommendations. I was part of assembling a "camouflage group" (a mixture of Greens [environmentalist group representatives] and Browns [representatives of industry]) to create a consensus, middle-of-the-road voting bloc.

This account illustrates the critical brokering role that some participants play as discussed in the earlier section on representation styles.

The question of minority reports is an ongoing possibility. In several cases, where consensus-building participants refused to go along with the group's agreement, others in the group were understandably upset. They talked about "violation of trust" that contributed to a significant setback within a group victory. The following quote illustrates how members felt a sense of betrayal (1):

> I would be dishonest if I didn't admit that I was really disappointed that one person wouldn't go along with the agreements. I felt personally betrayed by that. A lot of us had listened to a lot of speeches by that individual and worked very hard to find ways to compromise and include things that would make him comfortable. According to his arguments at the end, he was not going along because of what wasn't in the document, than because of what was in it. I didn't feel good about that. I have reason to believe that a lot of other people didn't feel good about that. I felt like he was grandstanding to some constituency.

An enormous amount of listening and "good faith negotiating" had been enacted and endured by all for many months. It was understood to be a process of give and take and to produce something everyone could support. Many expected to sign onto consensus recommendations "with a little bit of discomfort." A member's dissent was therefore a "betrayal" of the teamwork. It disrespected the goodwill and expenditure of the others on the team. The sense of teamwork and team victory is at the heart of the following assessments about a consensus outcome (1):

> *On how common will weathers dissent:* We had arrived at an agreement but at the end, one party did not support it. Worse than that, he went to the press with it and blew the horn that this was a faulty process. Well, ultimately the public was just too damn smart to buy that and the press had some fun with it for a month or two. . As always is the case, that kind of tactic basically does not work. There were a few people that tried to ride on the dissenter's tail. But the common understandings and common agreements were too strong to be sabotaged by one person or even a few people.
>
> *On pursuing ideals versus collaborating the best we can:* Collaboration processes tend to come out of litigation or the threat of litigation. The collaboration processes are not set up as visioning processes. We tried to make it into a strategic planning process and that's not easy to do.
>
> So one possible starting point is "let's sit down and come up with the vision for that, let's really be strategic about that together, and we're all out there living together. The other possible starting point is litigation or conflict negotiation. All the lines are drawn in the sand, we pretty much know where people stand, we know that who's coming to the table is going to be protecting an interest, and we also know, and here's a really key point, that they are coming to the table willingly because they know that if they're not there, things are going to be done to them.
>
> So here we are in the real world; how often do we really start strategic planning from scratch in these kinds of public collaboration things? Never. They emerge from the fire. They are out of a crucible, and what a facilitator is trying to do and hopefully what other people are trying to do is say, "Fine. We do have that issue alliance and those diverse interests, but let's seize this opportunity that is presented by us being together and work out a "hybrid" process. Let's be creative and strategic.

The facilitator participates in constructive consensus politics by making sure that the process belongs to the participants. Shifting the original script is a messy but productive professional obligation. Ultimately, the consensus is as good as the action that occurs after participants leave the table. For that reason, the process should be steered by those who must live with the outcome. The participants' sense of process fairness and relevance should be a key guide for facilitators.

The Politics of Public Documentation

A facilitator has a great deal of influence in his or her most invisible and silent role — writing up what happened. Representing the substance and spirit of the consensus deliberation is a subjective process no matter how the live session is recorded. Translating flip charts, legal pads, scribe minutes, tape recordings, memory, sticky notes, individual work sheets, and other raw records into findings, conclusions, and recommendations is a significant part of process politics. Consensus is always fragile. It can unravel like lightning for many reasons. One simple reason is not having a common public record of what happened.

The political challenge is to represent all sides fairly and accurately but be concise enough to be reader-friendly. Even the best consensus decisions can get lost in translation with an overly lengthy report. On the other hand, a brief summary may leave out key issues and views that will have to be rehashed during the implementation. A logger member of the forest management conflict process summed up the challenge: "I need the results of our work to be packaged into something I can have in the back of my pick-up!"

In addition to documenting results, a facilitator must make sure they are publicly accepted. As with parliamentary meeting minutes, it makes political sense for participants to review and refine the record of their consensus at every phase of the decision drafting.

The document is the main link between those who represented interest groups at the table and all the other members of those stakeholder groups. Therefore, consensus implementation is greatly enhanced by a report that enables all future readers to become insiders in the whats, whys, and hows of the negotiated decisions.

THE SPONSORS: THE POLITICS OF LINKING CONSENSUS TO MAINSTREAM DECISION MAKING

Project sponsors convene, commission, or otherwise initiate the collaborative process. They perform the functions of positioning a meaningful consensus process. They conceive the project, invite the players, and secure the funding and resources for process activities. In many projects, they play a significant role in developing the basic parameters, scope, and a rudimentary script for each consensus process.

Community and organization administrators, officials, managers, and other leaders have a pivotal role in positioning consensus success. If the collective process is not connected to real world operations in a meaningful way, motivation to participate is greatly diminished. Sponsors and conveners inhibit or enhance the power of consensus ventures by how they set up a participative exchange of ideas, urgencies, power, resources, convictions, opinions, and solutions.

A sponsor of an effective consensus process takes on the role of a process architect. The goal is to design group decision making that answers the question: "How do you equalize power and voice among various stakeholders at the table to promote an authentic dialogue between groups with inherently different roles? (10) This question was at the heart of Bauer's research, *Creating a Level Playing Field.* Twenty design teams from New York school districts were charged to develop "rules of the game" that would make the best shared decision-making policies for the needs and nuances of their district. The project trained sponsors to be architects who custom build meaningful forums for multiple-stakeholder decision making:

> Instead of looking at the routinized adoption of a *standard model* (i.e., site-based management means devolving decision-making authority over budget, staffing, and curriculum to a site council made up of the principal, teachers, and perhaps parents), research needs to focus on *how to fit site-based processes into existing school system cultures* and the ways to use this restructuring as a lever for improvement. This depends, in part, on devising ways to create forums that invite frank, open discourse on issues of importance to the school. (10)

Process sponsors give consensus participants a clear role in changing or influencing mainstream decisions and patterns. They do so by determining the *reasons* and *rules* for the collaboration game. They set the parameters for *roles* in the game. They allocate the support *resources* to carry it out.

Consensus building can be sponsored in several ways. Some common sponsorship formats include the following: 1) The leader of a team, department, agency, company, or organization calls together a consensus process for planning, problem solving, input, or other group decision-making effort. 2) One or more public entities commission a project. 3) One or more organizations convene a potential cross-boundary partnership. 4) A grassroots group initiates a consensus effort.

Leader-directed Process

The most common sponsor of a consensus process is the official leader(s) of a team, department, function, school, district, company, community, or any other group.

Commissioned Projects

In several policymaking situations, an official body funds and directs a group of people to develop consensus solutions to community problems. Here are some examples:

- A rural development agency invited key leaders of regional businesses, civic organizations, vendors, labor unions, educational entities, and all local governments to select key projects for reviving the economy and form an interorganizational partnership to pursue the project.
- A state legislature created a formal senate resolution for commissioning stakeholders of 40 organizations to develop recommendations for the state's forest policy. They specified the outcomes and began scripting the process. They appointed the meetings' managers and assigned the executive branch agencies to implement the process.

- A state agency sponsored several processes in order to get unified citizen consent about fish and fisheries management, trail use coordination, and forested land management.
- A district court directed a state agency for child services to institute a collaborative reform process to correct the major child services deficiencies that brought on a class action lawsuit.

Convened Projects

Many cross-organization partnerships are convened by a lead organization. The convening organization hosts and supports the consensus-building steps for launching a potential partnership. They assume that participating organizations will eventually share resources to launch and operate the partnership. In many cases, the stakeholders who join the consensus building are willing to contribute their time and other resources to help conduct the consensus decision-making efforts. What evolves is a "pot luck" model for self-supporting partnership development. Consensus builders share the costs of meeting space, meals, materials, and staff time. Here are a few illustrations:

- A school board and superintendent of the district convened meetings to begin a multiyear initiative to involve the entire "village" in education improvement. The PTA, community groups, public organizations, employers, and foundations who agreed to participate offered support and resources to plan and implement shared strategies for building a "world class school system."
- A nonprofit housing and counseling organization in a major urban area called together a network of over 100 affordable housing support organizations to expand and strengthen consistent and accessible access to first-time, low-income homebuyers across the state.
- A regional planning agency served as an "initiator" for a controversial effort to establish procedures for water quality decision making among 48 stakeholders including agricultural, industrial, recreational water users; local and municipal governments; federal and state agencies, water providers, and the water and sanitation districts. Due to past conflicts, all organizations were hesitant to step up as "the sponsor." Even the initiating agency wished not to take on the role because they often were litigants of the Water Court. A planning group representing a "microcosm" of the stakeholder system was created to steer the collaborative problem solving.

Grassroots Sponsorships

In some grassroots voluntary collaborations, a group of community leaders sponsor the process, lead the meetings, and serve as consensus participants. In their self-facilitated process, the members of the leadership group rotate meeting leadership. They invite other participants on stage at any time. On an as-needed basis, the group brings in other people and entities to present information, conduct research, lead meetings, and help with other meeting leadership and support duties.

- The Quincy Library Group is a famous grassroots group that has met for years to debate and resolve local environmental disputes. They are named after their meeting place. They chose the library setting to make sure everyone abides by the ground rules that require listening and never shouting or attacking other participants.
- A cadre of nine people representing important environmental interests in a large, forested watershed of northwestern United States launched a disciplined but flexible collaborative process that continues to this day. The chronic conflict between environmentalists, industry, federal land managers, farmers, ranchers, and community residents "appeared destined for terminal gridlock" (11) until a core group of people representing all the groups gathered on the back porch of a key community leader to begin the initiation of the Applegate Partnership in 1992. They began meeting weekly and invited everyone to join the dialogue. The cadre named themselves board members, and that's where the formal structure ended. Meeting agendas and leaders were suggested and selected at the beginning of each meeting, and committees were created as needed by the mission at hand. Restoration, education, forest products, agriculture, research, and monitoring have been the focus of work groups.
- A group of five rural communities have decided to form an operating alliance to share municipal and township public services.

Regardless of who sponsors the collaborative problem solving, the duties are the same. The sponsor sets the stage for the collaboration politics by determining the 1) *reason*, 2) *roles*, 3) *rules,* and 4) *resources* of the consensus game. If the effort makes sense to people, they are willing to play the game. I discuss the political implications of these duties in this section. Further clues about fulfilling them effectively are relayed in chapter 6.

Determining Reasons: Making a Compelling Case for Consensus Engagement

The importance of a meaningful mission applies to any project or endeavor. If you cannot easily answer why the process is needed, who needs it, and what it should achieve, it is better not to start. In order to attract stakeholders, there must be something at stake and a readiness to engage.

Without a concrete link between the "input, through put and output," (11) stakeholders cannot gauge their own incentives for participation. The diagram in figure

3.6 was used in one consensus process to help sponsors envision the project from beginning to end and identify the whats, whys, and hows essential to gaining buy-in and getting to a worthy outcome. Even when a dispute, problem, or partnership seems evident or urgent, a process should not be commissioned until there is a meaningful purpose for the consensus product. If the likely, projected, or promised benefits don't exceed the cost of involvement, consensus building will not have the incentives it needs to succeed.

Furthermore, credible purposes need clear champions to see the process through, receive the results, and assure implementation. Consensus projects were minimally effective when sponsors failed to clarify the ultimate uses or recipients of a consensus group's work. Often this happened because the urgency, continuity, and stewardship for a project was lost in the turnover of staff and leadership following an election, reorganization, buy-out, merger, or other major organizational transition. The completion and impact of consensus processes cannot be guaranteed, but they have a better chance of surviving organization changes if specific people or positions are listed as accountable, authorizing, and responsible parties.

Consensus needs to be integrated into mainstream operations instead of an "attachment" to official decision making and management. For example, at a large mining operation, assets were saved from a slow death when all 200 managers became insiders in the improvement effort. The mine and plant was transformed through a rigorous participatory planning process that identified improvement options, selected priorities, and lobbied for capital funds from the parent company.

A study of site-based management, *Avoiding Disaster While Sharing Decision Making*, underscores the importance of integrating consensus processes into the fabric of the organization. Researcher Sorenson warns against superficial empowerment on stakeholder participation in decision making (12):

> The term empowerment saturates the educational literature and evokes a variety of operational definitions. Sergiovanni (13) stressed that before empowerment can be meaningful, there must be agreement within the organization or a shared covenant.
>
> A covenant that is the product of consensus among a representative group of school stakeholders helps define the organization's collective values, vision, mission, educational objectives, organizational priorities, and operating principles. This comprehensive review of the system, beginning with the fundamental issue of purpose, represents a significant step in the redefinition of the learning community by its members.
>
> Developing consensus on a shared covenant and reshaping school culture requires open and honest communication among stakeholders and an honest assessment of organizational strengths and weaknesses as they relate to the preparation of students.

Once a process is mobilized, sponsors need to monitor it closely. They are the bridge between the temporary problem-solving process and the leaders of the institutional systems that must implement the solutions. Serving as an active political

Establishing Compelling Reasons for Consensus Decision Making

INPUT CONSIDERATIONS:

What and why people are being asked to participate

- What the focus questions are
- What is the need or urgency for answers
- What decision process will be used
- What will be the roles of various stakeholders

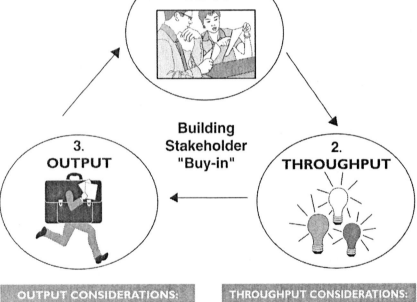

Building Stakeholder "Buy-in"

OUTPUT CONSIDERATIONS:

The difference participation made

- How results are reported
- How the results are acknowledged
- How participation is recognized
- How next steps are identified and delegated

THROUGHPUT CONSIDERATIONS:

The role of input on decisions

- How feedback will be communicated
- How input will be used in decision making

Figure 3.6.   Consensus Sponsorship Touchstones

link between the work of consensus builders and future results means staying visible and vigilant as the consensus builders carry out their charge. Regular visits to work sessions will encourage and reinforce the important purposes of the problem solving and its products. Updating key stakeholders that are not at the table will increase the likelihood that they will be prepared to accept and adopt the consensus plans, recommendations, and other decisions.

The linking role will be augmented by some of the consensus participants. Throughout the process they have the opportunity and power to keep their legislators, professional associations, advocacy groups, and other influential leaders apprised of the consensus developments. The more that all stakeholders and/or the powers that be know and understand, the easier it will be to make visible changes based on the recommendations. For example, the representatives of a large state agency that sponsored an environmental issues process built internal receptiveness to eventual recommendations by regularly debriefing over 25 agency managers and legislative stakeholders during a yearlong process.

Clarifying Roles: Assign Responsibility
Along with Accountability and Authority

Designating the individual and collective role for consensus builders is another major political decision for sponsors. One of the mistaken assumptions about consensual approaches implies democracy at every turn; that everyone makes decisions about everything. This is not the case. However, operating and decision-making loops should provide all stakeholders with clear, agreed-to mechanisms for participating in choices that affect them.

Problems arise when role expectations of the group and its leader differ. Nothing destroys group trust and productivity faster than false ideas about their responsibility, accountability, and authority. Also, frustration reigns if participants are given heavy responsibility and accountability for a task without enough authority to conduct the duties within their scope of work. Inviting people to serve in a meaningful role is a matter of respect and common sense. Everyone wants to spend time on activities that make a difference. Nobody wants his or her time wasted or intelligence assaulted. If input is sought, people will provide feedback if they know who will use it and how it will be used.

The same is true in developing site-based management and shared decision making for the first time. Rosann Sidener of Dade County Public Schools reminds us that setting up a shared decision-making forum is only a first step:

> Setting up a governance council does not, in and of itself, redistribute power and authority. . . . Time needs to be devoted to redefining roles so participants understand how the new roles differ from current ones. Accountability structures should then be put into

place that will reinforce these roles. For example, the principal's role should shift to a facilitator who builds alliances to accomplish goals. The principal's job descriptions and evaluation procedures should focus on demonstrating facilitative behaviors. In addition, staff at the central office and regional office need to understand changes in their own roles in relationship to the principal's role. They should not expect an "on-the-spot decision" about an issue if the school functions under a shared decision-making model and the principal needs time to build consensus. (14)

To avoid false expectations and invite targeted participation, sponsors need to decide and communicate what role the group plays in a given decision-making process. Is it a consulting group that asked for input? Is it an advisory group responsible for decision recommendations? Is it a shared decision-making group that is expected to make the action choices and implement the plan? Is it an action team assigned to execute decisions made by the sponsor? All types of roles are fair game as long as they are clear upfront.

In determining who will participate in a consensus process, sponsors are advised to identify players after carefully weighing up the benefits and consequences of involving people at various stages of the decision-making process, decide participant roles, and communicate them clearly. Remember the super clue from the first chapter: One way or another, people will participate or weigh in. They always will. If they are not in on the original planning or decision making, they will participate with their feet, money, time, complaints, sabotage, inertia, and rebellion. The only choice that leaders have with respect to participation is *when* stakeholders participate. Leaders can build buy-in before a decision is made or troubleshoot implementation issues caused by a lack of stakeholder ownership. There is no way to avoid stakeholder participation. There is an infinite number of valid delegation approaches, but I share two primary strategies for involving systemwide participation and overview the common costs and benefits of 1) *telling and selling* versus a 2) *partnering and involving* approach to delegating consensus process roles:

Telling and Selling Approach to Decision Making and Implementation

The sponsor or leader takes primary responsibility for formulating the issue, analyzing options, and making decisions. Stakeholders are briefed on the decisions and plans and delegated implementation roles.

Costs:

- Likelihood that key considerations or issues were missed in planning
- High potential for stakeholder unclarity, misunderstanding, conflict, opposition, and even sabotage
- Time-consuming role of pushing plan and troubleshooting implementation

- Short-term changes without sustainable gains
- Need for extensive and ongoing performance checking and controls

Benefits:

- Speed of planning and decision making
- Appreciated in crisis situations or when directions have obvious level of consensus
- Stakeholder appreciation and anticipation for changes in situations where an obvious problem requires resolution and change
- Stakeholder willingness to help minimize implementation issues

Partnering and Involving Approach to Decision Making and Implementation

Stakeholders are involved in every step of the decision-making process—to some degree they help assess the issue, analyzing options and constructing the ultimate decision. As in any approach, stakeholders are the key players in implementation action and alliances.

Costs:

- Need for substantial investment of time and resources to involve stakeholders

Benefits:

- Likelihood of developing a realistic plan
- High level of stakeholder understanding and buy-in
- Stakeholder willingness to work through the hurdles of implementation
- Broad-based desire to succeed and produce results

In either scenario, clarifying roles at the start enhances the results.

Setting Rules: Providing a Fair and Fruitful Political Forum

Once it is clear why a problem needs solving, who should do it, and what they need to end up with, the remaining question is how? As mentioned in an earlier chapter, litigation or parliamentary procedure comes with prescribed steps for conducting the process. Consensus engagements have some familiar building blocks, but each situation needs a unique, custom-crafted process.

Constructing effective consensus process means working closely with the process facilitator to assure a fair field of play. Close to 80 percent of a facilitator's time goes into translating the intents of the consensus mission into productive and meaningful decision steps, schedule, materials, ground rules, and meeting procedures. With or without facilitators, sponsors set the political parameters of the process including the following: protocols that constitute a consensus agreement; science, data, or background information needs to inform the discussion; and the procedures for creating and adjusting the meeting procedures. Chapters 5 and 6 provide clues for enhancing sponsors' and facilitators' duties in engineering and refereeing consensus game rules.

Securing Resources: Ample Time and Support to Build Credible Consensus Results

Securing resources may be the most challenging background duty for a sponsor. Previously, I likened the sponsor's role to a parent that endows the consensus project with authorization and resources. Until now we have talked about conferring authorization—developing consensus building reasons, roles, and rules. Without the other half of the role—securing resources—the quest for consensus will meet the fate of other unfunded mandates.

Bauer points to resource allocation as common pitfall of effective shared decision making in schools (10):

> Issues of "insufficient capacity" are often cited as explaining the failure of site-based management. "Capacity" equates to district support for site teams in terms of providing authority, training, time, information, and other resources necessary for team operation. Districts rush to implement site-based management without considering what it takes to make the transition from traditional decision-making structures. (15)

The securing of resources tests any project's importance in an organization, community, district, or other system. When organizations put money, staff, and infrastructure support into a project, it is no longer just a nice idea but an investment with an expectation for a return. The cost-benefit scrutiny is likely to be very intense at a time when most entities have few surplus resources. Someone must convince the budget gatekeepers that a collaborative problem-solving initiative is crucial enough to merit organizational resources. Negotiating, lobbying, budget adjusting, or other "creative financing" activities can be extremely difficult and frustrating. However, this political step helps transform a good idea into an institutional and/or mainstream priority.

CONCLUSION

Meeting sponsors can help reduce the negative image of politics and recover the essence of an inclusive political process. They do so by positioning a forum that enables people to engage effectively in the political work of sharing ideas, visions, beliefs, opinions, power, and resources through front- and backstage activities. History will continue to be made by resolves and relationships between human beings. Politics is the essence of the democratic political process. It is complicated and unpredictable, but it beats governance by rebel coups, military takeovers, war, bloodshed, or judgments by one dictator. Politics should be seen as a nonviolent act of waging peace.

If we want to rekindle trust in citizen participation, each public forum must be utterly meaningful. People will participate if they can see that their investment influences official decisions that affect them. As sponsors and leaders of consensus building, we are making up for lost time. No one can guarantee the outcomes of political activity, but failing to plan the input, through-input, and output steps of consensus decision making is a plan to fail. We need to build trust. Each meeting, planning session, committee meeting, or roundtable is an opportunity to build public trust in democracy or destroy it further.

What are specific clues for setting up, conducting, and engaging in consensus dialogue that makes a difference? How can participants, facilitators, and sponsors leverage the power of consensus to guide choices and directions in schools, organizations, communities, and society? Many clues have been implied up to now but are spelled out in the next three chapters: Sponsorship clues are featured in chapter 4, facilitation clues in chapter 5, and participant clues in chapter 6.

NOTES

1. Hanson, M. (2001). *Constructing sustainability policy through collaboration: A multi-site case study of decision making processes that seek sustainable solutions for statewide forests or local watershed development.* St. Paul, MN: University of St. Thomas.

2. Morgan, G. (1997). *Images of organizations.* Thousand Oaks, CA: Sage.

3. Smith, G. (1988). *Managerial problem solving.* Minneapolis, MN: Carlson School of Management, University of Minnesota.

4. Quinn, J., & Guile, B. (1988). *Managing innovation: Cases from the service industries.* Washington, DC: National Academy Press.

5. Berlin, I. (1953). *The hedgehog and the fox.* Chicago: Ivan R. Dee.

6. Thomas, K. W. (1977). Toward multidimensional value in teaching: The example of conflict behaviors. *Academy of Management Review, 12,* 484–490.

7. Albrecht, K., & Zemke, R. (1985). *Service America: Doing business in the new economy.* Homewood, IL: Dow Jones-Irwin.

8. Gerzon, M. (1996). *A house divided: Six belief systems struggling for America's soul.* New York: Putnam.

9. Argyris, C. (1985). *Strategy, change and defensive routines.* Marshfield, MA: Pittman.

10. Bauer, S. (1997, March 24–28). *Creating a level playing field: Structuring shared decision making to promote authentic dialogue.* Paper presented at the annual meeting of the American Educational Research Association, Chicago.

11. Harrington, Steve, Consultant, New York.

12. Sorenson, L. D. (1995, February 10–13). *Site-based management: Avoiding disaster while sharing decision making.* Paper presented at the annual meeting of the American Association of School Administrators, New Orleans, LA.

13. Sergiovanni, T. J. (1992). Moral authority and the regeneration of supervision. In C. D. Glickman (Ed.), *Supervision in transition.* Alexandria, VA: ASCD. Yearbook of the Association for Supervision and Curriculum Development.

14. Sidener, R. P. (1995, April). *Site-based management/shared decision making: A view through the lens of organizational culture.* Paper presented at the annual meeting of the American Educational Research Association, San Francisco.

15. Glickman, C. (1990). Pushing school reform to a new edge: The seven ironies of school empowerment. *Phi Delta Kappan, 72*(1), 68–75.

16. Institute of Cultural Affairs, *The Journal*, staff handout, 1979–1982.

17. Mencken, H. L. Retrieved August 4, 2005, from www.proverbia.net.

Chapter Four

Clues for Sponsors

We must devise a system in which peace is more rewarding than war.

—Margaret Meade

The overall role of a sponsor is to authorize and activate a consensus process to achieve a needed task. Sponsors can be:

- Superintendents launching a district school improvement or policy process
- Two neighbors initiating a regular block club council
- The vice president calling together a national business meeting for Division X
- The board chair organizing the annual board retreat
- The local churches convening a county forum on crime prevention

Why bother bringing people around the table? Answering this question in detail is the key political role of a sponsor. Even within a raging conflict, it is not sufficient to have a general answer such as, "we need to get together to figure out some solutions." As outlined in chapter 3, a worthy collective effort includes a 1) compelling *reason*, 2) well-defined participant *roles*, 3) fundamental *rules* of engagement, and 4) sufficient *resources* for getting the job done (see figure 4.0). Without strong sponsorship, collaborative efforts tend to be doomed from the start. This chapter identifies specific steps involved with each of the four major duties and discusses clues for optimizing consensus success.

FRAME A COMPELLING REASON

Clear reasons for bringing people together seem obvious, but a surprising number of meetings and committees are convened with ambiguous intents. Stakeholders will

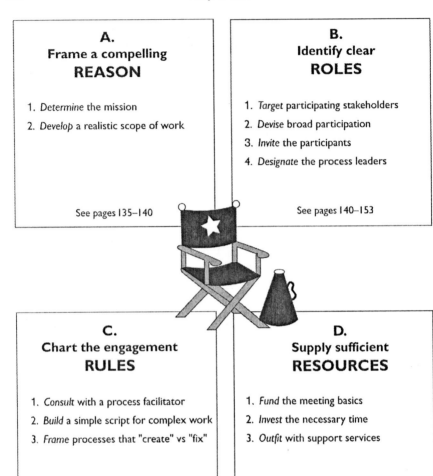

A.
Frame a compelling
REASON

1. *Determine* the mission
2. *Develop* a realistic scope of work

See pages 135–140

B.
Identify clear
ROLES

1. *Target* participating stakeholders
2. *Devise* broad participation
3. *Invite* the participants
4. *Designate* the process leaders

See pages 140–153

C.
Chart the engagement
RULES

1. *Consult* with a process facilitator
2. *Build* a simple script for complex work
3. *Frame* processes that "create" vs "fix"

See pages 153–156

D.
Supply sufficient
RESOURCES

1. *Fund* the meeting basics
2. *Invest* the necessary time
3. *Outfit* with support services

See pages 156–159

Figure 4.0.   Roles for Process Sponsors

participate actively if there is something important at *stake*. The first duty of consensus process sponsors is to create a compelling reason for inviting broad-based participation in decision making. This includes 1) determining the mission, 2) developing a realistic scope of work, and 3) clarifying measures for success.

Determine the Mission

A sponsor initiates the consensus process by spelling out the *"whys"* of the project: Why is this consensus project urgent? What is the purpose? Who owns or cares about the process? Without a clear or necessary mission, a venture is generally wasteful and extremely disrespectful of the people involved. Second, consensus needs to be integrated into mainstream operations instead of being mere "attachments" to official decision making and management. Laura Spencer makes this point plain in her book, *Winning Through Participation* (1):

> Participation is not just a "geegaw bolted onto the management machinery by social engineers," as Sasporito says many firms have done. Nor is it "installed" as if it were a muffler on a car, as Sashkin says quality circles often are. Thomas McKenna of Midwest Steel concludes that true participation "is not a program. It is a whole different way of dealing with people."

Develop a Realistic Scope of Work

If the mission passes the acid test of relevance, it needs to be translated into detailed *"whats"* for the task at hand. Most issues are complex, and consensus builders have wide-ranging expectations about the scope of the problem and/or the nature of the expected solutions. Ambiguity cannot be eliminated but can and should be reduced as much as possible before starting a consensus journey. To reduce unnecessary confusion, sponsors define and frame the "mess of issues" that is being addressed by a) setting boundaries for the issue; b) seeking action solutions versus principles; c) linking consensus solutions to ongoing problem management; d) mobilizing the mission with a focus question; and e) setting clear performance measures.

Set Boundaries

The key to consensus success is to define the task as concretely as possible. A project cannot be all things to all people at all times. Geography, time frame, audiences, level of solutions, or other boundaries are needed to maximize the chances of developing realistic solutions. This was the essence of successful community development projects initiated by the Institute of Cultural Affairs in villages, towns, and neighborhoods. Creating self-reliant, self-sustaining, and self-confident communities required adherence to five key principles (2):

1. *Operate within a clearly delimited geography* in order to produce visible results and assure community identity and ownership
2. *Deal with all the issues* because all community issue are interrelated and must be tackled simultaneously
3. *Involve all the people* because a broad-based resolve is the only way to get action on any plans
4. *Address the underlying issues* that keep community problems alive. Without addressing the "elephants in the room," issues will continuously reappear like dandelions

5. *Create community symbols and mechanisms to sustain consensus.* Keep the common agreements and commitments alive through writing, events, progress updates and recognition, celebrations, meetings, and other ways to keep the collective will and momentum alive.

Seek Action versus Principles

One big clue for scoping the consensus task is to seek advice about action rather than principles or concepts. This will minimize the debilitating tendency to get stuck in fights over ultimate truths that cannot be resolved. In the Middle East and British Isles those debates have gone on without closure for centuries and millennia. Stating the task in terms of specific action results will minimize the danger of falling into unproductive philosophical debates and generalities. Here are examples that compare and contrast vague and clear scopes of work:

Education Example:
> *Vague Scope:* Recommend solutions for increasing student academic achievement
>
> *Clear Scope:* Recommend actions and roles for administrators, teachers, parents, and students to identify and address the primary barriers in the short term (6–12 months) and long term (1–3 years)

Company Example:
> *Vague Scope:* Identify union/management responsibilities for improving the profitability of the mining region
>
> *Clear Scope:* Projects that will reduce the production costs of mining by x-percent without affecting safety and quality ranked and phased over three years

Community Examples:
> *Vague Scope:* Sustainable development directions to steer regional forest management
>
> *Clear Scope:* Steps and practices that public and private forest owners and managers need to implement in the next 3–5 years in order to reduce the rate of forestland fragmentation
>
> *Vague Scope:* Ways to reduce malnutrition in the province
>
> *Clear Scope:* Phased tactics for providing each child in a pilot village cluster with one meal a day

Link Consensus Solutions to Ongoing Problem Management

Avoid the illusion of "a solution to end all problems" or the hope that one meeting, one set of decisions, or a few priority policies will take care of a problem in one fell swoop. There are some tactics that have more visible effects than others, but most complex issues require a system of solutions that is launched and implemented over a period of time.

Each project should be constructed on the premise that one collaborative problem-solving process is an important, incremental part of ongoing attention to the mess of issues. Sponsors need to review the history of the debate, lay out the range of issues that need to be addressed in the future, and delineate a realistic focus for a given consensus process. As the consensus is building, the group can make official notes about implications for future decision making and submit concrete recommendations for the problem solving at hand. This eliminates the unrealistic expectation to solve all issues for all people.

Connecting the short-term activity to the long view is challenging and risky because public policy, issues, and organization development are moving targets. Local, state, and national governments are not structured to follow strategies that are longer than executives' or elected officials' terms in office. Each collaboration process is a unique political opportunity to get the most done while a particular window is open. I agree with the Solution Broker who said that, "all the stars have to be aligned to make an impact on the political scene."

In fact, my metaphor for public decision making is the game of football. There are a hundred variables that determine how far the ball moves: team strategies, the quality of the opposing team, referee temperament, weather conditions, individual biorhythms, audience support, etc. On a good day, the ball moves several yards and the audience cheers. On extraordinary days, when the "stars are aligned" and the team gains 10 to 20 yards, the crowd goes wild.

It would be great if every multiple constituency deliberation could occur on an extraordinary day. It would be wonderful if all the political stars aligned to create, approve, and implement all consensus recommendations. Given we live in a world that is not set up to follow long-term strategies, every project should do the best it can within the scope of influence to target feasible short- and long-term agendas to push and pursue.

Set Performance Measures to Steer the Process

The next step to creating a compelling reason for consensus processes is to answer the question: "How will you decide when the process is done?" or "How will you measure the success of the process?" The missions and scope of task may already clarify these questions, but usually they do not. The expected results may be implied but spelling them out makes a world of difference. The performance measures translate the mission and tasks into concrete terms that help the participants and facilitator better fulfill their roles: The diverse expectations of stakeholders will be easier to align if the sponsor knows exactly what types of products the consensus building needs to produce. The facilitator will have an easier time developing the process road map with well-articulated end products.

Mobilize the Mission with a Focus Question

The focus question summarizes the mission, scope of work, and expected measures. A focus question will serve as a rudder for keeping the deliberations on course and connect those who develop answers to those who want them. When confusion and chaos reigns, the focus question can rescue sidetracked conversations, remind people of the ultimate purposes, or help redirect the process steps. If you can't explain how an activity relates to answering the focus question, you better shift to a method that will. For example, rather than charging a group to create "recommendations for school district budget goals, strategies, and priorities," frame the task with the question "What are ways that the school board and superintendent can fulfill its services to students and parents in the next 2 years given the 2 million dollar projected deficit?"

IDENTIFY CLEAR ROLES

Once the compelling reasons for the consensus process have been established, the next order of sponsorship business is to assemble an effective and inclusive cast of collaborators. This includes at least three decision steps: 1) Targeting the stakeholder groups affected by the issue, 2) devising opportunities for broad participation, 3) inviting the participants, and 4) designating the meeting leaders.

Target Participating Stakeholder Groups

What does a system of stakeholders look like? Assessing and assembling the right group of "publics" is unique to every situation. The best way to start identifying key consensus constituencies is through informal, exploratory conversations with known stakeholders. Ask for suggestions about who needs to be involved in a given consensus-building project. If consensus is to be developed on a public affairs issue, it should be announced through various public channels and feedback invited from everyone about the mix of representatives required to address an issue equitably and holistically. Some push and pull from the constituencies should be expected and welcome. Sponsors will be able to discern a consensus about participating groups in the course of responding to both invited and uninvited stakeholder suggestions about stakeholders to include, exclude, emphasize, or de-emphasize.

No generic template exists for targeting stakeholder groups but experience provides substantive clues. I pass on some tried and true frameworks for pinpointing a "whole system" of stakeholders based on 1) geographies or operating functions; 2) degrees of stake in the issue; 3) levels and roles for providing care or services; 4) sectors, interests, perspectives, and beliefs; and 5) other ways.

Identify Stakeholders Based on Geography or Function

Established political or operational territories are often safe ways to cover a "whole system" of stakeholders for collaborative problem solving. Gather process participants that represent affected geopolitical units such as communities, counties, neighborhoods, states, or nations. For example, priorities for county childcare strategies should perhaps be decided by calling together representatives from each city and township in addition to key providers and experts. When a major city developed its first mass transit lines, geographic stakeholder representatives were called to help negotiate and select the designs for the city's first rail stations; officials and citizens of all the formal neighborhood groups were invited to participate in the design process.

In organizations, functions replace geography as a natural unit of representation. When developing strategic or operational plans, the heads of key functions, departments, and areas are invited to make sure all the parts are represented in organization-wide priorities. School improvement planning in larger schools brought together representatives of all teaching departments, specialist programs, support functions, and the administrative team.

Identify Stakeholders Based on Degrees of Stake in the Issue

A "whole system" of stakeholders can be identified by depth of various groups' stakes in a given matter and ranked according to the degree to which they are impacted or influence the problem (see figure 4.1). The *core players* are those groups whose lives and livelihoods are deeply tied to the problem and its outcome. The

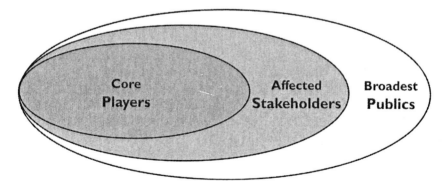

Figure 4.1. Spheres of Stakeholders

affected stakeholders are those who are indirectly related to the issue but influence its maintenance or resolution. The *broadest publics* include stakeholders who need to be kept in the loop in case they have or develop an interest in some aspect of the issue. The metaphor of the ham and eggs breakfast is a quick way to identify the different degrees of "stakes" between various stakeholders:

- The *broadest publics* are *related* to the issue. They are the potatoes, wheat, and tomatoes that made the side dishes possible—hash browns, toast, and ketchup.
- The *affected stakeholders* are *involved*. They are like the chicken that provided the eggs.
- The *key players* are *committed*. They are like the pigs that contributed the ham.

A waste management agency used this screen to divide their audiences into three tiers according to the following criteria: Primary stakeholders were those whose input "must drive" agency priorities. The secondary constituencies were those whose input needs to "be considered" in shaping directions. In the third tier were those publics that needed to be "heard and referred."

Identify Stakeholders Based on Roles or Levels in Delivery of Care or Service

Another way to identify all stakeholders in a system is by their role in a service delivery system such as education, mental healthcare, or delivery of services.

Sociologist Joan Tronto has an excellent way to identify service stakeholders in her book, *Moral Boundaries* (3). She combines political and moral considerations into a model based on four types of service or care (see figure 4.2): From the "big picture people" to the frontlines, the roles include the following:

1. Those who *care about* people: The policymakers of service and care industries
2. Those who take *care of* people: The managers of major institutions of service and care
3. The *caregivers:* Those providing the direct, hands-on help to people, customers, or clients
4. The *care receivers: The* clients, patients, students, and others who receive care

Here are three examples that use the levels of care model to identify their system of stakeholders.

The first example is a pilot partnership that sought ways to provide health care and housing to homeless people with AIDS/HIV, chemical dependency, and/or mental illness. Those who *care about* people were the housing and human service agencies and legislative committees that determine public policies and funding. Those who *take care of* people were the county agencies, HMOs, and state housing resources agencies that formed the backbone of the service delivery system. The Caregivers

Project	Example 1: **Making Homes and Health Care Affordable**	Example 2: **Community-Based Education Partnership**	Example 3: **City-wide Bus Service Improvement**
A. **The** **Policy Makers** Those who CARE ABOUT PEOPLE	• State housing agency • State human service agencies	• School board • Municipal leaders • Major employers • Civic organizations	• City Council • Metropolitan government • State's transit support division of the transportation agency
B. **The** **System Leaders** Those who CARE FOR PEOPLE	• County agencies • HMOs • State housing finance programs	• Building principal • Program administrators • College Deans	• Transit agency • Disabled persons transport • Subcontractors • School district bus operation officials and subcontractors
A. **The Providers** Those who are CARE GIVERS	Providers of care: • Supportive housing • Human services • Health care	• Parents • Teachers • Day care providers • Youth program staff • Coaches • Counselors	• Agency schedulers and other staff • Drivers • Labor union representatives • Neighborhood leaders
D. **The Clients** Those who are CARE RECEIVERS	Homeless who are: • AIDS/HIV positive • Mentally ill • Disabled	• Students • Adult learners • Preschoolers • All citizens	• Riders • Employers • Advocacy groups for people who rely on mass transit (e.g., elders, low income workers/ residents, etc.)

Figure 4.2. Assembling Whole Systems of Care

were the provider organizations that assisted clients with supportive housing, human services, and health services. The Care Receivers were represented by organizations that advocate for people who are HIV/AIDS positive, chemically dependent, mentally ill, or homeless (see figure 4.2).

Another example is a school district that was developing an authentic community partnership to identify, fund, and support a "world class school system" (see figure 4.2). They invited all levels of the education science sytem to the problem-solving table: The school board, municipal leaders, major employers, and civic organizations (those who *care about*); the building principals, special education, and other program administrators, preschool program coordinators, and community college deans (those who *care for*); the teachers, day care providers, preschool staff, youth program staff, coaches, counselors, police, youth, and parents (*care providers*); and the present and future students (*care receivers*).

The third example is a hypothetical one (see figure 4.2). If a city wanted to improve its bus service with broad-based thinking and support, the participants in the collaborative process should involve all levels of the service: policymaker representatives from the city council, metropolitan government, and the state's transit support division of the transportation agency. The system leaders would be the transit agency, disabled persons transport, subcontractors, school district bus operation officials, and subcontractors and other groups that operate transportation systems that could link with the basic public bus service. The providers would include all of the above joined by agency schedulers, other staff, drivers, and their labor union representatives. The care receivers would consist of the riders, employers, and neighborhood leaders, advocacy groups for people who rely on mass transit, such as elders, low-income residents, and any other groups that use or could use the bus system.

Identify Stakeholders Based on Sectors, Interests, Perspectives, and Beliefs

"Whole systems" can also be identified by the continuum of beliefs that surround the issue. This is the most common way to identify stakeholders in a conflict or crisis. Identifying stakeholders according to ideology or interest is clearly a very subjective criterion for selecting stakeholders. No group ever represents all the interests. Having said that, what are some clues for targeting the key interests and roles related to an issue? In reality, there are as many belief systems about a given subject as there are people.

Generally the interests and beliefs include stakeholders from three major sectors—the private, public, and community sectors (see figure 4.3). Controversies such as reproductive rights, school vouchers, welfare reform, airport noise abatement, land use disputes, or environmental clashes tend to have a similar pattern of stakeholders—two dominant and polarized interests with various degrees of moderates in between. In such cases, sponsors do the best they can to identify all major ideologies and interests and

**Typical Sectors, Interests, and Perspectives in a
multiple stakeholder decision-making process**

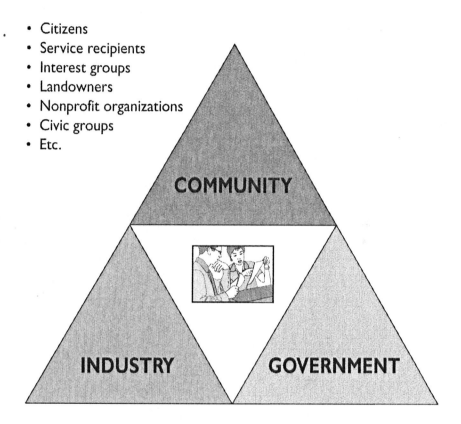

- Citizens
- Service recipients
- Interest groups
- Landowners
- Nonprofit organizations
- Civic groups
- Etc.

- Companies
- Employers
- Trade unions
- Economic groups
- Landowners
- Etc.

- Public agencies
- Elected officials
- Local governments
- Education
- Public land managers
- Etc.

Figure 4.3.   Getting the Whole System in the Room

find formal groups that would be invited to represent them. In newer social dilemmas, the stakeholders may be less clear and require more research to pinpoint. If the issue has been around awhile, the various stakeholder groups are more obvious and identifiable. The case studies in chapter 2 provide examples of interest groups that were involved with various consensus-building issues.

Identify Stakeholder Groups in Other Ways

I want to underscore that identifying stakeholders depends on the situation. One of the first steps in collaborative problem solving is to study the scope of the issue and determine the best ways to identify a microcosm of the "whole system." It may involve *one* of the three models I described, *none* of the above, or a *hybrid* of all three. The goal of consensus decision making is to assemble people that have the interest, passion, and willingness to resolve a problem that affects all their constituencies.

Devise Opportunities for Broad Participation

Once the primary stakeholder groups are targeted, sponsors have three important calls to make regarding how they can participate in the process. Only a few can come to the consensus table but more stakeholders can be involved in the process. Here are some clues for 1) maximizing the direct participation of all constituencies, 2) identifying the table participants, and 3) inviting players to the consensus venture.

Maximize the Direct Participation of All Constituencies

A collaborative problem-solving process gains power and credibility by involving hundreds of people beyond the tens that sit at the table. Follow-up and implementation of consensus solutions will be easier if a large base of people understand and support the solutions.

Connect the discussions at the table to a broad group of interested people through multiple mechanisms for sending and receiving ongoing input and feedback. The search for consensus solutions can be fortified through mailings, surveys, focus groups, public comment periods at official meetings, process briefings, and other methods; more human intelligence; passion; and ingenuity. A progress update mailing or news bulletin is a common mechanism for involving those not at or directly represented at the consensus table. Also, most processes have open meetings with public comment opportunities. In controversial deliberations, the meetings tend to be well attended by observers. Usually, stakeholder groups represented at the table take responsibility for informing and involving their constituencies on a regular basis. Examples for expanding the consensus debate and dialogue are shown in figures 4.4 and 4.5.

Identify the Optimal Number of Participants at the Consensus Table

It matters greatly who shows up at the table. If you were convinced of this before, hopefully the insider view of consensus building has reinforced the importance of selecting participants that are prepared for their formal and informal work. Participants

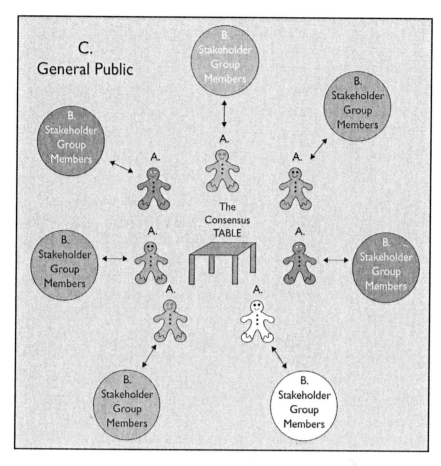

A 🍪 Stakeholder Group Representative

Figure 4.4. Involving Participants Beyond Those at the Table

determine their level and style of engagement but sponsors can select the 1) *size* and 2) *mix* of the groups who will represent the diverse stakeholder groups at the consensus-building table. Here are some clues and guidelines for determining who will represent a diverse group of stakeholders at the consensus table.

Group size: I have seen textbooks that recommend 8 to 15 people as an optimal size for group decision making or team operations. Group dialogue is easier with a small group, but I have encountered very few multiple-stakeholder situations in which a group of 15 people can adequately represent the diversity of perspectives. Given the large number of constituencies with a legitimate stake in any given issue,

Participation Avenues for...	*Tracking* **Process Output**	*Providing* **Process Input**
A. Stakeholder Group Representatives	• Meeting participation • Full meeting packet • Handouts • Informal and independent information gathering	• Meeting participation • Contact meeting leaders • Informal advocacy • Request to present information • Bring in materials
B. Stakeholder Group Members	• Receive information through an extended stakeholder mailing list • Stakeholder group meetings	• Talk to representatives to express opinions and submit input/output • Stakeholder group meetings • Contact meeting leaders and sponsors • Written suggestions at meetings or by mail, email, etc.
C. The General Public	• News media reports • Website communication • Provide information by request • Observe meetings	• Join constituency meetings • Contact meeting sponsors or leaders • Public comment period at the meetings • Written suggestions at meetings or by mail, email, etc.

Figure 4.5. Methods for Expanded Constituency Involvement

the number of people that should be invited to the table can easily add up to an unmanageable number. This is not unlike the problem of developing a guest list for a wedding. It is a struggle to reconcile the number of guests a couple would *like* at their wedding and the one they can *afford*.

Identifying the right number of individuals to represent the "whole system" of diverse stakeholders can be a daunting task for sponsors. There is no one way to assure that the process includes a microcosm of the affected stakeholders. The best advice is to do the best you can to balance inclusion and efficiency. Maximizing inclusiveness increases the chances for a broad-based buy-in on the product. Minimizing the participants eases the coordination of the dialogue.

Group mix: The correct mix of players depends entirely on the issue and the intent of the project. The goal is to surround the consensus table with people representing a continuum of perspectives, increase the group's capacity to exert its own balancing influences, and optimize holistic treatment of issues. It would be nice to invite a critical mass of Solution Brokers or Boundary Spanners to guarantee consensus innovation, but since sponsors cannot control the choices collaborators make regarding their engagement style, the next best thing is to concentrate on a team of diverse interests.

In assembling stakeholders, one temptation is to exclude stakeholders without direct ties to an issue such as "citizens at large" or groups that are neutral in a controversy. However, this would eliminate a major asset of collaborative problem solving. One reason collaboration works is because it involves the vocal minority as well as the silent majority affected by a complex and controversial set of issues. Finding common ground solutions is significantly improved by balancing the chorus of extreme voices with a steady choir of participants who have a deep stake in building bridges and fewer boundaries to defend. Think of a sixth grade class. Would you conduct class improvement planning by involving only the three bullies and the three shrinking violets?

A group that overtly represents the whole community is more likely to transform the diverse, polarized, or limited positions of a few stakeholders into socially palatable solutions that have broad-based backing.

Invite the Participants

Many collaborative processes have used some form of public invitation and self-selection to commission an ad hoc group of citizen leaders. In many cases the sponsor was a public agency that sent invitations and background materials to propose the project and request nominations for these citizen leaders. The call usually goes out to 50 to 100 stakeholder groups. The host organization chooses the collaborative process representatives from a list of candidates nominated by interested stakeholder groups.

Invite stakeholder groups to choose their representatives carefully. Truth in advertising is in order. Share an honest job description of the consensus participant role and ask stakeholder groups to choose people willing to serve as active advocates for their interests and ambassadors for consensus. Encourage groups to build a support system that helps their representative stay in close touch with them.

While there was some negotiating over specific candidates, the selection of representatives has been relatively harmonious, as reflected in this participant's account of the process:

> Well, I remember there was some jockeying around in the selection. I can't recall if there was much coordination with the environmental groups about whom they wanted. I'm pretty sure we knew that others were going to be putting in names, and we were putting in names. Given who we were and how we fit into the environmental community, we figured we'd get a spot.

In each case there is always some frustrations expressed by stakeholders that feel that the process was weighted in favor of a particular interest group. In general, however, the stakeholders were satisfied with the cast of actors selected and assembled. This is especially true if the process set up ways for the larger public to track the process and offer input from time to time.

As with any project, a good beginning sets the tone for a good process and outcomes. A letter, project materials, and a launch event symbolize the sealing of a temporary sociopolitical contract between institutions and individuals. Make sure you recognize people who will be donating precious time and talents to an important cause. Whether a participant is paid or a volunteer, the problem-solving effort would not be possible without them. Some key ingredients of the commissioning and orientation events and materials include those following.

Overview of Participant Roles

Review the participants' job duties and expectations with a special emphasis on the essential attitudes and approaches for acting collaboratively. Describe the dual responsibility of serving as advocates for special interests and ambassadors for common ground. Include examples of the formal and informal duties that consensus building is likely to entail. Clue participants in on their time and resources requirements and, if possible, offer ways to support them and/or get appropriate backing for their duties from their stakeholder groups. Require or strongly recommend attendance at all work sessions. Being present is critical. The controversy and consensus thicken in surprising and significant ways at each meeting. Missing work sessions usually sets the process back because time is required to "catch up" absentee members. Representatives are often allowed to designate one well-briefed alternate who can take their place in emergencies or nonnegotiable schedule conflicts. (These requirements should be addressed clearly in the ground rules; see an example on pages 182–184). Help participants tolerate, understand, and even enjoy the wonders and "bumps" of being part of a complex, high-stakes pioneering venture

Briefing on the Project

Describe and reclarify the whys, whats, whos, and hows of the projects. Review the purpose of the process and its relationship to mainstream dilemmas and decisions as well as the ground rules, guidelines, timelines, and steps of the joint venture. It helps to have the "knowns" of the process be clear to all since the task of finding consensus will involve plenty of "unknowns" and ambiguities.

Background on the Issue

The goal of the background information is to make all the players feel they are issue insiders. This element of the orientation is the bridge to the rest of the process. Getting on the same page about the state of the issue begins at the introductory session and continues throughout the first phase to consensus building. There will always be some degree of hierarchy based on participants' level of information, but it is good to educate representatives generously at the start about all the substantive aspects of the subject at hand—its history, surrounding trends, key political players, and the scientific knowledge (as agreed to by the process participants). Process sponsors are encouraged to customize the issue background orientation by surveying participants on what they know or seek to know and/or using their best intuitions about what participants need.

Introduction of the Consensus Builders

Take time to introduce the participants—their unique experiences, backgrounds, and worldviews. This provides consensus builders a chance to share each stakeholder group's "stake" in a given issue. It also offers participants a broad menu of subjects and angles to pursue informally. Extensive introductions will help jump-start the process of eliminating simplistic stereotypes, building relationships, and negotiating resolves.

Designate the Process Leaders

Sponsors decide what leadership roles will be needed to manage the consensus project. The process leaders' joint charge is to assure a fair, efficient, timely, and productive project. What leadership team has the trust and expertise to motivate, facilitate, and support the consensus process?

The three functions that are needed for process leadership include an 1) official leader, 2) process facilitator, and 3) support staff. Depending on budgets, competencies, convenience, etc., projects have handled the process leadership functions in different ways. Sometimes a different person serves each function, and in other situations, one person handled all three. Here is a description of the key functions:

The Official Leader

The official leader is the formal head of the project or its "chief operating officer." Chair, convener, or task force leader are some typical titles for this role. Those who serve tend to be trusted and/or familiar members of the stakeholder community related to the problem at hand. He or she often has a seat and even a vote at the consensus table. They serve as the symbolic leader of the process and provide an ongoing bridge between the project sponsor and the consensus effort. They work actively with the facilitator and staff to support the consensus process. Their role can range from opening and closing meetings to co-facilitating parts of the process.

The Process Facilitator

The facilitator's primary duty is to manage the meetings and adapt the process to meet evolving needs, changing circumstances, participant input, or recommendations of the official leaders. In many situations, the facilitator is brought in after much of the process had been constructed, casted, and scripted. Once on board, the facilitator has two tasks. The first is to translate process mandates and expected deliverables into a manageable group process. The translation challenge continues throughout the engagement. Prior to each meeting, the agenda and approach has to be adjusted to fit the consensus progress as well as anticipated process needs. The second is to coordinate the live discussions as they unfold.

In commissioned projects, the sponsor usually hires the facilitator with input from key facilitators. In consensus processes that have multiple sponsors, the parties typically agree on major outcomes and ground rules and then jointly hire a consultant to direct the process. In grassroots projects, an external facilitator may be used to launch the effort or conduct occasional special meetings, but participants take turns to facilitate ongoing meetings. Chapter 5 describes the tasks of facilitation in much more detail.

The Support Staff

The members of the support staff are usually personnel of the sponsor organization(s). They handle the logistics of hosting meetings as well as technical support for meeting management, documentation, and materials distribution to participating audiences.

In past processes, the staff of the agency, university, or other government entity connected to the sponsor served in the technical support roles. Again, every process handles the technical assistance differently. In one scenario, the sponsoring entities hired or borrowed research support, meeting space, information, project management, communication, and other administrative functions from participating stakeholder organizations in the most cost-effective manner possible. In the volunteer-based processes, the support, just like all the other roles, was carried out by the individuals that showed up around the partnership table.

CHART THE RULES OF ENGAGEMENT

The sponsor weighs in on the political process by choosing an overall process strategy for the consensus-building process. The way the game rules are framed makes an enormous difference in the way it gets played. The sponsor needs to be an active co-architect of the "due process" that will produce consensus results and connect them to mainstream governance or operations. Clues for effective design of the rules of engagement include 1) consulting with a process facilitator as early as possible, 2) building a simple script for the complex work, and 3) framing the process as "creating" versus "fixing."

Consult with a Process Facilitator as Early as Possible

At the risk of sounding extremely self-serving, the first clue to effective process is to work with an experienced consensus process designer at an early stage. They will help translate the urgencies, mandates, mission, and participation requirements of the project into a realistic group activity. Just like anything, group decision making benefits from the best technology. Experienced process professionals have hundreds of useful methods and the expertise to know when and how to apply them. They have a toolbox of feasible options to help sponsors make strategic choices about the most effective group methods for the resolving the issue at hand.

Even under the most placid circumstances, facilitating is a challenging job. Keeping the group on track is easier if facilitators are part of constructing a sensible track. Hiring a facilitator after the meetings and agendas have been set is the equivalent of asking a chef to prepare dinner three hours prior to a banquet with a set menu and ingredients. Another analogy for bringing facilitators in late is hiring an interior decorator after the furniture, carpet, window dressings, budget, and deadlines have been selected. A good expert will find a way to make the parts work, but the end product will not have the full benefit of their professional wisdom and expertise.

Build a Simple Script for the Complex Work

No process will ever substitute for critical thinking and hard work, but we must keep discovering and experimenting with simple but not simplistic constructs that enable participants to wrestle with intricate and interdisciplinary realities. Increasing the amount of processing time is a great way to support deliberations but difficult to do. Decreasing the demands on limited time is a very important alternative to produce quality results. A general guideline is to minimize the steps and requirements of the decision-making process. The subject matter is already complex. The process should not add extra noise to an already complicated debate. Simplifying group decision making is not easy when issues comprise an interrelated web of social, economic, political, historical, and other factors.

Here is one clue to keeping constructs simple but not simplistic. Don't squeeze too many agenda items into one meeting and don't pile on the deliverables. It pays to consider the wisdom behind various group dynamics guidelines that recommend amounts of time needed for a group of a certain size to share ideas, reflect on them, analyze the situation, and come to conclusions. Heed human limits to concentration, energy, and creativity. Scrutinize the intent of every planning or problem-solving step and select the activities that will most enrich the dialogue.

One consensus process, for instance, required the group to agree on five components in the first two meetings (definitions, concepts, benefits, goals, and indicators). Each component was an aspect of creating agreement about the desired future state of a community landscape. Focusing on one component would have enabled the 31-member group to have an in-depth conversation about common values and "ends" to be sought rather than five brainstorming discussions on facets of a desirable landscape.

Frame the Process as "Creating" versus "Fixing"

There are two basic philosophies for addressing a mess of complex issues. One is to see problems as ills to be cured. The other is to view them as situations people wish to change. Participants of consensus processes have referred to these approaches as the "issue-oriented" approach or the "planning approach," respectively. Once again, the best approach depends on the needs of a given situation. However, in my experience, the planning approach is more powerful because it puts everyone on the same team from the start. Resolving issues one by one encourages fault-finding and sets up an adversarial contest between differing tactical approaches. The planning approach directs energy toward things people are *for* rather than *against.* According to professor, scientist, and author Russell Ackoff, this means *creating* rather than *forecasting* the future. It requires addressing problems *synergistically* versus *discretely* (5):

> In a real sense, problems do not exist. They are abstractions from real situations. The real situations from which they are abstracted are messes. A mess is a system of interacting problems. The solution to a mess is not equal to the sum of the solutions to its parts. The solution to its parts should be derived from a solution to the whole—not vice versa. The question of priorities is misleading. All messes should be dealt with simultaneously and interactively.
>
> We waste too much time trying to forecast the future. The future depends more on what we do between now and then than it does on what happened up to now. The thing to do with the future is not to forecast it, but to create it. The objective of planning should be to design a desirable future and to invent ways of bringing it about.

The planning approach to consensus decision making involves questing for solutions through a series of agreements about the a) current reality, b) the shared goals, the c) challenges preventing achievement of the goals, and d) directions for moving toward the goals together (see figure 4.6). After clarifying the state of the problem and how it affects each stakeholder, the first step is to identify shared goals and destinations for the future. The goals become context and criteria for developing and selecting "good directions or solutions." "Good solutions" are those that can transform the current reality into the shared vision of the future. Making agreements takes time as people negotiate what is good for the whole in the midst of diverse views. The energy of the group is directed toward addressing the situation rather than fighting each other.

A handful of consensus participants I interviewed felt that the planning approach used in their deliberations was a key factor for finding common ground. One participant reflected on the importance of a "big picture approach" to resolving issues and

"Creating Common Directions vs. Mitigating Differences"

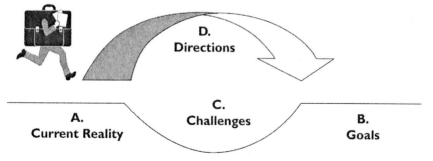

Figure 4.6   Basic Steps in Creating Futures vs. Fixing Problems

credited the systematic and often meticulous process as one of the reasons why the group was able to find some areas of agreement (1):

> There are two reasons for our transformation. First, many of the members were at least willing to listen and reflect on what others said. Although it took time, we began to trust each other and to clearly speak our minds. Second, many of us thought the facilitation got in the way of our discussions but it seems looking back now that it was the main reason for the common ground we established when we began talking to each other rather than shouting past each other. It wasn't easy as it required a high tolerance for ambiguity, but it may have allowed us to reach broadly supported recommendations.

Stay Visible throughout the Process

Sponsors add credibility and importance to the process and players by staying visible. Hands-on involvement of the administrator was cited as a key to successful group decision making in a study on site-based management and site-based decision making (SBM/SDM) in Dade County Public Schools composed of 296 buildings (4):

> The superintendent needs to maintain a high profile of commitment to the shared governance project. The study school experienced early success as the superintendent pushed the concept of SBM/SDM and gave it high visibility. He designated a person to oversee the project and provide support to SBM/SDM schools, sending the message that it was important to the central office. Successive superintendents professed support for the program but took actions that moved the district structure toward central control.
>
> This caused participants to feel uneasy, as they perceived that their efforts were being undermined by lack of support from top echelons of the administration.

The study underscores that people need to be convinced that the sponsor of a consensus process "has good faith in sharing some of the power vested in the position for trust to develop among those involved."

SUPPLY SUFFICIENT RESOURCES

Collaborative processes add new and untapped resources to address problems. However, as with any worthy investment, it takes riches to gain additional riches. Consensus building is not cheap. In fact, in many past processes, the investment caught leaders by surprise. Mad dashes were made along the way to secure more resources—everything from meals and meeting spaces to more scientific experts to shed light on controversial issues.

Funding the process costs may seem high but not if you count the added values and resources a consensus effort delivers. If they lead to real progress, they are worth every penny. Furthermore, a sponsor's resources can leverage a priceless donation of participant hours, ingenuity, backing, clout, access group resources, political connections, and other inputs that help achieve a needed function. Also, consensus decision making tends to avoid potential future costs of sustained conflict, constituency protest, litigation, or other consequences of unresolved problems.

Many public and private leaders have seen the investment in collaboration reap tangible rewards. For example, a decade ago, when the president of a bank within a major national corporation decided the bank could shift from a cost to a profit center, she made the risky investment of inviting over 250 branch managers for a national business meeting. She was convinced that getting broad-based strategic buy-in and building working relationships would be the only way to turn the business around. It worked. In two to three years, the bank transformed a million dollar deficit into its first million-dollar profit.

I say more in the following sections about the three primary resources needed to host an effective consensus process: 1) funding for the meeting basics, 2) carving out time for the effort, and 3) providing logistical support.

Fund the Meeting Basics

Process design must give adequate consideration for participant care and comfort. The environment makes a substantial difference in alertness, motivation, creativity, and general ability to participate. Also, a quality setting symbolizes respect for the individuals and their task.

Work environment expenditures need to be considered essential costs and not "frills." If great things are expected of participatory democracy, great resources must be invested to enable human beings to function effectively. Assuring participant dedication, creativity, and critical thinking requires basics such as comfortable seating, good view of all the actors, bright rooms, windows, invigorating décor, frequent refreshments, ample water, and frequent breaks for rest and rejuvenation.

Participant comfort is considered essential to good thinking and productive teamwork at an annual school district planning retreat (6). Good retreat space is a top priority. The site is a scenic ranch setting with spacious state-of-art meeting rooms, large windows, elegant dining, private rooms, plenty of sitting and social spaces, and inspirational artwork:

> On entering the grounds, participants immediately realize they are being given very special treatment. The grounds at Gainey are formal, quiet, and elegant. As soon as participants get off the school bus, nearly every person pauses briefly to admire the grounds, the buildings, and the general pastoral atmosphere. Some comment on the

honor of attending such an elegant center; a few decry the expense (which is not divulged to the participants).

Some may consider it overly lavish, but the superintendent considers a respectful environment as a key to shifting from "finding new ways to bang our head, to looking for new ways to use our heads" (6).

Meeting environment, personnel, and participant care are the three basics of hosting the forum for collaborative problem solving. The *meeting environment* includes such things as gathering spaces, equipment, tools, materials, mailings, meals, field trips, retreat facilities, transportation, and other elements that support the group activities. The *personnel* needs of process include retaining a facilitator, bringing in subject-matter presenters, or hiring special support staff, such as a sign-language interpreter, meeting equipment technicians, or record keepers. Travel reimbursements, per diems, room and board, recognitions, and social events are other typical budget items for assuring good *participant care*. The amount of funds depends on the process duration, number of participants, facility options, and specific process needs.

Invest the Necessary Time

Interview participants confirmed that consensus takes time. There are ways to speed up discussion and maintain some degree of depth, but every shortcut cheats the dialogue to some degree. Unfortunately, time and financial constraints tend to dictate process schedules and many consensus processes end up with minimal or inadequate time for in-depth hearing, listening, analysis, negotiation, and closure.

Sorenson's study of site-based processes in schools highlights the importance of managing the "precious resources of time" (7):

Participation in site-based management provides great potential for organizational improvement. . . . However, such involvement demands large quantities of an educator's most precious commodity, *time*. Extraordinary demands on time create stress, causing organizational members to be less efficient.

One's enthusiasm for inclusion in the difficult job of school reform is probably directly proportional to the time available to the individual. . . . One of the more difficult resource issues to resolve is the provision of adequate time in which to plan for school improvement. Some learning communities have begun to address this issue by rearranging the school day, the yearly school calendar, and the provision of release time for teachers.

In addition to the considerations referring to the limitations of personal time, one must give careful consideration to the time available to the organization collectively. The adoption of an overly ambitious implementation schedule, due to the enthusiasm of individuals, may lead to their disappointment because the system was unable to bring ideas to fruition quickly enough. (7)

Allocating enough time is one concrete way to respect the importance of the activity and individual efforts. Process participants wanted more time for collective front stage activities, but the insider accounts suggest that more time for backstage activities should be provided on-site as well. The space, duration, and orchestration of meetings should include generous places and times for informal interchange, distancing, thinking, and diplomacy. Another important consideration is to allot enough time between meetings to help representatives communicate and sell consensus work to their constituencies. Additional allocations of on-site time will not substitute for the informal duties, but they would acknowledge, validate, and support the human homework that is essential to producing agreements in a minefield of controversy.

As mentioned in the chapter on consensus politics, negotiating the time frame for meetings and processes is a critical political task for process sponsors and meeting facilitators. Time is money. We don't have the luxury of endless and extended timeouts, but we need to apply full-cost accounting to the principles of participatory decision making. The more controversial the topic, the more time is required to reach resolutions. The more players around the table, the more time is required to accommodate everybody's view on each topic.

Outfit the Voyage with Support Services

From facilities to technical support, many of the meeting basics—environment and personnel—are often an in-kind contribution of the sponsor or partner organizations. Even when the components are funded, support staff is needed for ongoing coordination of the meeting environments, personnel, and participants. In addition to coordinating the physical supports, support staff knowledgeable in the subject matter are critical to documenting results, inviting experts, facilitating small groups, accessing background materials, and receiving briefings about existing agency/organization services. In the next chapter on facilitator duties, I elaborate more about collaborative processes rely on a vast repertoire of staff tasks and talents.

CONCLUSION

Sponsors decide why, how, and when mainstream decision processes need help from collaborative problem solving. They structure, authorize, and support a forum where people can actively discuss issues and devise new ways to help hundreds of people affected or hurt by problematic situations. Some leaders use consensus forums for targeted needs and others have adopted them as mainstream operating mechanisms. Whatever the frequency, successful group ventures are the likely outcome of involving people intentionally and wisely.

NOTES

1. Spencer, L. J. (1989). *Winning through participation.* Dubuque, IA: Kendall/Hunt.

2. Institute of Cultural Affairs. (1975). *The human development consult manual.* Chicago: The Institute of Cultural Afffairs.

3. Tronto, J. (1993). *Moral boundaries: A political argument for an ethic of care.* New York: Routledge.

4. Sidener, R. P. (1995, April). *Site-based management/shared decision making: A view through the lens of organizational culture.* Paper presented at the annual meeting of the American Educational Research Association, San Francisco.

5. Ackoff, R. (1980). Quote mentioned in an early 1980s article of the *Telegram*, a publication of the Council for Urban Development. At the time, Russell Ackoff was a professor at the Wharton School of the University of Pennsylvania. Ackoff is a renowned writer and systems thinker including books such as *Re-creating the corporation: A design of organizations for the 21st century* (1999), *Redesigning society* (2003), and *Ackoff's fables: Irreverent reflections on business and bureaucracy.*

6. Bjorum, W. (1991). *Listening for voices: A leader in action.* St. Paul, MN: University of St. Thomas.

7. Sorenson, L. D. (1995, February 10–13). *Site-based management: Avoiding disaster while sharing decision making.* Paper presented at the annual meeting of the American Association of School Administrators, New Orleans, LA.

Chapter Five

Clues for Facilitators

In order to make participation work, it is essential to have good structure. Clear limits, ground rules, and leadership are important in making an empowering, freedom-generating process work.

—Rosabeth Moss Kanter
In Laura Spencer's *Winning Through Participation*

The overall role of facilitators is to guide and support collaborative dialogue, problem solving, planning, and decision making. Using their expertise in various participation technologies, they custom-make a consensus process that translates the sponsor's decision-making needs into a group decision-making forum. Collective genius doesn't just happen. A fair and engaging process needs a robust structure and referees.

Consensus-building facilitation requires several roles: 1) the official leader, 2) the process facilitator, and 3) support staff. Each consensus effort has a different way of fulfilling the roles. Sometimes process facilitators play all three roles. In many cases there is a formal "chair" of a process and a team of staff to work with the process facilitator. In yet other situations, members of the sponsoring organization(s) may lead the process on their own. Here are further details about the three roles that steer and support a successful consensus-building effort:

The Official Leader

The official leader's responsibility is to keep the project on course and ensure that the process meets the expectations of the sponsors and external audiences. They remind the group of their charge and accountability. If the consensus problem solving takes place within one organization, the official leader might be the principal, manager, executive director, department head, or supervisor who heads up that organization. In multiple-organization processes, representatives of the sponsoring or convening organizations may serve as the official leader of the process. In many

161

commissioned consensus task forces, advisory panels, or roundtables, a "chair" is appointed by the sponsors to fulfill the role of the official leader.

An official leader serves as a "first among equals." He or she is a member of the consensus group, while performing the duties of a coordinator and symbolic leader. In the processes I have encountered, their job description was usually light on specifics and heavy with accountability. One stated that the chair's duty was to "work with staff and the facilitator to develop meeting agendas, help focus the group discussion and direction, and serve as the group's designated media spokesperson on matters related to its official position." In another venture, the chair was assigned by the legislature to "ensure fair and adequate representation among the members; monitor and report on the progress; ensure recommendations are credible and based on authoritative, scientific, and factual data and conduct parliamentary procedure with respect to formal recommendations of the consensus group." In general, the official leader was to direct both the collaboration process and the interface between the process and external audiences.

The Support Staff

The staff helps do whatever is needed to make sure the participants and process leaders have everything they need for their roles. I alluded to their demanding and diverse job in the previous chapter. Most of their duties are backstage and behind the scenes.

They record and communicate the proceedings for the participants as well as the interested parties who are not at the table. They set and clear the meeting spaces, produce technical materials, and make sure the cast and crew have food, water, shelter, and other basics to keep the process going. Staff members will also make formal presentations if they have responsibility for service functions related to the issues in the problem solving. One formal job description specified the following: Staff duties were to "provide necessary support to assist the group in organizing, evaluating, and presenting information; assist in securing information and data as requested by the group members; coordinate meeting facility arrangements; promote identification of points of agreement as well as disagreement; encourage clear communication and discussion and maintain direction and focus." In another the description of responsibilities was broad and general. The ground rules charged the staff assistants to the global task of "administering the process and providing relevant background information."

The Process Facilitator

As with the official leader, the specific duties of the process facilitator tend to be defined differently for each situation. In general, process facilitators are expected to be the neutral, objective third party that leads the meetings fairly and efficiently. In one case the job was to "ensure all points of view are expressed by the process members and considered on particular issues and to help the group reach consensus on all its deliberations." In another project, the consultants were charged simply to "mediate the negotiations."

Many of the consensus processes I have known began with somewhat defined roles for the chair, facilitator, and support staff but as things moved along, the boundaries between their responsibilities, authority, and accountability merged, overlapped, or required a great deal of interpretation. The "crew" of each process worked together very closely to manage the volatile forum and support the participants' ability to meet the high expectations of the sponsors and external audiences. In this account, a process chair emphasizes the deep reliance on teamwork among the official leader, facilitator, and support staff (1):

> I cannot possibly overemphasize the importance of my support group. Driving over to [the meeting] we would talk about the process. I would say, "OK guys, shoot at what I'm about to tell you. Here's what I'm thinking about the approach for tomorrow's meeting." They would come back with things like, " I don't think that's too good of an idea," or "You know that may not work the way you think it might because it might elicit this response." . . . And then of course after meetings . . . we critiqued each other. Had I not had that, I would have gone under. I could not have handled [the challenge of managing the process] in a vacuum. It was beyond any one person intellectually, . . . emotionally, and spiritually.

I agree wholeheartedly with the statement that these processes "cannot be handled by any one person in a vacuum." Teamwork is not an abstract notion in conducting consensus projects.

I repeat a conclusion I have stated before: Method matters. Just like any other process, the quality and substance of the output is heavily influenced by how the input is used and organized to create a final product. For example, the same building materials such as cement powder, sheet rock, steel beams, workers, trucks, permits, etc., can produce a wide range of buildings depending on the who and how directing the drawings, steps, timing, and coordination of the construction process.

Similarly, method matters in putting on a school holiday concert with a group of 200 elementary school children, a pianist, and music scores. A great deal depends on the leadership that combines those components into a show. One year it can be a semi-chaotic succession of soft-voiced children's choruses. Another year the program can be a captivating two-hour pageant of bold singing, movement, and innovative stage effects presented by beaming little performers.

My favorite illustration of how process influences content is a *Far Side* cartoon showing the sheriff of a wild west town reviewing and reprimanding his deputy who proudly points to a pile of horses, bags, cowboys, guns, and lamps piled in front of the office. The caption reads: "Hey Charlie, don't you know you have to *organize* a posse?"

What does experience reveal about the best way to organize a collaborative process? As a team, the process leaders 1) *plan*, 2) *preside* over, and 3) *publicly document* a consensus process (see figure 5.0). This chapter provides clues for each of the three duties.

A.
Process
PLANNING

1. *Research* to understand the situation
2. *Engineer* a fair and empowering process
3. *Prepare* procedures for each step or session
4. *Maximize* value for sponsors and stakeholders

See pages 165–179

B.
Process
PRESIDING

1. *Facilitate* productive meeting
2. *Mediate* conflict resolution
3. *Cultivate* collegial working relations
4. *Remain* neutral and objective

See pages 179–186

C.
Public
RECORDING

1. *Document* the deliberations
2. *Communicate* decisions

See pages 186–189

Figure 5.0.   Roles of Facilitators

PLANNING A MEANINGFUL PROCESS

The facilitator is responsible for developing a participation framework that achieves the precise intents of the sponsor. It is an engineering role that involves 1) researching to understand the situation; 2) engineering a fair and empowering process; 3) preparing procedures and tools for each work session; and 4) constantly evaluating and managing the process to maximize value for sponsors and stakeholders.

Research to Understand the Situation

The process leaders should know enough about the subject at hand to avoid getting in the way of the process. The official leader and staff are generally selected due to their familiarity with the subject of the problem solving. Process facilitators should know enough about the subject to stay ahead or abreast of the information relevant to the group inquiry and dialogue.

The process facilitator is the designated "neutral outsider," but it helps to be an informed foreigner. If the facilitator knows too much about the underlying conflicts and histories, they may become more hesitant to probe ambiguous statements that shield sensitive issues from discussion. However, while it is helpful for a facilitator to be distant enough to ask the clarifying questions, they should be familiar with the basic status, issues, and jargon related to the consensus-building topic. Participants should not have to constantly stop and educate the facilitator. In order to provide equal airtime and avoid skewing the education toward particular views and opinions, a facilitator should know about the alleged "sides" and "positions" of stakeholders.

Self-education is an important preparation step for effective facilitation. Specific activities include reading all process-related materials to prepare for meetings, pursuing additional orientation on the underlying issues, and staying abreast of the content in order to understand the group's discussions.

Engineer a Fair and Empowering Process

Process design is an influential step in the process leadership and the primary reason for retaining a professional facilitator. Nobody can guarantee that consensus will emerge, but facilitators have a broad and deep reservoir of methods that are most likely to foster group agreements. To use a classic analogy, the horse may not drink if it is brought to water, but facilitators know the 50 ways of guiding the horse to the stream that maximize its desire and decision to drink. This saves a great deal of trial and error time on the part of those less familiar with the craft of guiding group discussion.

Constructing an effective consensus process means assuring a fair field of play. Specific tasks include a) determining the best methods and techniques; b) making sure the process is easy to understand; c) clarifying what constitutes a consensus agreement; and d) managing science and data proactively. It also means empowering the players by e) building in the time and mechanisms for the consensus builders' political work (see figure 5.0 for a diagram and summary).

Determine the Best Methods and Techniques

The most influential call a facilitator makes is determining the timing and method to be used for each step of crafting consensus. As with anything, the secret to designing consensus process is matching the best technology to a given audience and situation. Making process choices is no different than the judgment calls involved with any life practices—applying: the right club to a golf shot, the appropriate disciplinary action for student misbehavior, the best information system for an organization, the correct medication for a diagnosis, the strategic combination for football, the best combination of alternative routes home during rush hour, or the most influential marketing tactics for a product or political campaign.

Sponsors can and should rely on process facilitators for specific technologies and procedures, but they should know the basic elements of consensus building in order to evaluate process proposals. In this section, I describe what every sponsor should know about the elements of good process—the five "basic food groups equivalent" of process design that will enable sponsors to work wisely with process facilitators:

1. Building *shared awareness* about a situation affecting them
2. Producing *mutually meaningful analysis* to inform decision making
3. Making *mutually satisfying agreements* to resolve issues or work together
4. Initiating *collective action*
5. Developing formal or informal *working alliances*.

For each process, the order and emphasis of each element will vary, but I identify outcomes, activities, and clues for conducting each element.

Element 1: Creating Shared Awareness

Consensus building begins by acknowledging the full situation—the complexity of issues and richness of perspectives that gather around a problem-solving table. Without some degree of agreement about the status of the issue or situation, it is difficult to determine where to go. Whether you are planning a wedding, creating district-wide education standards, or setting up a women's business cooperative in a village, never assume that stakeholders have a similar understanding of the scope and dimensions of the topic in question.

Key STEPS	1. Creating **Shared** **AWARENESS**	2. Producing **Acceptable** **ANALYSIS**	3. Making **Binding** **AGREEMENTS**	4. Mobilizing **Collective** **ACTION**	5. Developing **Working** **ALLIANCE**
Focus QUESTION	What is the "state of the issue"?	What needs to be examined or considered?	What do we need to do and why?	What is the follow through?	What will lead and assure implementation?
Sample ACTIVITIES	• Task clarification • Participant introductions • Process orientation • Issue clarification • Background information • Sharing perspectives	• Probing key issues • "Unpacking" controversies • Targeted research • Developing scenarios • Cost/benefit analysis • Establishing criteria	• Generating solutions • Identifying options • Forming recommendations • Making choices	• Publishing results • Transmitting recommendations • Advising implementation • Monitoring follow-through • Resource investment • Adopting action plans	• Formal assignments • Coordination and communication mechanisms
Main OUTCOME	Common understanding of the issue and task	Collective explanations and implications	Resolutions which all stakeholders support	Plan for implementing agreements	Designated leadership responsibilities, accountability, and authority

Figure 5.1.   Elements of a Consensus-Building Process

The Outcome: This step is completed when there is a mutually satisfactory answer to the question: What is the state of the people, problem, and perspectives? Every participant sees parts of the whole, so the safest way to define the "state of the issue" is to combine all perspectives. The "right" reality to work from is the one that is described, named, assessed, and labeled jointly. The process facilitator's duty is to provide a comprehensive framework that allows people to share what they see and develop a common understanding of all the dimensions of the matter in question.

The Activities: Key components for creating shared awareness include an orientation to the purpose, process, parameters, and anticipated products of a given consensus venture and to receive a generous amount of information concerning the issues at hand.

The Clues: Due to time constraints and general impatience with "getting on with it," the most common propensity is to minimize the time spent on orientation to the consensus issues and participant perceptions. The tendency is to briefly cover what many sponsors or crew refer to as the "niceties" such as extended participant introductions and other steps to get to know the players.

Similarly, there is a propensity to shortchange what I call the "not-so-niceties"— the airing of diverse perspectives about the issue. Processes tend to jump right into setting common goals as soon as actors are briefed on the mission and game rules. As a result of minimizing the soft tactics and hard realities, participants tend not to get the benefit of hearing and understanding the depth of passion, unique experience, and full logic that each member brings to the table. As a result, the consensus builders' core beliefs tend to get revealed bit by bit as they discuss and debate specific topics.

Conflicts and tensions arise, in part, because people have determined their "rights" and "wrongs" or labeled the "good and bad guys" based on limited background data. Natural humility sets in when participants see that their concern is one piece in a very large and challenging jigsaw puzzle that involves many real persons and real lives.

Only one process I have worked with allowed time for representatives to overview their background, understanding, and "stake" in the focus problem. The presentations took a day and a half, but participants gained a more intimate understanding of the individual experiences, logic, and urgencies that gave rise to each of the diverse positions. The sooner the Solution Brokers, Boundary Spanners, and Team Players know where people stand, the sooner their minds can go to work on finding common ground for creating unexpected points of intersection.

Element 2: Producing Acceptable Analysis

The common understanding of an issue is developed in the awareness stage. It sets the context for probing the issue further in the analysis step. Collective analysis is an opportunity to inject the thought, inquiry, innovation, and insight needed to change a problematic state into strategies. Roy Hanson, former Associate Dean of the Humphrey Institute for Public Affairs at the University of Minnesota, set the standards for effective analysis when he said, "I believe analysis matters when it informs, offers alternatives, avoids the higher idiocy, wears well, and is presented in digestible proportions and in understandable language."

The Outcome: This step is completed when there is a mutually satisfactory answer to the question: What needs to be examined or considered before making choices and recommendations about solutions?

The Clues: Deciding what dimensions of an issue to probe and how to analyze them is often a controversial decision in itself. Since the time is limited, judgments must be made about which issues are examined in detail, whose data and research are introduced into the process, what science will be used for developing the "science-based" solutions everyone seeks, and when there has been enough analysis to move on to solutions. Many stakeholder representatives come with an arsenal of back-up data to support their view of the issues. Collective analysis often starts by making choices about the information that will drive all other consensus agreements.

If the group does not get a chance to weigh in about how to conduct issue analysis, they will often demand it. This was evident in many of the process turning points in chapter 3. In several processes the meeting sponsors/leaders' judgment about background presentations and briefings was not acceptable to all stakeholders. Consensus groups demanded that the analysis strategy be developed democratically. Participants listed their preferences, developed criteria for selection, and made choices about adding new information and analysis.

Limited analysis is an issue but so is the other extreme of over-examination. As in the awareness element, it is easy to fall into the trap of needing "more research" or "further study." There is no end to analysis that can be applied. The business school mantra is useful here: "Perfect information is hard to come by." There is not enough money to pay for the most information. Decisions would not be cost effective. All decisions are based on some version of imperfect information. Consensus builders need to decide the point at which participants feel they have enough information and inquiry to make choices.

The Activities: Any human or organizational dilemma needs a unique diagnosis strategy. A rigorous analysis process is especially critical when it is conducted by a diverse group of people. Analysis methods can include: public hearings, expert testimonials, review of research, trends assessment, SWOT evaluation (identifying strengths, weaknesses, opportunities, and threats), root cause analysis, issue ranking, vision development, goal setting, site visits, field trips, historical evolution scans, feasibility analysis, solution criteria development, cost/benefit studies, "unpacking" controversies, targeted research, developing possible future scenarios, cost/benefit analyses, thinking "out of the box," and many other methods for thinking through problems and possibilities.

Element 3: Making Binding Agreements

After careful analysis, consensus builders move to making agreements that everyone will support. This element is perhaps what many people have in mind when they refer to consensus building. It is the most visible and dramatic step: the culmination of a great deal of idea sharing, data gathering, digesting, and discussion. In fact, it is often difficult to pinpoint exactly when analysis ends and agreement making begins.

The Outcome: This step is completed when the group has answered the question: What do we need to do and why? The group makes judgments about conclusions, recommendations, action priorities, strategies, policies, project plans, and other consensus resolutions affected individuals and groups agree to implement and/or support.

The Activities: As with analysis, each group decision calls for custom-fitted set of methods for creating and sealing consensus agreements. Generally, the road to consensus involves some type of bottom-up approach to forming decisions. *First* participants generate suggestions that are examined and formulated into a series of solution options, a system of strategies and/or draft agreements. *Next,* the draft decisions are approved as official consensus choices using various means. *Finally* consensus decisions could mean editing strategies until everyone feels they can support the product, developing specific action details to implement high-level consensus, ranking and selecting courses of action based on common criteria, choosing options by secret ballot, a show of hands or hand signals indicating degree of support, and other voting techniques, etc. Consensus purists frown on voting because they see it as a divisive method. However, if we truly believe that consensus is an organic formula to be defined by each group, voting is a valid tactic if participants agree to use it.

The final step is to make the agreement official and show proof of support. As with all other elements and activities, this has been done in many ways. In one case, stakeholders signed a final document or transmittal letter to the entity that commissioned the consensus process. In other situations, stakeholder groups wrote letters of support. If the consensus produces a new interorganizational partnership, stakeholders show their support by investing their staff and resources or electing members to be part of an ongoing coordination team. Sometimes, agreements are formalized with head nods or listing consensus builders in the final report. Whatever the method, it is important to symbolize the collective will that was forged in the consensus process.

The Clues: The secret to achieving consensus agreements is the preceding two elements, pursuing shared awareness and mutually acceptable analysis. Common preferences for future directions are shaped continually in the formal and informal dialogue leading up to final decisions. Shortcuts and impatience with problem assessment will come back to haunt you in the form of incomplete plans or superficial accords. Consensus agreements without thorough inquiry are like marriage without substantive courtship or weight loss through quick-fix diets.

Another make-or-break variable in forming agreements is clear game rules. Participants must know the process for finalizing consensus early in the deliberations. This clue is so important that it merits its own section (coming up next). There is no faster way to invalidate the collective consensus that by discrediting the fairness of the process. On the other hand, when decision parameters and steps are explicit and internalized by all, group members will hold each other accountable for following through and supporting the consensus agreement.

I have a vivid example of the benefits of clear decision rules. In one long process, a group of very diverse stakeholders chose which of 20 possible recommendations they would endorse jointly. The plan was to use a hidden ballot to assess members' approval/disapproval for each recommendation, having them indicate their level of support using a three-grade scale:

1. Support wholeheartedly
2. Can live with
3. Over my dead body

After the results were tallied, all recommendations passed even though several proposals were alleged to be too centrist for some activist interests. A representative of one such group was shocked by the outcome and claimed she could not accept the outcome. Another member of the group spoke on behalf of the consensus group about the need to honor their agreements about making agreements. "What you are saying," he pointed out, "is as though requesting your money back after the bets have been made, and the horses have run the race!"

The "Fist to Five" is a popular method of consensus assessment and development. One community school that has instituted a wildly successful site-based management approach uses the "Fist to Five" with all members—from kindergartners to school policymakers (2) (see figure 5.2). When a proposal or draft decision is made, everyone indicates their support with their hands: A fist means they feel the idea is not good and want to block it. Putting up one or more fingers indicates various levels of support. One finger says, "I don't but won't block"; two means "I don't agree, but it may work"; three means "I'm neutral and will work"; four means "This is a good idea and will work"; and a full hand signifies a "It's a great idea, and I'll be one of the leaders."

The Fist to Five indicator provides the opportunity for further discussion. After the show of support, if 75 percent or more are not in agreement, there is not sufficient consensus. Those not in agreement suggest what it would take to move to a higher level of support, and everyone works together to expand the common ground.

Element 4: Mobilizing Collective Action

The proof is in the pudding. Consensus decisions worth their salt need to be linked to action in the lived world. Hopefully those who commissioned or convened the project have carefully built follow-up steps into the consensus process. However, this is not always the case. Specified or not, participants will demand that their expenditure and work goes somewhere and makes a difference.

The Outcome: This step is completed when there is a mutually satisfactory answer to the question: What is the follow-through to assure that the consensus products are

Assessing individual support for a consensus decision in process

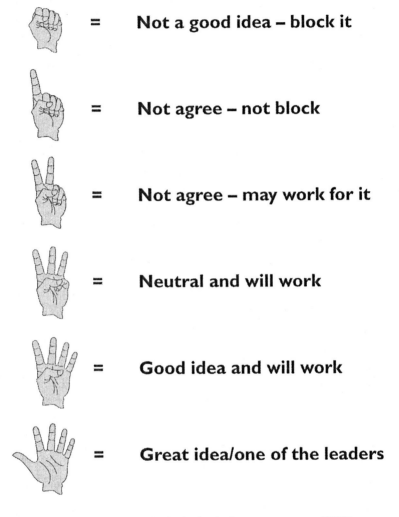

= **Not a good idea – block it**

= **Not agree – not block**

= **Not agree – may work for it**

= **Neutral and will work**

= **Good idea and will work**

= **Great idea/one of the leaders**

The Fist to Five indicator helps clarify the level of group consensus. If 75% or more are not in agreement, there is not sufficient consensus. Further discussion is needed. Those not in agreement suggest what it would take to move to a higher level of support. Then, everyone works together to refine the common ground.

Based on the work of A. Fletcher (2002). *Firestarter youth power curriculum: Participant guidebook.* Olympia, WA: The Freechild Project.

Figure 5.2.   Fist to Five Consensus Support Indicator

used to solve the problems? The stakeholders establish the actions and roles for reconnecting the solutions to the original problem. In many cases, all the stakeholders will have some role or responsibility for implementation. One major benefit of collaborative problem solving is not simply sharing ideas but pooling support, power, and resources to mobilize the consensus solutions.

The Activities: Translating agreements to action can vary greatly with every process. It can range from a short discussion about next steps to a detailed road map for long- and short-term priorities. A typical way to link consensus solutions to implementation is formally publishing and transmitting products to leaders who will incorporate them into a mainstream decision process in the legislature, city agency, school district, or other existing institution. In such a case, the consensus builders may retain a monitoring role by receiving regular progress reports and advising the implementation. If the consensus product is the formation of a multiple-entity partnership, the partner organizations set up a coordinating mechanism and invest in a shared action plan.

The Clues: Action planning worksheets, methods, software, and techniques are extremely abundant. Every situation has a unique set of requirements and preferences for the time frames, specificity, format, and measures in a "good" action plan. The most useful workshops and worksheets are tailored to produce the exact answers a group needs to get going: identify action steps, define success measurements, assign responsibilities, and specify monitoring mechanisms.

Element 5: Developing Formal or Informal Working Alliances

The final step in consensual decision making is establishing personal or positional responsibility for follow-through. If the consensus has been built deliberately, the planning relationships will naturally translate into sound capital for implemantation. In otherwords, working alliances evolve as a result of the trust and relationships developed during the consensus process.

The Outcomes: The result of this final step is to establish who will lead and assure implementation. The action needs to be linked to specific people that have clear leadership responsibilities, accountability, and resources.

The Activities: The action planning in the previous element becomes the venue for formalizing ongoing alliances. This step is about formal assignments, shared budget implications, and setting up coordination and communication mechanisms for action partnerships.

Merge the Steps into a Manageable Process

When the best techniques for each step are selected, the facilitator's process design duty is to package the pieces into a meaningful and manageable whole. As a start, a user-friendly schedule is created to show what topics, agenda items, and procedures will be used at various stages of consensus building. Of course, the final act or acts of a process facilitator are to track the process and be prepared to change it as needed.

Keep the Process Understandable and Sensible at All Times

Every step and exercise of a consensus process must make sense to frontline consensus makers. Participants have a lot on their hands without having to devote extra time to "figuring out the process." As suggested in the sponsor's clues, streamlining tasks and deliverables is a good start. Another suggestion is to minimize confusion about the process by replacing jargon with questions in plain English. Earlier in the study, I discussed how words such as "consensus," "collaboration," and other "plannerese" terms such as "objectives," "goals," "strategies," and "mission" have thousands of perceived meanings and uses. For example, instead of labeling an agenda item as "goal setting, " replace it with a question such as, "what do we want to achieve in addressing the homeless in this city in the next three to five years"?

Questions are amazing tools for staying on task. Translating purpose to focus questions forces clarity on the part of process designers. Questions quickly communicate the scope, intent, and desired results of each step. They also help order chaos: If the dialogue strays from planned forum procedures or mutates in other unexpected ways, the stated question on the agenda helps steer the deliberation back on task. (See p. 138 for examples of focus questions.)

Clarify What Constitutes a Consensus Agreement

Consensus decision making protocols are not universally defined so how do we know and show that we have made an agreement everyone can live with and support? How does consensus become official? Traditional processes have clearly defined ways to closure. In parliamentary procedure, a decision is a proposal that has been motioned, seconded, discussed, and put to a vote. In litigation, the decision is the jury's verdict after all the evidence has been heard from each side. In consensus processes the decision-making steps are up to each process.

As indicated in the previous section, clear criteria for making binding public agreement is a make-or-break variable in consensus building. I have seen protocols range from head nods and raised hands to voting on jointly crafted recommendations by secret ballot. One legislature charged a collaborative problem-solving panel to come back with "minority and majority recommendations." They specified the percentages of votes required for each category. Again, this smacks of consensus heresy for some practitioners, but I believe that every group has the right to decide how they decide.

Consensus decision rules need to be customized and can be very innovative, but once established, the protocols must be clear, explicit, and logical to all players. People cannot participate fully if they do not know how they weigh in and influence the decision at every stage. The process facilitator makes sure that the steps to consensus agreement are understood and enforced.

For example, one yearlong process followed a three-step process—discussing, drafting, and deciding—in working through each major set of recommendations:

Step 1: Discussion: Information or input is presented; diverse ideas, options, and views are shared; and key areas of conflict and common ground are identified

Step 2: Drafting: The elements of assessment are analyzed and formed into proposed consensus decisions

Step 3: Decision making: The draft is written up, reviewed, debated some more, refined, and finalized and formalized as shared decisions using signatures, show of hands, head nods, or other agreed-to ground rules

The meetings had a predictable rhythm. Participants knew when the records would be published, when to input formally and informally, and how to contribute stakeholder ideas and suggest consensus proposals.

Manage Science and Data Proactively

Many consensus processes seek to construct a "science-based" collective agreement. However, each of the multiple stakeholders will have different convictions about the sciences and scenarios that explain the true condition and needs of the issue.

For sponsors and meeting leaders, determining what background information to use requires as much thinking and planning as identifying the mix of participating stakeholders. What background information will inform consensus decisions? Stakeholder efforts to prove that "my research can beat up your research" should not be a surprise in any problem-solving process. The use of data needs to be carefully planned.

Dueling scientific facts were at the heart of a recent failure to achieve consensus about all-terrain vehicle (ATV) use on public lands and/or state parks. Environmental protection stakeholders and ATV users could not agree on how much impact riders have on the natural resource.

Sorenson's research into shared decision making in school districts confirms the need to make sure that participants have the working knowledge needed to be a meaningful player in decision making (3):

> The knowledge and experience required to make quality decisions on some topics that have been traditionally deferred to administrators is not necessarily possessed by others.

In some site-based systems, teachers are asked to make decisions on budgets, personnel, and noninstructional issues about which they know very little.

Weiss, Cambone, and Wyeth (4) interviewed approximately 180 people from 45 high schools in 15 states and found frustration among some teachers involved in shared decision making was significant. One teacher commented . . . "How can I, who's never dealt with school budgets, make intelligent decisions about the budget? . . . So simply giving teachers an opportunity to vote, that is not the answer."

Making quality decisions on issues such as school finance, auditing, personnel, school law, and collective bargaining requires the information and training usually possessed by a specialist. The provision of staff development to enhance the requisite knowledge of those being asked to make quality decisions is essential.

The challenge is to acknowledge the bias of all information and decide what is the most perfect version of the imperfect information that should inform consensus decision making. Specific clues for managing the science/data base of problem solving include the following:

- Balance the request for "objective information" with the reality that there is no such thing as objective information. The "truth" to guide decisions needs to be negotiated by the consensus players.
- Work with the group to access the experts, technical information, consultants, and presenters which are needed by the process.
- Build in meaningful methods for jointly selecting and reviewing technical documents and educating group members.

I want to recount an innovative method for handling the science that was included in chapter 3 as a great example of political turning points in consensus process (see pp. 119–120). In a clash over wetlands protection needs and flood control on agricultural fields, the process designers acknowledged that (a) the quantity of information that representatives had to master was too much to achieve. Participants could and should not be required to be scientists in order to be effective in a public decision-making process. They also understood that (b) all information is biased. They came up with a very effective mechanism for negotiating collective scientific "truths."

Each stakeholder representative was asked to appoint his or her own "science ambassador" to a technical advisory group. This technical advisory group was charged with interpreting the voice of nature or "best science" regarding issues appearing in the process of developing policy consensus. The "interfaith" team of scientists produced background papers that were accepted and used by the policy group to inform critical decisions. The strategy worked and the consensus outcome was well received (1).

I believe there are many tried and yet-to-be discovered ways to use science to support holistic consensus decisions. Use your imaginations and best know-how to create a science strategy that all ideological camps can live with.

Build in the Time for the Consensus Builders' Political Work

Effective consensus processes foster resolve and relationships, not just reports. As we have seen, the formal and informal politics build such resolves and relationships. Furthermore, the public conversation involves far more people and parties than the delegates at the table. All processes should structure time and vehicles for everyone to be active in the consensus politics.

Some specific clues for building positive political momentum include the following:

- Build unstructured or small group venues into official work sessions. Field trips or overnight retreats are excellent, work-related opportunities to make contacts, make alliances, or make sense of the issue at hand.
- Offer representatives (who need it) more assistance with constituency relations.
- Schedule public meetings several weeks apart in order to allow time for representatives to interact with their constituencies.
- Conduct well-advertised and open meetings, progress bulletins, newsletters, distribution of meeting minutes, and now, e-mail forums as a way to expand the formal conversation beyond the inner circle of collaborators.
- End each with a joint discussion reviewing the result of the collaboration dialogue and discussing best ways to communicate the work to those not at the table. Each meeting should begin with a debriefing on the reactions and feedback of outside stakeholders.

Prepare Procedures and Tools for Each Work Session and Step

An overall process design guides the planning of each segment, but the process facilitator develops procedures for each meeting by considering many other factors including the progress of previous meetings, intervening events, participant feedback, available time, and other situational factors. Developing a detailed road map for each work session is very similar to teachers' lesson plans. Careful planning and rehearsing is critical. A general guideline is that every hour of group work requires about four hours of preparation. The preparation steps include:

- Analyzing the state of the audience
- Assuring adequate space for interaction and needed stage props for tracking the discussion
- Preparing a time-lined "lesson plan" for robust dialogue and meaningful closure
- Preparing materials to assist individual and group thinking
- Identifying and rehearsing roles of process leaders, resource people, and participants
- Arranging and setting up the physical environment prior to each session

- Evaluating work sessions through formal mechanisms and information communication channels
- Scheduling and coleading extensive process planning meetings in between consensus work sessions
- Comparing results with objectives
- Adjusting the process to respond to emerging opportunities and unforeseen events
- Responding to changing circumstances by adjusting the timing, phasing, or structuring of group sessions
- Coaching process leaders, sponsors, and participants in implementation of consensus solutions

As illustrated in the following comment, all the consensus builders I interviewed struggled to understand the steps of the consensus process at some point, even after regular explanations (1):

> I felt in the early part of the meetings that we didn't know where we were going. We were basically throwing ideas up there on the board and those got filtered down through the hourglass into a smaller pile, and then those went through another screen. There was so much of that happening in the early part of the process . . . . There was no way to understand it unless you were there. Even when I was there, I didn't understand it half the time and asked, "Why are we doing this?" But, after a period of time, it all began to filter down, nail down, and come to a direction.

There were those who continued to push for clarity and others who entrusted the process staff, chair, and facilitator with guiding and refereeing. In this quote, a participant defends the case for letting the leaders lead (1):

> I was vexed at the start that there wasn't more of a template; that the goals weren't clearer . . . that the sheet of paper was so blank. Certainly there was a document to work from, but I think the process continually begged next things. What have we accomplished today? So, what are we going to work on tomorrow? Well, I think behind the scenes there must have been an outline, but that was not apparent to most of us day by day. But we seemed to make progress because there was a progression to the deliberations . . . . So there were these steps—the goals, priority directions, specific recommendations—but I think that we were basically always guided along meeting to meeting. That took the place of having a template.

Few participants thought the process was confusing by design. Maybe it was a technique for breaking people out of old ways of thinking. One member reflected on his yearlong experience and concluded that there may have been a positive role for confusion:

> The first three-fourths of the process, I was in the dark and said to myself, "The facilitator is doing it on purpose to encourage us." I felt that I never quite understood the

process and that made it more difficult to prepare for each session. In the end, the unclearness was actually an asset. It forced spontaneity.

I wish the facilitators could take credit for such intentionality. The truth is that each day's decision-making procedures were a product of meshing planned steps, audience reactions, professional wisdom, and common sense to identify a route that might help achieve the best results.

Maximize Process Relevance for Sponsors and Stakeholders

Another critical role for facilitators is maintaining the vitality and relevance of the consensus effort for the stakeholders. Facilitators need to remain open and eager to adjust the process, leveraging emerging momentum and internal issues that can help or hinder the successful completion or implementation of consensus solutions. The consultant is a temporary helper, but they must live with the results and relationships after the project is over.

As described in chapter 3, many of the successful deliberations included one or more midcourse corrections triggered by members of the process. Many unified recommendations may not have had majority support without the process modifications requested by participants. Process managers should prepare to consider and accommodate shifts in the original process roadmap if needed. Since the decision process impacts human judgment, participants need to have a significant role in determining how they will collect, analyze, and judge the situation before them. Start with a formal opportunity for participants to understand and refine the original meeting plan so it makes sense to them. Schedule midcourse correction points that allow the group to change their process if necessary. Again, I am not suggesting that the deliberations be constantly up for grabs. Participants need to develop criteria and protocols for making midcourse changes.

PRESIDING AT CONSENSUS SESSIONS

Once the decision path is developed for the full process and a particular work session, a facilitator assumes his or her most visible duty—guiding the dialogue at the table. Specific responsibilities include 1) managing productive meetings; 2) developing and enforcing ground rules; 3) mediating conflict resolution; 4) assuring collegial working relationships; and 5) remaining neutral and objective.

Facilitate Productive Meetings

The process facilitator referees the public discussion, simultaneously monitors the meeting's vital signs, and adjusts the procedures or pace in order to deliver on the session goals. The official leader, chair, host, or sponsor representative often opens and closes the meetings. At times, they may preside over sections of the meeting where participants vote or formalize consensus recommendations. Beyond those activities, the official leader's role as a facilitator is limited by the fact that the leader is often a "voting member" of the consensus process.

The backstage activity of process design continues even in the midst of leading meetings on front stage. Process changes must be made if the content loses its focus or clarity; timeframes exceed their planned limits; participation is minimal or unbalanced; brainstorms slow down to a drizzle; recording space is constrained; unexpected events intervene; obvious conflicts need attention; the room is too cold, dark, or otherwise uncomfortable; people show signs of physical discomfort; or any other factors negatively impact the collaborative work. Specific components of facilitating productive meetings include the following:

- Develop meeting agendas that clarify objectives, present clear procedures for achieving them, identify key focus questions that guide discussion and premeeting preparation, provide a productive but comfortable timeline, and identify specific roles for participants, presenters, staff, facilitator, and others.
- Present and get agreement on the agenda and road map for each meeting.
- Plan and set up meeting spaces that support effective hearing, seeing, thinking, interaction, and dialogue. Discussion is useless if people cannot track what is being said and recorded. Specific features of good meeting environments include:
  - A good view of the front of the room and other participants
  - Comfortable seating that enables long sitting
  - Good lighting for reading papers and group graphics
  - Windows and natural lighting as claustrophobic spaces constrain thinking
  - Decor, plants, color, and other tools that minimize sterility, offer a respectful human environment, and stimulate whole brain thinking
- Facilitate all meetings.
- Make sure the methodology provides useful process not just process for the sake of process. Carefully screen any gimmicks, games, and indirect techniques and choose those that enhance group thinking and communication.
- Provide formal avenues—written and oral—for "reality checking" that invites participants to help assess, evaluate, and adjust the proceedings of each meeting and the process as a whole.
- Prepare multiple approaches to reaching meeting objectives in order to adjust deliberations to the unique needs and nuances of a group's dynamics.
- Always stay attentive to the state of the participants. Know when it is essential to stick to the planned procedures, make minor refinements, or shift course in order to assure a meaningful consensus process.

- Optimize ways to capture information visually during the discussions and deliberations. The latest comments tend to sway perceptions and decisions unless the whole conversation stays visible to the group.

Develop and Enforce Ground Rules

Facilitators should never assume that the rules of engagement are "common sense." Like the rest of the process, they need to be tailored to each consensus setting. In the next chapter, I share my research on universal ground rules but there is no such thing. Some rules such as "don't dominate the conversation" or "listen to others" are obvious to collaborative practice, but the best practices, protocols, and operating guidelines for each group should reflect the common cultures, backgrounds, and traditions of the stakeholders as well as project needs.

In daylong engagements, ground rules focus mainly on discussion parameters. Processes that last many months or a year need a more extensive code of conduct for participation at and off the table. The ground rules clarify expectations about official roles for meeting leaders and members in communicating/relating to constituencies, media, external stakeholders, and the public. They spell out mechanisms for submitting input to the process as well as procedures for administering logistics and expenses (see table 5.0 for an example).

Mediate Conflict Resolution

The essence of problem solving is to work through complexity and conflict. Unlike traditional conflict resolution processes, the process facilitator is not the sole or even the primary agent for transforming conflict into constructive solutions. As I have stressed many times, the participants and overall method are the primary agents for delivering consensus results. Debilitating conflicts or food fights over symptoms and principles shift to a joint inquiry for answers if participants agree to serve in the dual role of interest advocate and consensus ambassadors.

There are varied and appropriate conflict management techniques. Some conflict resolution methods include the following:

- *Interest-based negotiation:* Identify desired outcomes and interests and establish mutually beneficial goals to strive for. Develop criteria for solutions that achieve the common goals, generate alternatives, and choose the best options according to the agreed-to criteria
- *Common ground method:* With a process in which individual issues, solutions, etc., are shared using a brainstorm list or idea cards, related elements are identified to form a common direction everyone can support. Do this on at least two levels:
  - Agreement on the issue
  - Agreement on the needed solutions

Table 5.0.   Sample Ground Rules for a Policy Consensus-Building Forum

Member Input

Roundtable members may submit background information to the Roundtable process. Materials may be brought to the meetings and provided to members at a designated table. All material made available at a particular meeting will be listed in a bibliography attached to the meeting summary. Members can submit material to the chair for inclusion in meeting packets and/or staff background papers. Members may be asked to obtain copies for all members. The chair has the discretion to use or summarize the materials submitted.

Public Input Opportunities

Individuals wishing to address the Roundtable can do so at each Roundtable meeting. The chair has the discretion to determine when during the course of a Roundtable meeting this public input opportunity will be provided, as well as the amount of time allocated to such input.

Distribution of Materials

The agency will be responsible for distributing all materials to the Roundtable and alternates, and distribution will occur as soon as practically possible. The Roundtable will not be asked to reach consensus on any items from which relevant materials were not received at least 48 hours in advance of such decision.

Media Relations

Members may express personal opinions to the media on matters or activities related to the Roundtable's discussions or agreements. However, the Roundtable agrees the chair will be the designated spokesperson for the Roundtable on matters related to its official position.

Post-Report Activities

At the pleasure of the commissioner, the Roundtable may continue to meet after submitting its report. The Roundtable conveys its interest to the agency and environmental oversight group in playing an active role after its report is submitted.

Agreement

The Roundtable agrees to reach decisions through broad agreement. The goal is to make recommendations all members can live with. Where possible, agreement will be made by consensus. At the discretion of the chair and facilitator, roll call voting can be used to arrive at agreement. When roll calling is used to reach agreement, a Roundtable decision will be identified if no more than one-fourth of the members dissent. Members and alternate absence will be equivalent to not dissenting. In articulating any decisions reached, the Roundtable will hold the value of a group report that is concise, helpful, and represents the areas of agreement and common ground. Roundtable decisions will also identify minority opinions authored by holders of those opinions. Any minority opinion counts as a minority opinion. Any written record of minority opinions will identify the author(s) of those opinions.

The chair and facilitator will determine when to table agenda items and/or revise the meeting process; when to keep working on a decision; when to declare a stalemate and record the result; and when to vote and record the status of the major and minority agreement. Meeting summaries and the final report will describe the process used to arrive at decisions of the Roundtable.

The Roundtable will strive to create agreement in an iterative process. Agreements will be made each step of the way, but prior agreements will be tentative pending a final package agreement.

Ground Rule Support

Roundtable members agree to abide in good faith by the ground rules identified in this document. These ground rules may be revisited by the Roundtable as deemed necessary.

Mission Statement

The mission of the Roundtable will be to advise the commissioner of the Natural Resources Department how to implement the strategic recommendations identified in the timber harvesting generic environmental impact statement. It is expected that the implementation direction identified by the Roundtable will affect a variety of public and private land managers and other stakeholders.

Product

The major product of the Roundtable will be to develop a written report that identifies a comprehensive strategy for implementing the impact statement strategic recommendations. This report will be prepared and submitted to the commissioner no later than _____, unless otherwise specified by the commissioner. Once prepared, the report will be broadly distributed to individuals and organizations with responsibility for or interest in implementing the impact statement recommendations as suggested in the report.

Membership

All members of the Roundtable are appointed by the commissioner environmental oversight group. Members are expected to attend all Roundtable meetings and to keep their alternates current on Roundtable matters. The following individuals have been appointed to serve on the _____: (list members)

Resignation of Members

Members may resign from the Roundtable at any time. The commissioner and environmental oversight group chair may appoint a replacement for the resigning Roundtable member.

Selection and Use of Alternates

Each member of the Roundtable may designate an alternate to serve in his or her absence. An alternate may participate in Roundtable discussions and agreements

(continued)

Table 5.0. *(continued)*

when the appointed member is not present. Roundtable members are expected to indicate who their alternate will be by the third Roundtable meeting and prior to their actual participation in Roundtable deliberations. The Roundtable chair has the authority to limit the participation of specific alternates if it becomes apparent that their participation is not consistent with the intended use of alternates.

Chair

The commissioner and environmental oversight group chair have appointed _____ as the chair of the Roundtable. The role of the chair will be to work with staff and the facilitator to develop meeting agendas and help focus the Roundtable's discussion and direction.

Vice-Chair

The commissioner and environmental oversight group chair have appointed _____ as the vice-chair of the Roundtable. The role of the vice-chair will be to serve as chair of the Roundtable when the chair is not in attendance.

Facilitator

_____ has been assigned to facilitate the Roundtable. The agency is responsible for retaining the facilitator's services. The role of the facilitator will be to ensure that all points of view are expressed by Roundtable members and considered on particular issues and to help the Roundtable to reach consensus in all its deliberations.

Meetings

All meetings of the Roundtable are open to the public. The chair, facilitator, and staff will be responsible for arranging Roundtable meetings and establishing meeting agendas. Staff will be responsible for preparing brief summaries of all Roundtable meetings, which will be approved as the official public record of the meeting at the beginning of the subsequent Roundtable meeting. The agency will circulate notices of upcoming meetings as well as summaries of such meetings to those individuals wishing to receive such information.

Staff

_____ is responsible for administering the Roundtable. _____ will assist in providing relevant background information to the Roundtable for their consideration.

- *Monitored dialogue:* In the refinement and editing phases, it may be best to walk through proposed recommendations slowly and invite participants to flag needed changes, clarifications, and lingering controversies. The facilitator calls on people who raise their hand, records their feedback, and facilitates a problem-solving discussion wherever necessary.
- *"Unpacking issues:"* Conduct an in-depth, "remedial" listening to each others' positions by understanding the deep experiences and motivations behind strong and opposing positions at various levels:

○ Facts Level Perceptions: Reveal differences in basic information
○ Reactions Level Perceptions: Share differences in feelings and gut reactions
○ Analysis Level Perceptions: Air differences in making sense about an issue
○ Convictions Level Perceptions: Disclose differences in stances on the issue

Cultivate Collegial Working Relations

Fostering healthy group relationships is an important component of leading productive meetings. When participants are able to take their task seriously without taking themselves so seriously, minds and hearts are likely to open up for greater insight and innovation. The "chair" or "convener" can do a lot to encourage or discourage collegiality through role modeling and leadership. As a process facilitator, I appreciate working with the official leader to foster a collegial working environment. The official leader can bring people back from breaks and coach the group through intense and exhausting phases with inspirational reminders about the urgencies of the task or humorous interludes that acknowledge everyone's humanness and effort.

At their annual retreat, one Minnesota school district intentionally builds relationships (5). The process begins with the journey to the site. Everyone, from school board members to support staff, ride together in a yellow school bus provided courtesy of the district. Here is a participant's view of the effects of the two-hour bus trip:

> The group is a mix of previous attendees and some new to the retreat, so there is some "Gainey Grouping" togetherness right from the start. Also, since there is a mix of staff represented, there are bound to be some in attendance who do not like or get along well with others. The bus ride, says the superintendent, tends to break down some of the animosity since they all begin the retreat by facing the same experience together.

Each process facilitator can catalyze working relationships by using his or her unique personality, talent, tools, and accumulated knowledge to fulfill the following responsibilities:

• Orchestrating interactive and fair dialogue
• Making sure everyone can hear, see, and track the proceedings
• Using group methods that involve everyone and support diverse learning styles
• Preparing models, stories, and examples that enhance group thinking
• Enabling and supporting participants' communication and relationships with their constituencies
• Recognizing and incorporating personal or constituent group events, incidents, and opportunities that relate to or affect the group process . . . Allowing participants to bring up process-related news or views during opening introductions always adds interesting clues, inspiration, or urgency to the ongoing consensus inquiry.

- Linking the process to parallel efforts or activities going on in participants' organizations or constituencies

If the facilitator and official leader set a supportive, human tone for the process, participants will take the initiative to add honesty, humor, eventfulness, and personal touches to enhance the quality of the teamwork.

Remain Neutral and Objective

Being a trustworthy and fair convener of the public forum is a cornerstone role of process facilitators. Losing neutrality and objectivity can cause severe career setbacks. Participants of a consensus process constantly evaluate the impartiality of a facilitator. It is both a front and backstage duty.

The field of facilitation does not have licenses or universal certification (yet) so the rules of "neutrality and objectivity" are interpreted individually. However, the "Statement of Values and Code of Ethics for Group Facilitators" (6) was recently drafted and approved by the International Association of Facilitators. It includes a strong downbeat on commitment to unbiased service, attention to conflicts of interest, and maintaining confidentiality of information and other rules for "setting aside personal opinions in order to support the group's right to make its own choices" (see table 5.1). The code is based on the input of hundreds of professional facilitators worldwide.

Serving in a neutral and objective way includes the following practices:

- Tracking the evolving consensus and/or the total picture
- Summarizing the emerging group consensus visually and verbally as needed
- Reminding people about previously formed areas of consensus to prevent the unraveling of existing agreements or the rehashing of old ground
- Arriving well prepared, well rested, and ready to be an attentive, neutral objective, positive, and energetic meeting coordinator
- Developing rapport with all members while maintaining enough distance in informal relationships to ensure professional neutrality

PUBLIC DOCUMENTING OF CONSENSUS RESULTS

The third major role of a process facilitator is to create an official record of the group discussion and decisions. A consensus-building session is not complete until the substance and spirit of the agreement has been articulated to everyone's satisfaction. Consensus documentation minimizes possible misconceptions about shared understandings and agreements and time spent repeating prior conversations. The process

Table 5.1. Statement of Values and Code of Ethics for Group Facilitators

Preamble

Facilitators are called upon to fill an impartial role in helping groups become more effective. We act as process guides to create a balance between participation and results. We believe that our profession gives us a unique opportunity to make a positive contribution to individuals, organizations, and society. Our effectiveness is based on our personal integrity and the trust developed between ourselves and those with whom we work. Therefore, we recognize the importance of defining and making known the values and ethical principles that guide our actions.

This Statement of Values and Code of Ethics recognizes the complexity of our roles, including the full spectrum of personal, professional, and cultural diversity in our membership and in the field of facilitation. Members of the International Association of Facilitators are committed to using these values and ethics to guide their professional practice. These principles are expressed in broad statements to guide ethical practice; they provide a framework and are not intended to dictate conduct for particular situations. Questions or advice about the application of these values and ethics may be addressed to the International Association of Facilitators.

Statement of Values

As group facilitators, we believe in the inherent value of the individual and the collective wisdom of the group. We strive to help the group make the best use of the contributions of each of its members. We set aside our personal opinions and support the group's right to make its own choices. We believe that collaborative and cooperative interaction builds consensus and produces meaningful outcomes. We value professional collaboration to improve our profession.

Code of Ethics

1. Client Service

    We are in service to our clients, using our group facilitation competencies to add value to their work.

    Our clients include the groups we facilitate and those who contract with us on their behalf. We work closely with our clients to understand their expectations so that we provide the appropriate service, and that the group produces the desired outcomes. It is our responsibility to ensure that we are competent to handle the intervention.

    If the group decides it needs to go in a direction other than that originally intended by either the group or its representatives, our role is to help the group move forward, reconciling the original intent with the emergent direction.

2. Conflict of Interest

    We openly acknowledge any potential conflict of interest.

    Prior to agreeing to work with our clients, we discuss openly and honestly any possible conflict of interest, personal bias, prior knowledge of the organization

(continued)

Table 5.1. *(continued)*

or any other matter which may be perceived as preventing us from working effectively with the interests of all group members. We do this so that, together, we may make an informed decision about proceeding and to prevent misunderstanding that could detract from the success or credibility of the clients or ourselves. We refrain from using our position to secure unfair or inappropriate privilege, gain, or benefit.

3. Group Autonomy
   We respect the culture, rights, and autonomy of the group.
   We seek the group's conscious agreement to the process and their commitment to participate. We do not impose anything that risks the welfare and dignity of the participants, the freedom of choice of the group, or the credibility of its work.

4. Processes, Methods, and Tools
   We use processes, methods, and tools responsibly.
   In dialogue with the group or its representatives, we design processes that will achieve the group's goals and select and adapt the most appropriate methods and tools. We avoid using processes, methods, or tools with which we are insufficiently skilled or which are poorly matched to the needs of the group.

5. Respect, Safety, Equity, and Trust
   We strive to engender an environment of respect and safety where all participants trust that they can speak freely and where individual boundaries are honored. We use our skills, knowledge, tools, and wisdom to elicit and honor the perspectives of all.
   We seek to have all relevant stakeholders represented and involved. We promote equitable relationships among the participants and facilitator and ensure that all participants have an opportunity to examine and share their thoughts and feelings. We use a variety of methods to enable the group to access the natural gifts, talents, and life experiences of each member. We work in ways that honor the wholeness and self-expression of others, designing sessions that respect different styles of interaction. We understand that any action we take is an intervention that may affect the process.

6. Stewardship of Process
   We practice stewardship of process and impartiality toward content.
   While participants bring knowledge and expertise concerning the substance of their situation, we bring knowledge and expertise concerning the group interaction process. We are vigilant to minimize our influence on group outcomes. When we have content knowledge not otherwise available to the group and that the group must have to be effective, we offer it after explaining our change in role.

7. Confidentiality
   We maintain confidentiality of information.
   We observe confidentiality of all client information. Therefore, we do not share information about a client within or outside of the client's organization;

nor do we report on group content or the individual opinions or behavior of members of the group without consent.
8. Professional Development
We are responsible for continuous improvement of our facilitation skills and knowledge.

We continuously learn and grow. We seek opportunities to improve our knowledge and facilitation skills to better assist groups in their work. We remain current in the field of facilitation through our practical group experiences and ongoing personal development. We offer our skills within a spirit of collaboration to develop our professional work practices.

facilitator takes primary responsibility for recording the discussions and decisions without skewing the results in favor of one or more players

The written record is the primary mechanism for keeping track of the consensus status and actively involving the direct and indirect participants in the problem-solving process. There is nothing more frustrating than repeating old conversations because meeting proceedings were not recorded and reviewed. Official materials need to be clear enough to be understood by those who were not involved in the discussions at the table.

Recording and communicating consensus progress occurs mostly behind the scenes. Writing on the flip chart is often perceived as a primary facilitator function but it is merely one important detail in documenting group work. Facilitators must do more than record. Brainstorming lists and other raw data from a session must be quickly and accurately translated into sentences and paragraphs. The official leader and support staff assist by taking detailed notes at the session and helping protect the integrity of the technical/scientific information in the report. The key responsibilities in fulfilling the documentation duty include the following:

- Recording proceedings as thoroughly as possible with the help of sponsors and support staff
- Translating the raw meeting records into a clear account of discussions and results of group work
- Developing, drafting, and producing a thorough yet reader-friendly final report of consensus session
- Presenting and reviewing the outcomes of previous work sessions before beginning a new discussion
- Getting buy-in on consensus minutes and/or decision reports
- Coaching sponsors and participants to communicate process results to all affected publics

CONCLUSION

The facilitator's role in collaborative decision making is to initiate or speed up the self-organizing capacity of civil society. When each consensus process participant sees him- or herself as a leader, the most complex problems and troubling trends can be addressed in organizations, communities, and our planet.

NOTES

1. Hanson, M. (2001). *Constructing sustainability policy through collaboration: A multi-site case study of decision making processes that seek sustainable solutions for statewide forests or local watershed development.* St. Paul, MN: University of St. Thomas.

2. Valley Crossing Community School. (2002). [Site council materials]. Woodbury, MN.

3. Sorenson, L. D. (1995, February 10–13). *Site-based management: Avoiding disaster while sharing decision making.* Paper presented at the annual meeting of the American Association of School Administrators, New Orleans, LA.

4. Weiss, C. H., Cambone, J., & Wyeth, A. (1992). Trouble in paradise: Teacher conflicts in shared decision making. *Educational Administration Quarterly, 28* (3), 350–367.

5. Bjorum, W. (1991). *Listening for voices: A leader in action.* St. Paul, MN: University of St. Thomas.

6. The International Association of Facilitators. (2002). *Statement of values and code of ethics for group facilitators.* St. Paul, MN: International Association of Facilitators.

Chapter Six

Clues for Participants

Democracy is measured not by its leaders doing extraordinary things but its citizens doing ordinary things extraordinarily well.

—John Gardner, Common Cause

The overall role of consensus participants is to work with others to develop mutually beneficial solutions to a situation or dilemma that affects everyone. Political work that participants do between and at meetings is a key to achieving adequate or innovative solutions. The *way* in which a consensus builder engages in the task matters greatly, just as it does for any other elected, appointed, hired, or voluntary position. They do the heavy lifting that converts impossible problems into positive directions. If sponsors and facilitators do *their* jobs properly, a representative group of stakeholders can do their jobs effectively.

The responsibilities of consensus participants are usually described formally but briefly in the invitation letter or meeting ground rules. In most cases, however, not many details are given about the duties of the representative. Much is assumed under general process mandates that call for consensus participants to represent their constituency's perspectives in the discussion and work actively to find mutually agreeable solutions (1). There are exceptions, of course. I am aware, for example, that when federal mediators came to mediate a dispute about use of motorized transportation in federal wilderness areas, they devoted two days to orienting participants about their role in the mediation process.

What does it really mean to serve as a consensus builder? Many participants of consensus processes discovered that they had signed up for much more than they had imagined when they agreed to be a representative for an interest group, organization, or constituency. Early on, they realized the lonely nature of the role. After the hustle and bustle of nomination, selection, and appointment, 15 to 40 people of all "faiths" are left sitting at the table, introducing themselves as representatives of XYZ stakeholder groups and pondering how to execute their brief and demanding job.

In theory the task seemed clear. In practice it was vague and uncharted. It is hard enough to represent one's own views. When participants are charged to influence decisions on behalf of tens, hundreds, or even millions of people, the challenge of advocacy increases manifold. Can you imagine representing an ambiguous stakeholder group such as the "citizens of the state," "urban dwellers," "the real estate industry," "district teachers," or "nonindustrial private landowners"?

Individuals were nominated as official representatives for certain interest groups because their worldview aligned with the group's positions and convictions. However, each advocate is a person with a unique character, history, and lifetime of experiences related to the issue at hand. They struggled with an appropriate way to balance group beliefs with personal beliefs. As participants engaged in the fast-paced problem-solving conversations, several interview participants indicated that lines began to blur between personal ideas and group positions. In the following soliloquy, one representative reflected on the solitary nature of his consensus duty and the dilemma of determining what a representative should *represent* (1):

> *On the complexity of the quest:* I think it's always a problem, the question, whom am I representing? Am I representing myself? Am I representing my organization? What exactly am I representing? And the answer is not simple.
>
> *On speaking for all citizens:* I feel, however, that when you get on this group, you are on here as a citizen. You have special sets of connections, you have special knowledge and background, but what you say in the consensus discussion is your best judgment on the situation. We already know what the pork butchers or clean water activists think as an organization. What we would really like to know is what a thoughtful, committed person thinks as a citizen even though they lobby for some group.
>
> *On thinking beyond your interest in the issue:* It's not an easy thing to do. . . . People have to play to their own commitments and to their jobs in certain cases. . . . However, in future processes, I would strive to get people who are willing to think like citizens rather than parrot for their particular interests.

As is evident, this representative made a choice about what representation meant: speaking on behalf of his interest group was only one dimension of his duty. Other members made opposite choices. They felt their sole duty was to be a mouthpiece for official stakeholder group beliefs. Most representatives fell somewhere in between.

Through the experiences and observations of insiders, this chapter examines the actual roles and adventures of individual participants in a consensus process. I describe in the following pages participants' activities and tips for fulfilling their main duties: 1) serving effectively as aggressive *advocates* for their interests and 2) becoming effective *ambassadors* for negotiating consensus solutions (see figure 6.0).

A. Serve as **ADVOCATES** of diverse views	B. Serve as **AMBASSADORS** of consensus solutions
1. *Represent* unique "stakes" at the table 2. *Actively* voice opinions 3. *Conduct* constituency feedback	1. *Absorb* background information 2. *Develop* participant relationships 3. *Participate* in consensus deliberations 4. *Promote* collaborative solutions 5. *Respect* collective and individual efforts
See pages 193–197	See pages 197–208

Figure 6.0.   Roles of Participants

SERVING AS ADVOCATES FOR DIVERSE VIEWS

Advocating for unique interests or beliefs includes three primary activities: 1) preparing to communicate views at meetings, 2) actively voicing views at the consensus table, and 3) conducting constituency feedback.

Prepare to Represent Unique "Stakes" or Views at Consensus Sessions

Identifying the interest or "platform" to be represented varied greatly among the consensus participants and is usually more ambiguous than clear-cut. Narrower or well-defined positions lend themselves to advocacy more readily than representing interests of a broader group such as the "neighborhood," the "parents," or the "faith community." Those with well-defined agendas enter the consensus process with a clear advocacy task identified. Spokespersons for more amorphous but important interests have to work harder to identify the critical views that they hope to contribute to the dialogue. The consensus advocate seeks to find a voice that blends the stakeholder group's belief with his or her individual convictions.

The collaborative approach implies that a participant advocates aggressively for their views. Unlike the accommodating or avoiding approaches, participants are encouraged to be optimally assertive and cooperative in the consensus deliberation. If everyone brings their honest convictions to the table, the consensus building is more likely to avoid diluted analysis and superficial compromise. The two primary activities for representing a unique stake at the table include: 1) preparing formal stakeholder positions and 2) talking with like-minded consensus participants to better communicate perspectives at the table.

Preparing Formal Positions

Some went to great lengths to find extra background information to help them better understand the issues being considered at the table. Others took the time to prepare comments, issues, or questions to raise at the upcoming meetings. Usually this was a solitary activity but those who represented organized stakeholder groups had more support. They discussed past decisions and upcoming agenda items with their peers and those who were paid representatives of interest groups had staff identify materials and platforms that enabled them to present opinions succinctly and persuasively.

Talk with Like-minded Consensus Participants to Better Communicate Views

Many of the consensus participants I interviewed lobbied actively to influence the consensus work in much the same way that an advocacy occurs in a legislative process, labor contract negotiation, company business planning, capital allocation, and other organizational decision processes. They reported pulling together like-minded interest groups to strengthen their voice.

The collaborative process often intensified solidarity within ideological camps. The intervals between official consensus meetings allowed like-minded organizational representatives to dialogue together offstage. Carpools and breaks were the most common venues for caucus meetings. Many traveled alone, but if they shared rides, they tended to be with colleagues in their ideological camp. Carpooling between like-minded representatives strengthened the development of special interest positions as illustrated by this account (1):

> *On small group huddling between and on the way to meetings:* It seemed to me that a
> lot of stuff was happening in between the meetings that I didn't know about. There

seemed to be things happening in the car rides to the meetings. Because you'd see people get out of a car after having been riding for two or three hours, they are all smiles and then suddenly they're all talking the same way in the meeting. Obviously something happened on the way to the meeting.

Breaks were another popular time for forging small-group consensus. Sometimes the small groups involved opposing parties, but more often they were huddles between representatives within one ideological camp. Most interview participants reported participating or observing the special interest gatherings. They felt it was an important part of the process that should be formalized more in future group processes (1):

> *On the importance of "dyad" and "triad" discussion off-line:* Providing time for private discussions helps groups move along. Breaks are critical. If we didn't have them we wouldn't get anywhere. We have public discussions, but at any point in time, you'll see the frustration arise over the issues. That's a sign that there's been enough general discussion. The chair has to pick up on that and strategically call a break so people can go off and do their private dyads or triads and get through the tough pieces that they don't want to get through publicly. . . . When they come back together they almost inevitably go to a vote and things move along.

In addition to huddling in and around consensus-building meetings, representatives also organized ad hoc meetings or conference calls between like-minded organizations when they perceived that a united front would strengthen a particular position in the collaboration debates. These occurred in response to major conflicts or turning points in the process.

Participants generally felt that group networking was inevitable but somewhat stifling to consensus building. When the positions of these "caucuses" were proposed at the main table, they had a negative effect on the collaborative work. According to these and other interview participants, well-developed special interest positions eroded trust by making participants feel that one group was "co-opting" the process to their advantage or steering the collaborative discussion into unproductive impasses over details. After voicing these concerns, former consensus builders knew it would be naïve to think that the special interest alliances formed between meetings could or should be controlled. It is a natural part of any political discourse.

Actively Voice Opinions

Once a representative formulates his or her major "stakes" and views, they have the responsibility of playing their constituencies' stakes in the consensus deliberation. Specific activities include 1) adding stakeholder input to the dialogue *content* and 2) keeping an eye on the *process* fairness and effectiveness.

Add Stakeholder Input to the Dialogue Content

Participating in the substance of the consensus conversation is perhaps the best understood participant role. Since the dynamics of being active at the table applies to both advocacy and ambassadorial influencing, this duty is covered in the "Participate Fully in Consensus Deliberations" section later in this chapter (pp. 202–203).

Keep an Eye on the Process Fairness and Effectiveness

Participants can be strong advocates by influencing the consensus *process*. People were encouraged to express themselves on front stage, but participants always offered feedback in their own way, with or without ground rules. It seems to be an inevitable and important part of consensus building. I have several files crammed with the letters, memos, phone message slips, and e-mail from participants during various consensus projects.

The chair, staff, and facilitators must do their best to make sure the informal lobby influences the process fairly. In many of my meetings, the chair opened the session by acknowledging the informal feedback and letting the full group in on the key concerns raised in the private conversation. Unlike litigation or arbitration that have a fixed process, consensus building is customized and the process can change in the midst of the deliberation. Often the facilitator adjusts the procedures to keep on time. Sometimes the process must shift because the participants demand it. They questioned the procedures when they were unclear or seemed unfair. The leaders had to be prepared to redirect if necessary.

The clue to participants is to keep the opinions and proposals about the consensus content and process coming. Since process affects the content results, participants need to stay vigilant and vocal in assuring that the process assures a level playing field with a strong voice for every stakeholder. In chapter 3, the stories about process turning points illustrate the many ways in which participants helped increase process inclusiveness by insisting on additional information or avoiding superficial deliberation by lobbying to change the method of inquiry.

Conduct Constituency Feedback

The political duty of "carrying water" between interest groups and the consensus process involves formal and informal activities. A consensus participant needs to keep the lines of communication open between the affected groups by reporting back emerging consensus results; soliciting reactions, views, or positions of a stakeholder group; and preparing written updates in stakeholder mailings or meetings.

Consensus representatives reported communicating back to their stakeholder groups with varying degrees of frequency and intensity. For many, the feedback with their boards and constituencies was a major front stage duty as well as a significant backstage activity. Others interacted with their constituents on an ad hoc basis and still others did not even do that. They felt they could represent their constituencies intuitively and informally.

All consensus participants agreed on one thing: Communicating results was a challenge. It was impossible to appreciate and understand the inner workings of collaboration unless "you were there." Neither the minutes nor the draft working papers captured the verbal and emotional intensity of the meetings as described by these two testimonials about conveying messages back and forth (1):

> *On communicating what really happened:* Even the visible aspects of the work were difficult to communicate to constituencies verbally. We should have had public hearings and videotaped the sessions in order to describe what really happened.

> *On knowing how to catch constituent attention:* I tried to explain at the board meetings that took place at a six-hour meeting. There was no way to understand it unless you were there. . . . I know my board probably didn't bother to read everything. I brought to the meeting what I thought was important. . . . I told them that the language was a little wishy-washy and then showed them where our positions were included and not included. I wanted to point out that we at least got part of what we wanted. Generally, they felt fairly satisfied about the consensus and the something they got out of it.

As these accounts suggest, the reporting went hand in hand with soliciting input for the next consensus session. According to one player, "I had regular communication with my constituency—perhaps twice in between meetings to convey the results—got input for future meetings, and predicted the direction the process was going to head." Solution brokers went beyond these two connecting roles. They adopted the two-way messenger strategy. They lobbied for their stakeholder group positions in the consensus sessions and returned to sell the emerging collaborative agreements to the stakeholder group. The stressful nature of this approach comes through in this next section that features participants' stories about performing their ambassadorial duties.

SERVING AS AMBASSADORS OF CONSENSUS SOLUTIONS

In consensus building participants are expected to do more than contribute their unique points of view. By agreeing to be "collaborators" they acquire the added role of serving as the third party peacemaker. As discussed in the first chapter, this is the fundamental difference between adversarial and consensual problem solving.

Producing "win-win" solutions calls for everyone to act as an ambassador for common ground directions. According to experienced consensus process participants, the ambassadorial role consists of five key duties: 1) Absorbing background information; 2) developing participant relationships; 3) participating in consensus deliberations; 4) promoting collaborative solutions proactively; and 5) respecting each other and the collective effort.

Absorb Background Information

Information is a power source. Well-informed participants are more likely to excel at selling their interests as well as detecting entry points to common ground solutions. Schooling up on one's own side of the issue was covered in the previous section. As ambassadors, consensus participants are also expected to have a working knowledge of the wide world of views related to the consensus-building task and topic.

A good process includes time to brief everyone on the essential background information, but the clue is that participants study up on their own as well. The minimal ambassadorial requirement is to keep up on the issue briefings and meetings and record the state of the "common will" at every stage of the process. The sky is the limit when it comes to voluntary self-education about the parts, sum of the parts, and the whole web of complexity related to the consensus quest. Specific activities include tracking meeting plans, handouts, minutes, draft conclusions, and decisions; mastering the data, information, science, and propaganda of other interests; and staying open to diverse and ongoing input.

Participants of various consensus processes reported that absorbing and internalizing the abundance of information about the subject matter took enormous time and concentration. Premeeting packets were thick with reading materials. Handouts piled up. Each presentation and discussion produced volumes of lists or drafts. In addition to the official process materials, other representatives distributed new information (or propaganda) at the back tables on a regular basis. If that was not enough, representatives were required to "keep an open mind" as they listened to all the stakeholders' perceptions about the issue at hand. Every conversation added a new layer of content to the discourse. Each meeting report was anywhere from 5 to 20 pages long. The sheer quantity of deliberation-related data was overwhelming. Here are some examples:

- A school district task force charged to recommend millions of dollars of budget cuts had to master the complicated machinery of a public education enterprise. To illustrate the complexity, one urban high school principal said a minor part of his job was to manage relationships with 25 unions connected to keeping the building supported and staffed.
- The members of a timber harvesting consensus group had to familiarize themselves with a 5-year scientific study that produced 14 technical documents total-

ing 4,000 pages and an extensive arsenal of recommendations for statewide site- and landscape-level forestry practices.

• An interorganizational partnership for providing housing, services, and health care to a hard-to-serve population of homeless people, required participants to be conversant in the working vocabulary and understanding of three systems—affordable housing, human services, and health maintenance organizations. It was too much to do alone. Two days worth of "time-out" was called to have staff teach a "Housing 101, Supportive Services 101, and HMO 101" to overview *the* rudimentary history, policies, practices, and financing mechanisms of each universe.

We ask a lot from consensus builders. The problem solving is difficult even for veterans with extensive experience in the subject matter.

The information overload distorts a level playing field. Consensus representatives that were paid staff or represented organizations with deep pockets had technical staff and in-house knowledge to assist them. Those members who had less experience with the subject or were volunteer representatives of less structured constituencies such as "the parents," "local landowners," or "homeless HIV/AIDS patients" battled an enormous learning curve while trying to simultaneously participate in the fast-moving dialogue. Here is one participant in a forest management problem-solving process describing the tendency for setting up a power hierarchy based on access to information:

> *On the unfair gaps in keeping on top of information:* For volunteer citizens to participate in forums where industry pays representatives to participate is not a fair situation. . . These kinds of activities should be set up so that the volunteers are paid for their time. . . and are provided with some technical or professional resources. I can think of technical papers that we could write if we had some technical staff support. . . . I can frame the questions but don't have the good technical support. A person representing the industry or other organized interest can go out and get staff to write a so-called analysis. Even though it's mostly garbage, it comes across as authoritative and effective at the table—it's got graphs, it's got the whole works. We don't have the ability to do that.

Participants did as best as they could individually to stay on top of the issue. Those with the knowledge base had more power to present and persuade. Those without it burned the midnight oil to keep up with the conversation.

On a positive note, participants reported that some teamwork emerged in navigating the complex details of consensus development: In situations where the issue at hand required very technical or scientific knowledge, those at the less-resourced end of the information hierarchy took on the role of a jury. They listened carefully to the dialogue and formed their opinions based on the players that were most informative or compelling. They relied heavily on other members or staff to construct draft agreements for the full group to refine in subsequent discussions. In this excerpt, a member acknowledges how those with less background knowledge relied on the "wordsmithers" to help their analysis and move the agenda along (1):

> We had what I call the "wordsmithers." They can sit down, draft stuff, and think about it. I'm not very good at it. However, after I see what they have drafted, I can see and understand where we've gone and where we are going. I'll raise hell about it if I don't like it, but I'm not very good at sitting down and picking it apart. We had some very good "semi-moderates" who could work out details. Then the government people came in. They were good at wordsmithing and writing up agreements also. But we didn't just let them determine the decision. If we didn't like the direction we were going, one side or the other would shove them and say, "Wait a minute. We don't like this!"

Thus, necessary codependencies formed to support the give and take process in the consensus building discourse.

Develop Participant Relationships

All the veteran participants agreed on the importance of good working relationships. Getting to know the personal background, experiences, and motivations of other participants was the single most important mechanism for understanding the issues more fully. Encountering other participants "up-front and personal" and cultivating connections proactively shifted attention away from opposing others to exploring ideas jointly.

The consensus participant interviews revealed that everyone engaged in the development of relationships to some degree. Those who chose a less intense representation approach limited the relationship building to informal opportunities during the meeting. However, surprisingly many went out of their way to reach out between meetings. Participants 1) used informal time during meetings and some even 2) cultivated relationships with other stakeholders between meetings.

Use Informal time During Meetings to Discuss Agenda

Most participants talked about the "off-line" interactions with other representatives as one of the more rewarding aspects of the process. This occurred during meal times, breaks, field trips, carpools, and evenings between two-day meetings. Some explained that this was the one time they could hear each other's unabridged worldviews. The interchange often involved nonwork topics, and many reported finding personal connections and making friends with people from all interest groups. Establishing personal relationships enabled participants to stay open to opposing views at the table. One participant felt that "putting a face to an organization makes it hard to criticize, especially when it is a very nice person." The value of the informal exchange is reflected in these specific comments about the value of offstage mingling (1):

On how lowering one's guard leads to gaining real understanding: Once, twice, or thrice, there were moments when participants would see something they had never realized before; moments when they said, "Boy! I never saw something like that." . . . . The large majority of the times that took place, not during a formal session, but during a breakout, during the evening, or during lunch hour or dinner; when folks could talk more one-on-one and let their guard down and not be viewed by other members of a similar group as a traitor. I saw some of that going on, and I thought, "Hey, I don't care if this goes on officially, unofficially, in class, or outside of class (so to speak), as long as it's happening!"

On meal gatherings, trust, and learning: Whenever you break bread with people, you increase trust. Eating and drinking together is a critical part of the process. We could have been more successful if there were even more time for informal discussions. Most learning takes place in nonformal settings.

On the benefits of informal ties for increasing teamwork: The informal tie was most important. Being isolated together for two days and staying over a night was a key aspect in being able to work with people of differing views.

On the value of speaking "off the record": The opportunity to exchange information outside the formal meetings was the main thing that promoted the group members' ability to work with those holding different views. The coffee breaks enabled productive mingling, and overnight trips provided useful interaction between stakeholders—people who were not "speaking on the record."

On the link between social activities and consensus progress: Most of the understanding took place in social settings away from the process itself—the van rides on the field trips and postmeeting socials. The effort to mix van participants helped deepen working relationships.

Many participants suggested that future processes increase opportunities to allow participants to get to know each other as people. As one said, "I don't care how much you know, until I know how much you care." Field trips received high marks as venues for getting acquainted with each other and getting up to speed on more personal perspectives on issues surrounding the consensus dialogue. They were described as less awkward than purely social events, such as receptions and other official celebrations. The field trips were task-oriented. They offered many work-related but informal opportunities for collaborators to exchange ideas in person and, according to one participant, "time to complete sentences and conversations."

The power of building human relationships is one of the better-advertised and minimally applied ingredients in group work. Senator George Mitchell of the United States Congress understands and acknowledges this power. According to a source close to the peace talks in Ireland, informal dialogue was an official part of his formula for engendering respect at the tense negotiations. He asked that members focus their lunch conversations on their own lives, families, and other personal topics and refrain from discussing the peace-building issues directly. Many observers and participants credit the lunch interludes for increasing trust and openness during the official peace talks.

Cultivate Connections with Other Members

In addition to the free-form conversations in and around the meetings, a handful of members in each process went out of their way to see other members between meetings. They were convinced that relationships are key to searching for solutions that have buy-in. Several participants told stories about making an appointment to visit another consensus process member with a very different view of the issues including this scenario (1):

> *On deepening understanding during self-initiated visits with others:* The prep for the meetings provided an opportunity to talk to people you normally don't get a chance to talk to. I went to see one member who was not someone I would normally talk to for a variety of reasons. I went to see him, sat in his office, and we talked about some upcoming issue. I came away from there with at least some acknowledgment from him that he understood where I was coming from. There was that kind of opportunity at the margins to have those talks. And I think that helped move people toward a sense that, "Yes! We have to do something."

Another participant shifted her opinion of another stakeholder after a personal learning moment that occurred informally (1):

> *On seeing another side of a person in an informal exchange:* I had a chance to talk extensively with one forester. This fellow took me out in his pick-up truck and he showed me how he lays out roads. He explained how you have to be careful going over the streams. You don't want to run the roads too straight for too long because it's dangerous for the wolf. Did you know that? I sure didn't. You put a curve in the road so the wolf can hear you coming. Just that little fact from talking to a person I could trust, I understood that consulting foresters aren't all bad. I could see the other side of the issue, and the good things that were being done by good people.

This was one of many stories about how self-initiated, one-on-one encounters shattered stereotypes about opponents. They fostered understanding about the deep causes and circumstances behind the positions of players in the consensus debate.

Participate Fully in Consensus Deliberations

The responsibility of interest advocacy and consensus ambassadorship is most intense at the table. The *table* has become a symbol for working things out together.

How often do you hear people saying things like, "both sides need to *come to the table* with their ideas," "let's *sit down* and work through our differences," or "everything has to be *on the table* if we want to find solutions."

As we have seen, the table is not the sole place where consensus is conceived and nurtured, but it is the forum for translating informal discussion into formal public decisions. Consensus meetings are the culmination for all related discussion around the table. They are the places where the findings, conclusions, and recommendations of many people are acknowledged, argued, and formulated into the official will of the group. As one anonymous leader said, "democracy is the counting, not the voting." Specific responsibilities of serving at the table include keeping up with the content of the discussion, staying open to diverse and massive input, and making judgments about the cumulative results and decisions of the group

As a facilitator, this front stage activity is familiar and intense, but the participants shoulder the primary burden of identifying common ground within the diversity. Veterans of past processes agreed that meetings were a full contact sport. Hands-on participation influenced discussions. Meetings were eventful and draining for all involved, including the meeting leaders.

In many postmeeting evaluations, participants acknowledged the struggle of staying alert and active in the content of the discourse. One member confessed that the "long hours spent in formal discussions often made me tired and irritable and caused knee-jerk reactions." Another participant quoted earlier in the book assessed that the most powerful players were those that could endure the long hours of sitting, listening, debating, questioning, proposing, and co-constructing.

Keeping up with the discussion is indeed challenging. Some discussions are a free-form exchange of reflections and comments prompted by questions from the chair or facilitator. Other sessions are more structured. Either way, the task of listening to viewpoints and gauging the best time for jumping into the fast-paced conversation is not easy. Even though the facilitator kept track of raised hands and allocated speaking turns as democratically as possible, participants expressed frustration with the timing. More often than not, when their turn came around, the conversation had shifted to a new focus.

Equal airtime for everyone's content was a constant battle. In many sessions, after the group identified and sorted areas of common ground, little time was left for what some participants called the "negotiation" on substantive issues. At times there was a perception that the "other sides" were overloading the discussion with too many "irrelevant views." On a more diplomatic note, a participant observed the same phenomenon this way: "Everyone has a chance to present their views. Some do it too often and repeatedly." The implied advice for future participants of controversial dialogue is to expect impatience in hearing and rehearing from not-so-like-minded participants. The secret to success is simply to hang in there.

Promote Collaborative Solutions

Some participants went above and beyond the call of duty in being behind-the scenes ambassadors to promote solution options or proposals. They engaged in advocacy with a different intent. Instead of pushing a particular view, they worked behind the scenes to help search for common ground. They took the initiative to sell the work of the collaboration to their constituencies, broker solutions between diverse players, and promote the credibility of collaborative agreements. Many insiders of past processes were convinced that this behind-the-scenes activity made a huge difference in devising good recommendations, achieving buy-in, and building the political capital required to translate consensus into mainstream decisions, funded mandates, and other implementation support.

Specific ambassadorial activities involved 1) "selling" emerging consensus proposals and drafts back to stakeholder groups, 2) suggesting, sounding out, or floating consensus proposals with several other process participants known to have diverse and even opposing views, and 3) promoting the logic, benefits, and credibility of collaborative agreements to key external audiences.

Sell Collaborative Results Back to "Home" Constituencies

In the previous section I relayed the tough duty of taking consensus conclusions back to their constituencies. Some participants felt that reporting was their main function, but many admitted that consensus building is hard to describe in written or oral reports. Therefore, participants chose not only to communicate but also sell consensus progress to their stakeholder groups. They took on a two-way salesperson role. They worked hard to reconcile the collective results with their interest group's original positions. Those who chose to take on this challenge of lobbying for the newly constructed consensus faced the likelihood of being accused of "selling out."

One person confessed to the conundrum of participating freely in the collaborative dialogue while "understanding very well where my folks wanted to be." This representative explained how she had to "get to know what my constituencies' hot buttons are, have a pretty good idea of what they would agree to, what would take some selling, and where there wasn't much chance of selling-it-back-home." Juggling their loyalty from their interest group to the collaboration process and vice versa was intense and even risky. Here is how two consensus participants described the challenge of being two-way salespersons (1):

> *On the trickiness of cutting some slack and facing the tough questions:* Walking the fine line between losing credibility and figuring out a way to give your interest and meet other people's interest at the same time is tricky. Ultimately that became almost a down-

fall for some; they can lose credibility with their own constituents. I learned going into the process that when you have these kinds of groups working on contentious issues, and they're representing a segment of society, it's pretty important for the whole group to give each other some slack. You have to be able to ask the tough questions and make the tough statements that represent the viewpoint of the people you are representing. If you put it under the table, it's going to come out sometime. It's better to grapple with it up front. Sometimes you have to get your constituents together in a side meeting, help them redevelop their confidence in you, and help the whole process.

On the fears and hardships of enabling your own people to see the common good: There were tumultuous times on stakeholder group boards when it came down to the end. When people had to cast their vote and say, "I'm in favor of this final report," it was hell. It took a lot of leadership ability to be able to go back into one's group saying, "You guys need to take this bad medicine because if you don't take this bad medicine now, you're going to get poison next time and you're going to die." So the reality is that members have to be able to go back to their groups and do that and be really good at it. Some members publicly admitted that they had failed in their efforts to go back into their constituencies and make the case for what it is that was agreed to by the entire consensus group. One told me he was just unable to do that; he just couldn't do it. He didn't say why he couldn't do it. He just couldn't do it.

Consensus participants were aware of the different choices that representatives made regarding this salesperson role. Here one member reflects on the salesperson duties and speculates about the reasons why many representatives opted not to do them (1):

I actively informed my constituencies about the progress made in the collaboration discussion including the criticisms others had of our interest group. I also described what misconceptions our group had about other groups. . . . It was difficult to bring my constituents along. I noticed that some members of the collaboration group retreated between meetings. Possibly they were discouraged because their group's evidence was misrepresented at the table. Or they just plain believed their point of view was right.

As hinted in this account, some representatives did not have the time, incentive, or emotional capacity to campaign actively on behalf of evolving consensus and controversies. These stories confirm that consensus success relies heavily on participant willingness to invest intellectual and emotional energy, brokering new ways of thinking, doing, and believing.

Suggest Proposals That Everyone Can Support

In the final phases of the successful consensus processes, the tough got going when the going got tough. Members of many different stakeholder groups took a leadership role in helping the group arrive at acceptable and realistic agreements. One representative defined brokering as "looking for things we could all agree to and include something for everyone. He felt every member must be able to go back to their own group and say 'I got this for you.'" Another described the brokering task as deal-making and picking battles to create mutually acceptable solutions (1):

> *On creating win-win situations by focusing on the war not battles:* Trying to create "win-win" situations is important. Sometimes you have to make some deals. "Win-win" means being able to see the whole war and not just see the battles. If you can get some wins toward battles you're going to fight in the future, and create some understanding or agreement, that's something that you can take back to your group. You can make your group feel good because it is something of interest to them.

The *Solution Broker* section of chapter 3 recalled further adventures of consensus players that made it a point to engineer win-win solutions formally and informally.

Convince External Parties of Process Credibility

At least a third of the participants in consensus processes I have known considered themselves experienced practitioners in public or political dialogue. They were usually thinking ahead and reported being in constant contact with school board members, lawmakers, opinion leaders, and other key community stakeholders who would be important players in implementing the consensus recommendations once they were identified. In communicating to key people they hoped to increase the chances of broad community support for the products of the process. Often, these consensus participants remained active after the formal process in order to assure follow-up. In one state, several members of a policy consensus group helped herd the proposals through the legislative process. In the following excerpt, one participant analyzes the powerful role that backstage attitudes and actions played in scoring group victories (1):

> *On keeping the process the best alternative for all stakeholders:* There's been a number of consensus groups since ours, and I don't see any of them achieving anywhere near the success. . . . And the question is why? With us there was no debate. They passed the entire document, literally lock, stock, and barrel. With other [processes], a small group of legislators, who—because of an end run by members of the collaboration process—have basically gutted the document that the group produced . . . Our process faired well because we stuck together. It didn't mean that we didn't talk to legislators during the process and try to convince people of our position. It did mean that the work that we did together was important enough to keep doing.
>
> No matter what we did on the outside, we kept working together inside. I mean it's fascinating. It's so fundamental. And why is it? You know that thing about BATNA (Best Alternatives To Negotiated Agreement). . . . Something in our process kept the interest of those who were being paid to represent their groups at the table. I believe it was because, at every point, they saw that it was better to stay than to do an end run on the process. That is the crux of sticking with a consensus activity.

The sponsors of the process are officially responsible for linking the ad hoc effort to official decision making. However, the political power of consensus building mushrooms when all participants actively promote the collective process and products to the powers-that-be.

Respect Individual and Collective Efforts

The facilitator has the responsibility for keeping the dialogue civil and productive, but the journey will be 10 times more effective if everyone self-regulates according to the operational ground rules. At the heart of most codes of conduct is the notion of *respect*. Process participants advise that building "win-win" bridges over complex conflict takes 1) respect for others in the group and 2) respect for the collective process.

Respect for the Process

"Everyone must negotiate in good faith" is a commonly used phrase to describe the need to respect the process. "You have to listen and be patient" was another way interview participants summarized the core activity of being respectful. There was no uncertainty about this point. Points of view must have an opportunity to be expressed and heard genuinely. Participants should be given a chance to reflect on the realities of respectful interchange early in the process.

Respect is a tough principle to practice. Most consensus-builders confessed to the frustration of staying open-minded while receiving endless inputs of all kinds: comments, background information, field trips, ad hoc conversations, venting, outbursts, repeating speeches, and multiple drafts of working agreements. Many admitted to losing their patience. Even the best of the *Boundary Spanners* talked about the rigors of continuing to pay attention and give people the benefit of the doubt meeting after meeting.

Respect for Each Other

Respect for each other meant avoiding all naiveté about differences. Participants agreed that before focusing on common ground, it is essential to provide time to share and acknowledge unique and diverse perspectives. In the rush to get to similarities, it is easy to gloss over the difference. As one participant observed, "You can get people that think alike together. That's easy and that's not what we are talking about. What we are talking about is bringing people that don't think alike together."

The earlier that participants face the deep diversity in beliefs and the grayness of "truth," the better. Hopefully many will see that there are no obvious heroes or villains and decide to get out of the conversion business. Once that reality is understood and accepted, the problem-solvers face the task of finding what makes "common sense" within a confusing mix of deeply-held "rights" and "wrongs."

Frank debate is another component of respecting others. Many players felt that a good process must address underlying conflict boldly and openly. If that is not done, issues will fester and reappear at a future phase or venue of the ongoing conflict.

Straight talk is easier requested than realized. The briefing needs to invite participants to be as assertive as possible. Open disagreement often goes against deep-seated social norms about politeness. It is surprising how hard it is to shake off the influence of lifelong messages such as the advice, "If you can't say something nice, don't say anything at all." Consensus building invites individuals to be ready and willing to be more aggressive than they may be used to. The meeting methods and facilitation will do their best to encourage formal discussion about deep and undiscussable issues, but individuals can make the final difference. Once problems are surfaced, people need to work hard to make sure that the inquiry addresses the underlying controversies.

UNIVERSAL GROUND RULES

Consensus builders determine their own right way to collaborate. A universal consensus code of ethics may someday be needed and available but for now, we have an honor system in effect. In the absence of a participant code of ethics, I conclude this chapter by sharing possible elements of universal ground rules—a set of *Golden Ground Rules* for consensus building (2). It offers another set of clues for participants, facilitators, and process sponsors:

The *Golden Ground Rules of Participation* identify essential elements of effective teamwork that were common to 50 different "codes of conduct" from various organizations and applications around the world. A decade ago, I gathered sets of rules, group norms, and team standards used by real groups, companies, public sector settings, nonprofits and recreational clubs, facilitators, trainers, group work consultants, and community researchers.

Ten major principles for succeeding in collaborative work emerged from the research. I call these the *Golden Ground Rules* because they represent worldwide wisdom and grassroots convictions about what it takes to build common awareness, analysis, agreements, action, and alliances. The two overarching themes reinforce the duties of consensus ambassadorship—help unite the group and help mobilize solutions. Five common elements and further sub-elements emerged within each of the theme as shown in table 6.0.

CONCLUSION

The participants are the magic to collaborative problem solving. According to author Starhawk (3), they practice magic by envisioning what they want to create, clearing the obstacles in their way, and then directing energy through that vision.

Table 6.0.   The Golden Ground Rules

*The Golden Ground Rules represent the 10 common elements for effective meet-
ings and teamwork drawn from 50 different "codes of conduct" of organizations
from around the world.*

Note: Numbers in parentheses show how many Golden Ground Rules from 50
"codes of conduct" around the world included the listed element.

A. Help UNITE the group

1. Require MUTUAL RESPECT
   - *Accept all input.* Respect equality of all ideas and be fair in providing time
     for everyone's right to speak.
   - *Maintain privacy.* Allow each person their personal space through appropri-
     ate confidentiality, distance, and sensitivity.
   - *Honor humanness.* Relate to others as fellow human beings who strive and
     struggle to live effectively in a challenging world.
2. Realize INTERDEPENDENCE
   - *Acknowledge interdependence.* Recognize and accept the reality that indi-
     vidual survival and success is dependent on collective well-being. Coopera-
     tion is in our self-interest. (6)
   - *Appreciate diversity.* Understand diversity as the raw material of society and
     welcome varied experiences, talents, and perspectives as assets to creating a
     strong whole. (9)
   - *Bias for synergy.* Go beyond minimal cooperation. Seek collective efforts that
     produce results that are greater than the sum of the parts. (6)
   - *Collegial Relationships.* Relate to peers with courtesy and support. (13)
3. Keep an OPEN MIND
   - *Spirit of inquiry.* Stay alert, be curious, pursue analytical contemplation, and
     seek collective discovery. (13)
   - *Possibility thinking.* Maintain hope and faith in an open future and belief in
     the ability to accomplish the impossible. (6)
   - *Receptiveness to change.* Recognize the inevitability of constant change and
     embrace new ideas. (4)
   - *Ability to let go.* Review, affirm, and learn from the past but don't be bur-
     dened by it. (5)
   - *Take a chance.* Be willing to take some risks and go where no one has been
     before. (5)
   - *Accept group outcomes.* Believe in unlimited solutions and ability of the
     group to find the "right" one. (3)
4. Contribute THOUGHTFUL EXCHANGE
   - *Active listening.* Listen to all participants actively, patiently, and with empa-
     thy. (8)

(continued)

Table 6.0. *(continued)*

- *Proactive disclosure.* Contribute your knowledge, questions, feelings, insights, and convictions openly, confidently, clearly, and honestly. (12)
- *Ongoing exchange.* Keep lines of communications always open and operating. (3)
- *Encourage sharing.* Actively seek other's ideas. (7)
- *Give and receive feedback.* Assure that positive contributions are acknowledged, and negative participation is redirected in a sensitive and timely manner. (11)
- *Avoid hurt.* Be sensitive to people. Address the issues without attacking, sarcasm, blaming, judgment, and personal criticism. (8)
- *Process observation.* Be aware of group progress and actively improve group interaction. (5)
- *Clear language.* Use words, materials, style, and body language that is clear—say what you mean and mean what you say. (6)
- *Channel information.* Assure that all relevant information is surfaced and flowing between the group and all related stakeholders. (12)
- *Mutual support.* Actively assist the group, think together, and implement the task. (13)

5. Seek COMMON GROUND
   - *Seek win-win agreements.* Actively seek mutually beneficial solutions and be willing to bend and compromise. (17)
   - *Explore disagreements.* Tolerate disagreements and strive for ways to "fight with dignity" and bridge differences with integrity. (7)
   - *Proactive critique.* Provide alternatives and synthesis. Don't sit back and criticize and complain about others' input. (3)
   - *Uncover underlying interests.* Suspend assumptions and negotiate based on understanding. Seek fulfillment of each stakeholder's deep, human interests and needs. (5)
   - *Enlightened self-interest.* Commit to a systemwide view as a way to benefit individual interests. (7)
   - *Bridge factions.* Serve as a gatekeeper to actively facilitate cooperation between levels, functions, and all stakeholder groups. (4)
   - *Search for truth.* Focus on the substance of the decision rather than personalities, favoritism, assumptions, and administrative procedures. (14)
   - *Shared power.* Build strong decisions through mutual influence and shared power. (5)

B. Help MOBILIZE solutions

6. Strive for RESULTS
   - *Seek outcomes.* Focus attention and energy on achieving the desired common future, success, or end product. (7)
   - *Plan for action.* Interactively develop action strategies that enable everyone to assure follow-through of the group mission. (5)

- *Mutual benefits.* Assure group decisions, plans, and actions that deliver shared rewards and benefits for all. (5)
- *Maximize ownership.* Define standards and outcomes that are desired, understood, and accepted by all stakeholders. (10)
- *Progress evaluation.* Relentlessly track and test group progress against original mission and standards. (4)

7. Share RESPONSIBILITY
   - *Individual commitment.* Accept responsibility to help implement the consensus. (22)
   - *Clarified accountability.* Ensure collective success by establishing clear and shared accountability for results. (4)
   - *Delegated roles.* Enable everyone to contribute equitably to the common effort through various roles that are clear, acknowledged, and optimize member talents. (11)
   - *Shared leadership.* Attend to the big picture and group process and take responsibility for the welfare of the whole venture. (12)
   - *Personal effort.* Contribute to high quality through hard work, timeliness, confident communication, thoughtfulness, and good judgment. (22)
   - *Model behavior.* Practice the mission, code of conduct, or philosophy, which the group aspires to. (3)
   - *Personal mastery.* Optimize and support individual development in the midst of the collective effort. (3)
   - *Care for yourself.* Do things that are good for your mind, body, and soul in order to sustain your ability to participate effectively. (5)

8. Choose EFFECTIVE PROCESS
   - *Status review.* Build in regular "check-in" points to orient, clarify, and summarize group work for everyone. (6)
   - *Shared information.* Empower everyone to make informed decisions by sharing all the relevant facts, status, and knowledge about the task at hand. (8)
   - *Appropriate analysis.* Avoid jumping to conclusions. Don't skip steps for considering multiple perspectives, verifying facts, and fostering innovation before making final choices. (6)
   - *Effective process.* Carefully choose the most timely and effective method for assuring focused group work which everyone honors and follows. (10)
   - *Play by the rules.* Accept that effective participation takes time and discipline. Show up on time and follow agreed-upon norms and protocols. (7)
   - *Designated leadership.* Choose process facilitators carefully and respect their leadership. (6)

9. Help ORDER CHAOS
   - *Expect chaos.* Get comfortable with ambiguity and help order chaos. Be ready to encounter the fears, fascinations, challenges, and dynamism of a collective effort. (9)

(continued)

Table 6.0. *(continued)*

- *Face tough situations.* Be willing to embrace conflict, wrestle with complexity, and encounter endless problem-solving duties. (6)
- *Perspire and persist.* Be clear about the ultimate secret to success—sweat equity and not giving up. (2)
- *Learner mentality.* Understand that living is learning. Adopt a "no failures" approach. Evaluate and affirm setbacks and use every experience as a means for constant improvement. (4)
- *Roles flexibility.* Be patient and poised to adapt with the changing needs of the group effort. Be prepared to assume various roles. (5)

10. Employ HUMAN SPIRIT
- *Mix business with pleasure.* Insist that people enjoy the journey to the destination—laugh, be aware of wonder, and maintain a sense of humor. (11)
- *Positive attitude.* Maintain and enliven group productivity by fostering a motivating vision, unifying story, and team spirit. (10)
- *Deep human relations.* Have the courage and respect to address the deep human needs, fears, concerns, anxieties, and longings that underlie surface tensions and conflicts. Support individual potential and empowerment. (6)
- *Life balance.* Stay true to the task but take time to break, rest, and replenish energies. (4)
- *User-friendly culture.* Make everyone feel welcome and maintain a comfortable environment. (4)

NOTES

1. Hanson, M. (2001). *Constructing sustainability policy through collaboration: A multisite case study of decision-making processes that seek sustainable solutions for statewide forests or local watershed development.* St. Paul, MN: University of St. Thomas.

2. Hanson, M. (1996). *Golden ground rules: A leader's guide.* Minneapolis, MN: Meeting Needs.

3. Starhawk. (1987). *Truth or dare: Encounters with power, authority, and mystery.* San Francisco: Harper and Row.

Epigraph

One crucial quality of creativity is an ability to hold fast to confusion until confusion becomes clear.

—Anonymous

If creativity is the capacity to create new capacities, constructing a consensus-building project is nothing but sheer creativity. There is no other way to address the serious and ambiguous issues we face today. No process substitutes for critical thinking and hard work. This book shared the experiences and clues of consensus veterans, but the main message is the permission to create new ways to make binding public agreements and work together.

I recall a problem-formulation course in business school where we identified "creative processes." I raised my hand to add one to the list—setting up complex projects or orchestrating problem-solving processes. It did not make the list. According to the professor, it failed to meet criterion five—"the creative activity is not tightly proceduralized but rather uses heuristic strategies, insight, association, abstraction, and adaptive revision to pursue its goal." At the time I did not argue but, 20 years later, I beg to differ. Consensus building meets the criterion; designing and implementing an effective consensus process requires multiple players to navigate in a terrain of very few constants and hundreds of variables.

Devising effective forums for solving complex problems collaboratively means finding creative ways to augment and supplement official decision-making processes, practices, and protocols. Project sponsors, meeting leaders, and consensus participants embrace existing structures as stepping-stones and apply generous doses of creativity to pioneer collaborative ways to achieve meaningful analysis, agreement, and action. Here is one agency commissioner's recipe for creative problem solving:

Yes there are rules, but we all operate in regulated society and come face to face with some kind of rule almost every minute of our waking lives. Rules exist for a reason—simply to define the acceptable limits of behavior. We wouldn't think of playing tennis

213

on a court without lines or driving on a freeway without speed limits. The rules in state government are really no different . . . . I regard them not as constraints but as the white lines on the tennis court. As long as I operate within those lines, avoiding even the casual foot fault, I can be as creative or as flexible as I choose to be (1).

Every person can be a pressure point for creating new forms of public discourse and social engagement. However, those in formal positions of leadership have a unique role in accelerating collaborative problem solving. Large-scale change will happen if pilot demonstrations succeed and show the way. Societal patterns can be changed one meeting, one project, and one dispute at a time. According to the theories of tipping point and critical mass, a growing number of pioneering efforts can catalyze a societal sea change. You have seen it in small scale in your own neighborhood. One household sets up a fetching three-pot flower arrangement in front of their front door. In a few weeks, several other neighbors customize the idea in front of their own houses. Within the summer, it becomes a fad around the neighborhood.

My hope is that more and more leaders will adopt a collaborative option to address organizational dilemmas, develop community, break out of conflict, and move beyond simply surviving our problems. By unlocking the human capacity to build new capacity, workplaces, cities, governments, schools, associations, partnerships, and nations, we can not only survive but discover ways to thrive and flourish as a human community.

NOTE

1. Badgerow, D. B. (1991, April). On my mind. In *Administration*, a newsletter from the Minnesota Department of Administration.

Index

absolutes, 9. *See also* truths

accomodating mode of interaction, 5–9, 11, 89–90, 91–92, 194

action through consensus: accountability, 26, 94, 131, 135–40, 186–89; benefit, 37–42, 55, 73–76, 77; between sectors, 21, 39; conflict resolution, 10–11, 138–39; developing, 168, 174–75, 212; power generated by, 37–42; reactive/proactive, 28; results, 2, 3, 5, 32, 40, 44–45, 215; social change, 32; successful examples, 12, 13; support, vii, ix, 16, 32, 33–34, 138. *See also* case studies and examples, education; case studies and examples, nonprofit; case studies and examples, private; case studies and examples, public

advantages of consensus. *See* benefits of consensus

adversarial methods and approaches, 5, 6, 8–9, 11–12, 29, 154–56, 197

advocating: consensus solutions, 11–12, 197–208; dual role of advocate and ambassador, 11–12, 88–92, 100, 191–208; positions, 11–12, 88–89, 109, 192–97; styles, 86–104

agents, 79; constructs, 1, 11–12; collaboration, 102–3, 181

agreements: benefits, 37–42, 55, 68–76; definition, 1–5, 42–43; documenting, 186–89; input for, 128; pitfalls, 21–30,

42–51; process, 89, 99–123, 154–59, 165–190, 191–208

aggressiveness. *See* assertiveness

alliances, 5, 27, 34, 38, 39, 45, 50, 54, 58, 76–79, 130, 131, 167, 173, 177, 210; creating collegial relationships, 25, 77–79, 166, 179, 185–86, 194–95, 209

ambassador, 11; participants serving as, 89, 176, 198–208

analysis, consensus building, 5, 28–29, 38–39, 45, 51, 54, 84, 101, 166, 167, 168–69,170; benefits, 61–68, 194; collective intelligence, 63–65; data overload, 62–63; innovative solutions, 65–68; pitfalls, 194, 199–200. *See also* awareness; data; information for decisions; judgment; objectivity; politics

arbitration, 11, 70, 111, 196

Argument Culture, 9

assertiveness, 5–10, 53, 89, 90, 91–92, 94, 97, 192

avoidance mode of interaction, 5–8, 11, 89–90, 91–92

awareness, 5, 45; benefits, 38–42, 45, 55, 56–61, 68; process, 45, 166–68, 169, 170, 208

backstage activity: facilitators (process leaders), 104–5, 110–23, 161–64, 165–79, 180, 185–90; importance, x, 86–88; participants, 86–89;

About the Author

Mirja P. Hanson, EdD, has three decades of experience facilitating group decision making in hundreds of communities, school districts, agencies, nongovernmental organizations, and corporations. Her consensus education began informally while growing up in Japan as the daughter of Finnish missionaries. Her formal education includes a doctorate in education from the University of St. Thomas in St. Paul, Minnesota; an MBA from the Carlson School of Management, University of Minnesota; and a BA from the Metropolitan State University of Minnesota.

Mirja Hanson is affiliated with Millennia International Consulting Group, Inc., a worldwide network of independent firms providing customized consulting and facilitation services in all nations, markets, and cultural contexts. She specializes in multiple-stakeholder decision making, policy consensus building, conflict resolution, interorganizational partnership, and strategic planning. Recent clients and projects include over 50 state, federal, regional, and county agencies in the U.S., numerous K–12 and higher educational institutions, the U.S. House of Representatives, town meetings in more than 100 U.S. municipalities, U.S. Steel, 3M Corporation, United Nations Sustainable Development Program—Environmental Facility, and Habitat for Humanity.

Prior to private practice, Mirja Hanson was a senior consultant with the Institute of Cultural Affairs and Management Analysis and Development, an in-house consulting group that is a division of the Department of Administrating of Minnesota State Government. She served as coordinator for STEP (Striving toward Excellence in Performance, the state's award-winning quality improvement program.

Dr. Hanson is a founding member of the International Association of Facilitators, a member of the adjunct faculty at the University of St. Thomas, a Master Trainer of the Institute of Cultural Affair's Technologies of Participation, and a contributing author for *Beyond Prince and Merchant: Citizen Participation and the Rise of Civil Society* (1997, John Burbidge, Ed.) and *Government Works: Profiles of People Making a Difference* (1995, James Troxel, Ed.).

223